# *Occupation and Quality In Later Life*

## **Sharon Green**
### *PhD, MEd, DipCOT*

# Dedication

*This book is dedicated with gratitude to two inspirational women:*

***Jessie Taylor*** *was a pioneer occupational therapist, born in 1914 on the Cherokee Indian Reservation in North Carolina. She was one of the first occupational therapists to graduate from Western Michigan University. I first met Jessie when she was working in a Nursing Home setting in San Francisco in the early 1970's. From the outset I recognised her deep commitment to her profession. Every one of her frail older clients was an important person and every encounter one of encouragement and assistance to make the most out of each day. Jessie's enthusiasm and devotion was instrumental in my selecting elderly people as my chosen specialist area of research and clinical practice.*

***Beaulah Bentley*** *was and always will be an excellent teacher. Although retired from her profession for over 30 years, she has embraced many new challenges and throughout has retained the ability to inspire and encourage others to do more, learn more and generally make progress. She epitomizes the importance of time, never wanting to waste a precious moment for herself, and always wanting to share knowledge to enable others to do likewise. I have been privileged to know Beaulah in her $90^{th}$ and $100^{th}$ decade and from who else could I possibly have learned the names of 47 different varieties of viola! Her passion has been an ongoing impetus for the research of this book.*

*Sharon Green*
*5th April 2009*

# *Acknowledgements*

*I am grateful to many people who have given help and support in the initial preparation of the research, and then the compilation of this book.*

*Able mentorship and colleague support was provided by Andrew and Judith Sixsmith and Barbara Acheson Cooper. Abhi Mantgani and Mary Waldron and Phyllis Jones assisted in my gaining access to research subjects who are listed here under their pseudonyms to protect their ongoing privacy. I remain indebted to the willingness of the following people who shared their homes and lives with me as part of the research: Ann, Beatrice, Cath, Doris, Edith, Fay, Gladys, Horace, Ian, Joyce, Karl and Lucy.*

*Richard Green has been my technical advisor; without his assistance this final volume may never have surfaced.*

*Along the way too, I have been ably supported and encouraged by many friends, colleagues and family members, not least by my husband and photographer. I am thankful to them all.*

# OCCUPATION AND QUALITY IN LATER LIFE

# OCCUPATION AND QUALITY IN LATER LIFE

## PART 1   THE BACKGROUND

***Synopsis****:    A book devoted to later life occupation: the curious general reader may well pause here and ask why this is necessary. After all is not the long-awaited period of retirement with its release from the essentials of working to earn one's living, both eagerly awaited and gratefully embarked upon, and if so then why is a book on occupation necessary for this phase in life? Other readers, with a more immediate involvement in later life issues, whether due to personal or professional reasons, may well be grappling with some of the knotty issues associated with the topic. After the book's key terms are introduced, this first Part of the book introduces research and popular theories connected with the subject; namely quality of life, the links between occupation, personal health and quality of life, and the arena of successful ageing. To conclude Part 1, chapter 4 brings research in the area up to date by describing research methods which have been used to explore the subject more fully. At the close of chapter 4 readers will meet the twelve older people who took part in this research and who provided the case studies to follow in Part 2.*

### Key Terms

***Occupation****: is viewed as individually meaningful use of time. It encompasses any goal directed activity that has meaning for the individual (Creek, 1990) and is composed of skills and values. Sabonis-Chafee (1989) stated simply: "occupation refers to all purposeful activities that fill a person's waking hours. Purposeful activity is thus more than just doing, it is doing that involves the person on many levels" (p.13). Although there is much recent debate, neatly summarised by Pierce (2001b), that seeks to distinguish between "activity" and "occupation", such theoretical discussion relies heavily on semantics. A recent distinction is suggested by Royeen (2002) when she suggested that "occupation should be considered as the process of doing with meaning, and that activity should be the outcome" (p.111). Throughout this book, occupation is viewed as synonymous with purposeful activity and it incorporates the three broad and overlapping areas of self-maintenance, productivity and leisure activities.*

***Quality of life****: is a complex concept; definitions are explored in chapter 1 which follows. Put briefly, quality of life addresses subjective well-being*

1

*and its constituent domains. It encompasses both health and sociological perspectives.*

***Later life and old age****: does not commence at any specific chronological point, although there are acknowledged points at which the terms come into use. The earliest uses are found for people over the age of fifty, for instance the "Later life Convention", held in Wirral September 2007, and advertised as "a spotlight on services for people aged 50 plus in Wirral", and the Strathclyde University's "Centre for lifelong learning which offers a learning in later life programme to the 50 plus age group. It is however more usual to hear of old age issues arising after the age of retirement which in the UK, by 2010, will be 65years for men and women. Research papers tend to use the term "younger old" when referring to people aged between 65 and 84 years. However it is amongst the "oldest old", i.e. those people over the age of 85 years where much research interest lies, commensurate with the increased life expectancy now experienced in many countries. Whilst advanced chronological age does not necessarily equate with being frail it is normally accepted that the oldest old are more likely to experience frailty, illness and dependence in comparison with younger old people. Seshamani and Gray (2002) add: "It follows that the oldest old are the main per capita users of health services compared with other age groups of the population. In the USA similar findings are also evident: "although not necessarily frail or dependent, this group of people consumes disproportionate amounts of health and long term care services" (US Bureau of the Census 1999). People within the oldest old age group may then be seen as being at risk, or vulnerable, when confronted with the challenge of keeping pace with elements of successful ageing, namely: low risk of disease and disease related disability, high mental and physical function, and active engagement with life (Rowe and Kahn 1998). Case histories presented in this book are drawn from both the younger old and oldest old age groups.*

***The Environment****: is an important concept, closely related to the book's topic. To a large extent the local environment determines possible activities and occupations, and this is especially important when any degree of frailty is present. The General Household Survey of 2001 when reporting on the living arrangements of the oldest old at this time indicated that 12% of men and 23% of women lived in any form of communal establishment, with all others living in their own homes in the community. (Tomassini 2006). Own homes include both sheltered living and independent living arrangements. Beyond the physical or built environment there are additional important environmental characteristics of a social and organisational nature (Letts et al. 1994) to be considered. The three environmental perspectives namely:*

*physical, social and organisational provide the context for the setting of this book and are explored further as the text unfolds.*

## CHAPTER 1 WHAT IS QUALITY OF LIFE?

It is necessary to take a theoretical look at this topic, before we examine how occupation may influence a person's experience of quality of life. During the 1970's the term quality of life became popular and a topic of much academic and professional debate. An example of one study that reached the media headlines was the *Fickle Finger of Fate Award* of a popular television show of the time. (Lawton 1991). The award was given to a group whose $300,000 grant concluded that healthier and wealthier people were happier than sick and poor people. Such a finding may appear naive thirty years on, but it was an indicator that along with numerous studies that reported medical-related quality of life, there was growing interest in publicising the equally important sociological components. Terms such as 'social well-being' and 'social health' entered popular use and, together with the term 'quality of life', they became recognised components of the concept of positive health. As health at this time was no longer a mere absence of disease, wellness became equated with ingredients such as high morale and life satisfaction, psychological well-being and even levels of physical fitness (Lamb *et al.* 1988). Quality of life sat neatly with this group of terms, and some professional health groups appeared to have a clear vision of the essential ingredients in relation to specific client groups. The Royal College of Nursing (1975) for example, published the following views:

> *Quality of life for the elderly requires the recognition of the old person as a unique individual with a need for creative activity, for privacy and fellowship at appropriate times, and with the right to be consulted and to choose in all matters affecting his health and welfare.*
>
> *(Royal College of Nursing 1975:11)*

Interest in the concept of quality of life grew at a steady rate during the 1980's. As an example, citations in *Index Medicus* listed 77 articles in English in 1985, and 149 articles in 1988. *Psychological Abstracts* first listed such an entry in 1985 (38 articles), and by 1988 the number had risen to 80. In the 1990's interest burgeoned and in 1997, *BIDS, Social Science Citations* listed 4,393 entries.

As interest grew, so did the debate about defining the components of quality of life. Hughes (1990:47) neatly summarised this as: "The concept of quality of life is multi-dimensional and has no fixed boundary". Hughes went on to cite George and Bearon's (1980) work in which they suggested:

> *On the whole, social scientists have failed to provide consistent*
> *and concise definitions of quality of life. The task is indeed*
> *problematic, for definitions of life quality are largely a matter*
> *of personal or group preferences; different people value*
> *different things.*
>
> *(George and Bearon 1980:1)*

Medical practitioners continued to make much use of the term quality of life. Many measures of quality of life resulted from identified areas of clinical concern. For example Habu *et al.* (1988) studied quality of life in relation to older patients after surgery for gastric cancer and Wenger (1988) investigated how the diagnosis and management of hypertension affected the quality of life of the patients concerned. In the late 1990's, there was a large volume of medically-related literature purporting to address quality of life for specific groups of patients, as for lung cancer patients (Montazeri *et al.*1996), patients with multiple sclerosis and their carers (Aronson 1997), adults with growth hormone deficiency (Wallymahmed *et al.* 1996) and elders with mental health problems (Kupfer and Weyerer 1995). Schreiber (1996) debated the ethics of some geriatric surgery and strongly urged that the elderly person's quality of life must not be objectively judged by others. Slovick *et al.* (1995) also pursued the elderly patient's interpretation of life quality in their work of testing alternative hypertension medication. They suggested that:

> *determination of the effects of treatment on the quality of life*
> *requires special tests that are sensitive to small changes in*
> *patients' daily activities, psychological well-being and*
> *cognitive function.*
>
> *(Slovick et al. 1995:139)*

All these writings used a broad set of interpretations of the term quality of life and its links with health, sometimes apparently regarding quality as synonymous with quantity, so that for example, extra years or quantity of life following surgical or medical intervention was expressed as increased quality. There are some health-related areas however, in which there is little debate over the inclusion of areas of core medical concern. Health and freedom from pain or discomfort, for examples, are always essential. Rokeach (1973) carried out a study to explore the most valued components of living, and he removed health from the rank order because every one of his subjects valued it more highly than any other item.

## What is Quality of Life

On moving beyond a medically-related interpretation of the term quality of life, the debate over essential constituents expanded in almost all directions. Some definitions, arising in the 1970's, still have wide appeal. Mendola and Pelligrini (1979:457) defined quality of life as: "the individual's achievement of a satisfactory social situation within the limits of perceived physical capacity". Around the same time Shin and Johnson (1978) provided a fuller definition, suggesting that quality of life is dependent upon previous experience and knowledge and that it:

> *consists of the possession of resources necessary to the*
> *satisfaction of individual needs, wants and desires,*
> *participation in activities enabling personal development and*
> *self actualisation and satisfactory comparison between oneself*
> *and others.*
>
> *(Shin and Johnson 1978:476)*

Other authors of the time, for example Patterson (1975), compiled lists of characteristics thought necessary for quality of life. Bowling (1991) later summarised this body of literature with the following comment:

> *Basically quality of life is recognised as a concept representing*
> *individual responses to the physical, mental and social effects*
> *of illness on daily living which influence the extent to which*
> *personal satisfaction with life circumstances can be achieved...*
> *It is an abstract and complex concept comprising diverse areas,*
> *all of which contribute to the whole, personal satisfaction and*
> *self-esteem.*
>
> *(Bowling 1991:9)*

A little later, Mayers (1995) was another of the many authors to comment upon the elusive definition and assessment of quality of life. After an extensive review of literature, she favoured the following definition provided by Niemi *et al.* (1988):

> *Although the concept has been only loosely defined there is*
> *agreement that quality of life refers to a person's subjective*
> *well-being and life satisfaction and that it includes mental and*
> *physical health, material well-being, interpersonal*
> *relationships within and without the family, work and other*
> *activities within the community, personal development and*
> *fulfilment, and active recreation.*
>
> *(Mayers 1995:147)*

Interest in defining the concept continued. Gill and Feinstein (1994) completed an extensive review of 25 articles in order to evaluate how well quality of life was being measured. They concluded that as quality of life was a uniquely personal perception, which reflected how a person felt about both their health plus other non-medical aspects of life, that most measurements in the medical literature aimed at the wrong target. The authors, both physicians, went on to present the bold suggestion that:

> *Quality of life can be suitably measured only by determining the opinions of patients and by supplementing (or replacing) the instruments developed by experts.*

> *(Gill and Feinstein 1994:619)*

More recent authors (Scherer and Cushman, 2001; Lau and McKenna, 2001), continue to support the principle that the subjective aspect of quality of life must always be recognised. Lawton (1991), specifically addressed the meaning of quality of life for frail elderly people. He provided a comprehensive overview of the potential components, and suggested that much emphasis is placed on medical quality of life and on negative deviations from the accepted norm. He noted that quality of life should include "every aspect of life", and he wondered whether a person's hierarchy of values in determining quality living may be rearranged in the face of frailty. One of his earlier studies (Lawton 1985) supported the same hypothesis. It showed that very impaired, homebound older people had established "control centres" from their living room chairs. From here they retained control over television, telephone, reading materials and mementos from the past. Lawton's study highlighted the connection between quality living and positive reports of time use and occupational control. He advocated further research to assess the positive features of life and to determine how people's environments can maximise opportunities for positive experiences.

There is limited literature that gives the floor entirely and directly to older people in defining their quality of life. Such that there is, suggests that meaningful occupation continues to be important to individuals as they advance in age. Lansdown (1994) described the eloquence of Mary Stott, then aged 80 years, and a former editor of the Women's Page of *The Guardian*. Stott spoke of the value to her of painting, gardening and music. She remarked that it was of little consequence if her voice had become lower over the years. She always had a low voice and could continue to sing the bass parts along with the men. Lansdown also illustrated a challenge to the unfortunate "what can you expect at your age" line, with a story about an elderly man who, having complained about a pain in his leg, was told that he could expect it at his age. At this point the man pointed out that his other leg was 104 years also and that had no pain!

Until the 1990's much research on the quality of life of older people had been conducted amongst the minority who were residents of nursing homes (Fletcher *et al.*1992). In such protected environments at this time the emphasis on quality of life was directed towards avoidance of the negative consequences of institutionalisation, making such research incapable of direct translation outside the nursing home surroundings. This body of research did however highlight the difference that environment can make to an individual's perception of quality of life. Lansdown (1994:636) phrased this as "the complex interaction between the characteristics of the individual and his or her environment".

Hughes (1990) and Law *et al.* (1996) both discussed the importance of studying the environment in relation to quality of life. Hughes described a model of quality of life for frail elders, in which she cited both purposeful activity and the quality of the environment as essential components. She moved the debate on by suggesting that further research "could usefully investigate connections and relationships between the different subsystems" (p.55). Law *et al.* (1996) introduced the 'Person-Environment-Occupation' (PEO) Model. This model addresses the important relationship between the environment and an individual's level of occupation and portrays the outcome of the relationship of these components as occupational performance (OP). The authors suggested that this is a dynamic relationship, such that a change in any one of the model's three components can influence the resulting occupational performance, either negatively or positively. Green and Acheson Cooper (2000) utilised the PEO Model to examine occupation and quality of life in Nursing Homes and highlighted the key role of the Matron in the environment. Residents whose abilities were fostered tended to reside in Homes where the therapeutic value of non-traditional activities was recognised and ingenuity and a flexible use of resources employed.

Work continues in the complex area of attempting to define and measure quality of life, with the field still attracting academics of many disciplines. It is interesting to note too that whilst new measures are under ongoing development, there remain valuable studies returning us all to some basic concepts. Anderson & Burckhardt (1999) summed up the situation in their comprehensive study of the concept and measurement of quality of life. Here they concluded that non-medical factors ought to be central and they suggest ongoing support for Flanagan's (1978) five quality of life domains which are: physical and material well-being; relations with other people; recreation; social, community and civic activities; and personal development and fulfilment. It is interesting to find a return to domains identified more than 20 years earlier. Perhaps researchers would do well to note the strength and rigour of Flanagan's earlier work. He arrived at his resulting fifteen categories in five domains only after he had collected 6,500 critical incidents from almost 3,000 subjects across the USA. In the collected incidents, he explored events over the preceding five years, which had produced pleasure or a strong positive or negative emotional response. Flanagan makes several references in his categories to "activities" and embedded in his personal development and fulfilment domain is a category entitled occupational role.

To conclude this chapter on a practical note we should take a look at current ways of assessing and addressing quality of life:

A major international project conducted by the World Health Organisation (WHO) on the conceptualisation and measurement of people's subjective quality of life, began in the mid 1980's (WHOQOL Group 1996). Twenty five centres globally were involved at this time and their instrument for assessing quality of life included the following domains: physical, psychological, level of independence, social relationships, environment and spiritual. A WHOQOL-100 questionnaire resulted (Skevington SM, 1999) and work continues in developing and standardising various versions of the WHOQOL, with the research team in Bath indicating that the scales have been administered to more than 16,000 people in over 40 countries world-wide.

One of the core instruments, the WHOQOL-100 contains 100 questions covering 25 facets or dimensions of quality of life that have a high level of international consensus. Some socio-demographic and health information is also obtained with an optional appendix of questions about the importance of these facets to quality of life. The UK-WHOQOL-100 includes two additional national questions covering issues that are important to people in UK. A short form of 26 items - the WHOQOL Bref - has now also been developed. The research teams note that current versions of the WHOQOL have good properties of reliability and validity both in UK and internationally with sensitivity to change still being fully investigated. To satisfy measurement requirements in certain diseases and conditions, some modules of specific items have been created for addition to the core instrument. For instance, the WHOQOL-SRPB contains 32 further questions covering 8 facets on spirituality, religion and personal beliefs related to health and quality of life.

Also a version of WHOQOL modules has been developed for research with older adults (WHOQOL-Old), and details of this can be found in the article by Power M, Quinn K, Schmidt S and WHOQOL-OLD Group (2005). In developing the special add-on module for use with older people 22 international centres were involved in the pilot phase, with older adults, carers and professionals working with older adults all contributing to focus groups. Items arising from the focus groups were then tested in over 7,000 respondents, a large scale field trial conducted and a 26-item 6-facet module resulted. The authors suggest this should be used in conjunction with either the WHOQOL-BREF or the WHOQOL-100 when assessing quality of life with older people.

## *What is Quality of Life*

Lastly let us look at an example of how the assessment of quality of life for older people is being put to practical use. East Sussex has produced a comprehensive document which aims to begin bringing together and guiding their work over the next three years for supporting a healthy and active later life in East Sussex. Their Consultation process, completed in October 2007 involved both older people and related agencies, and established the following:

"Older people in East Sussex have told us that good quality of life cuts across the following seven areas:

- *Access to activities that promote a healthy old age*
- *Health, social care and housing support services that promote older people's quality of life and wellbeing*
- *Feeling safe and secure*
- *Opportunities to continue to learn and develop in later life*
- *Playing an active part in community life and having a strong collective voice*
- *The ability to get out and about*
- *Having healthy finances"*

*(Time of our Lives Strategy, 2007)*

It will be interesting to note the impact of strategies such as this in the next decade. Will policies be driven by such strategies, and most importantly will older people report their quality of life needs as being addressed?

In the next chapter we will take an in-depth look at our understanding of occupation and how it has evolved over the years. We will examine links between occupation and quality of life and personal health status.

## CHAPTER 2   PERSONAL HEALTH, QUALITY OF LIFE AND OCCUPATION

> *Here I sit at this great big loom making God knows what for*
> *God knows whom*
> *(Anon. Patient, in Turner et al. (eds.) 1992: 6)*

It appears from the above quotation that whilst this patient was occupied, he/she understood neither the meaning of the activity nor its personal relevance. No quality is associated with the occupation and the experience is potentially both negative and unhealthy: a poor state of affairs for both the patient and the therapist!

On looking back into literature we are reminded of an early recognised link between health and occupation. In 2600 BC, the Chinese taught that disease resulted from organic inactivity, and they used physical training to promote health (Levin 1938). The earliest written references to the therapeutic value of activities predate 600 BC. At this time, Aesculapius who worked at Epidaurus in Greece, claimed that he could sooth delirium with "songs, farces and music" (Le Clerc, 1699). Shortly after this, from 600 BC to 900 AD, music was reported as therapeutic by many, among them Pythagoras, Thales and Orpheus. Hippocrates too made many references to a mind-body link and suggested that wrestling, riding and "labour" could all be used to aid recovery from a variety of ailments.

The word occupation comes from the Latin root *occupacio* which means "to seize or to take possession", implying action (Englehardt, 1977: 668). Wood (1998) takes this theme further and suggests that *occupacio* is "that wellspring of creativity that energizes life-giving and life-renewing actions from within" (p.320). Wood reminds us that Plato believed that all men and women instinctively needed to make and do, and that Aristotle suggested that well-being radiated from desirable and satisfying activities. Much later, by the eighteenth and nineteenth centuries, the early supporters of the positive effects of occupation were followed by such great humanitarians as Phillippe Pinel and William Tuke. They strove to improve the conditions in asylums, by substituting involvement in occupation for the restraint and immobility of the shackles (Bing, 1981). From this time onwards, there was regular recognition that being occupied was a good thing, although there was little early evidence as to exactly how and why this should be so. A very influential figure in the early twentieth century, Adolph Meyer, a well respected American psychiatrist, provided some of the first case examples of patients who benefited from involvement in purposeful occupations:

## Personal Health, Quality of Life and Occupation

*Groups of patients with raffia and basket work, or with various
kinds of hand-work and weaving and bookbinding and metal and
leather work, took the place of bored wallflowers and mischief
makers. A pleasure in achievement, a real pleasure in the use
and activity of one's hands and muscles, and a happy
appreciation of time began to be used as incentives in the
management of our patients.*

(Meyer A 1922, in: Englehardt 1997:667,668)

Turning to more recent times, the last decades of the twentieth century have
witnessed a growing interest in the value of being occupied and the paucity of
quality of life when there is no accessible and meaningful occupation.
Csikszentmihalyi (1993) goes beyond this point to describe the state of chaos that
can arise in minds that are left unoccupied. He suggests that when humans do not
have access to ordered stimulation, "the mind begins to drift in random patterns,
and usually ends up bringing up depressing thoughts, whether we like it or not"
(p.38). In this same paper he also reminds us of his earlier research into 'flow' or
occasions when a high level of enjoyment is reached (Csikszentmihalyi, LeFevre
1989). The 1989 paper reports subjects who are happily participating in diverse
activities ranging from chess to rock-climbing or composing music whilst
common phenomena are recognised. For instance, no matter what the activity
was, it was most enjoyed when the subject was able to meet a complex
opportunity for action.

Indeed recent writers have acknowledged that occupation always encompasses
complexities; it never exists in isolation, being intimately connected to both the
individual concerned and the environment in which it takes place. Nelson (1997)
purported that occupation is seen as the relationship between its two parts:
occupational performance (the doing) and occupational form (the thing that is
done). Law *et al.* (1996) highlighted the situational context in their work,
suggesting that occupational performance is at the point of intersection where the
person, the occupation and the environment are in contact and in fact overlap.
Their subsequent work uses case histories to illustrate how views of occupational
performance can be harnessed therapeutically to enable clients to successfully
engage in meaningful occupations in chosen environments (Strong *et al.*1999).

Occupational therapists as health professionals, place a strong emphasis on
harnessing the potential benefits of meaningful occupation. Mary Reilly, herself
an occupational therapist, delivered the Eleanor Clark Slagle Memorial Lecture in
1962 and took as her topic: *Occupational Therapy can be one of the great ideas
of 20th century medicine* (Reilly 1962). In her lecture she addressed a vital
question, shared today by all followers of the profession: "Is occupational therapy
a sufficiently vital and unique service for medicine to support and society to

reward?" This lecture, to an international audience, covered some rich topics for debate. She included the following suggestion:

*That man, through the use of his hands as they are energised by mind and will, can influence the state of his own health*

(Reilly 1962:2)

Reilly's words have been quoted on many occasions, and to a large extent her hypothesis continues to be addressed regularly in all clinical fields, as therapists seek for evidence-based practice. She also discussed "the vital need to be occupied", and gave examples of research into sensory deprivation, concluding that data indicated that "the mind cannot continue to function efficiently without constant stimulation from the external world" (p.5).

Wilma West (1916-1996) was another ardent student of occupation, who stressed that therapists must be ready to change with new service demands in order to realise the profession's huge potential contribution to society (West, 1968). A visionary, she was one of the earliest supporters of the concept of a foundational science, distinct from the occupational therapy profession. The foundational science became known as 'occupational science' and followed an earlier American concern with the development of models for practice and a revived interest in the concept of occupation that surfaced in the 1980's. Kielhofner's original work was instrumental here, as it was widely publicised and it re-awoke pride in occupation and also began to influence research studies. Mounter and Ilott (1997) also described some of the international liaisons that were developed around 1990, as interest grew in the exploration of the knowledge-base to the occupational therapy profession. The impetus to do this was fuelled by incorporation of professional training into higher educational institutions, which was taking place at the same time. With the validation of degree programmes, it became necessary to demonstrate a more rigorous theoretical approach, and in 1993 occupational science was included as a core aspect within the 'Curriculum Framework for Occupational Therapy' (College of Occupational Therapists, 1993). With a multi-disciplinary audience, this foundational science attracts researchers from wide-ranging backgrounds, from anthropology to sociology and occupational therapy. Wood (1998) described occupational science as "an academic discipline dedicated to a wide-ranging scholarly inquiry of occupation and the occupational human that is today nurturing the occupational therapy profession" (p.322). The *American Occupational Therapy Association* neatly summed up some of the paradoxes involved in the study of occupation: "Occupations are the ordinary and familiar things that people do every day. This simple description reflects, but understates, the multi-dimensional and complex nature of daily occupation" (A.O.T.A.1995:1016). Additionally, the burgeoning interest in the development and publication of research centred around the science of occupation, has become heavily invested in the semantics. Debate has yielded many articles considering "activity" and "occupation", frequently striving to publish fine semantic differentiations (Golledge 1998, Hagedorn 1997, Wood 1996). Whilst such theoretical study has been underway, it may be argued that investigation into practice and the real meaning of occupation to those who undertake it, has received insufficient attention. In a recent review of selected literature on the effects of occupation on health (Creek and Hughes 2008), the authors found only 17 of 38 potential papers from 2000-2006 contained valid evidence and further research is still necessary. As Stenhouse (1975) suggested, such a gulf is frequently noticed in educational institutions, where occupants of the "ivory towers" pay insufficient attention to what really happens in the outside world.

The literature that focuses on occupation in relation to elderly people, reminds us of some elementary concerns. Whilst academics wax eloquent about occupation: "Meaningful occupation animates and extends the human spirit" (Peloquin 1997:167), and repeatedly suggest that:

> *For us, in occupational therapy, the most fundamental area of*
> *research is, and probably always will be, the nature and*
> *meaning of activity.*
>
> *(Reilly 1960, cited in West 1984:17)*

there are those who have portrayed a more practical stance and urge that rather than waiting for "occupational science to expand our thinking and horizons" (Richards, 1998:297), there is "some urgency in the profession to move on from its constant preoccupation with its internal state of affairs". At this time, the Occupational Therapy Officer for the Department of Health, Sheelagh Richards, was well aware that there is a constant need for applied research to "improve the quality of occupational therapy practice and the outcome for service users". Nowhere is this more essential than in the area of health and social care provision for older people: the client numbers are increasing, and in many areas resources are stretched.

Practically there are some excellent accounts of health benefits for older people arising from occupational involvement. For example Baum's (1995) work illustrated the positive effects of occupation in her study of seventy two couples where one partner had Alzheimer's disease. Here the occupationally active subjects showed fewer disturbing behaviours and needed less help with self care. Green's (1995) study revealed the "enjoyment, animation and colour" of an organised activity programme for elderly mentally ill nursing home residents, and found the residents "enjoyed having something to do", because it "helps to keep your wits about you". In support of Baum and Green's studies, Perrin (1997) illustrated what happened when meaningful activity was not offered. Perrin provided an example of the results of occupational deprivation amongst elderly people with severe dementia, in hospital and residential settings. Through the use of dementia care mapping, she demonstrated a severe dearth of occupational provision and correlated this with the minimum level of well-being which most of the 109 subjects experienced, for most of the time. An interesting account of the benefits of horticulture is found in Milligan, Bingley and Gatrell (2003) They report their research with 93 people aged 65 to 91 years, carried out in Carlisle over a nine month period. Whilst suggesting they had little quantitative evidence from their small sample of gardeners, they report qualitatively: "Evidence from this study suggests that gardening and social activities have profound and positive effects on a person's sense of worth and mental well-being. These effects support older people to cope better with chronic or debilitating physical ill health" (Final Report , page 7).

A further well-reported study is that of Clark *et al.* (1997). The team conducted their well-elderly randomized control trial in Los Angeles between 1994 and 1997. Their subjects were 361 African-American, Asian, Caucasian and Hispanic men and women with a mean age of 74.4 years. Based on a strong belief in the value of occupational science, the study set out to illustrate the critical role that occupations play in affecting health and psychological well-being. One of the three experimental groups was treated by occupational therapists who focussed on preventing health risks and developing individual lifestyle redesigns, another group received a non-professionally led social activities programme and the third group received no treatment. At the close of the nine month treatment programme, a mixed battery of tests, revealed improvements in physical and social functioning, vitality and life satisfaction, in the occupational therapy group members, with all tests bearing a probability value of less than .05.

Taking a close look at the relationship between physical exercise and quality of life, the research results are again positive. McAuley and Rudolph (1995) reviewed 38 studies which examined the effects of exercise and physical activity on the psychological well-being of older adults and suggested the results were overall "overwhelmingly positive". They also found that results became increasingly positive when exercise programmes were continued for longer.

Rabbitt (1997) went further in his large, ongoing study of 6,500 elderly people, when he found that cognitive ability is preserved more frequently in those who take physical and mental exercise, although Angevaren M'Aufdemkampe G'Verhaar HJJ'Aleman A'Vanhees L (2008) whilst supporting the beneficial links between physical activity and cognitive function, express reservations about any added influence of aerobic exercise over cognitive skill retention. Looking specifically at cognitive abilities and depression, Rabbitt P, Lunn M, Ibrahim S, Cobain M, McInnes L, (2008) tested whether scores on depression inventories on entry to a longitudinal study predicted mental ability over the next 4-16 years. With 5070 volunteers aged 49-93 years the team reported a new finding that, in old age, increments in life satisfaction are associated with better cognitive performance.

Such research results demonstrating the positive effects of both physical and mentally stimulating activities will be of interest to an increasingly large number of older people. Predictions for the immediate future suggest that more people will be interested in how to occupy their increased free time as a higher percentage of people elect to take early retirement. In the UK there is reported continuing growth in the proportion of economically inactive people, particularly in the late middle-aged population group (Phillipson 1997) and more recently (Blair, 2007) reported that the number of teachers taking early retirement in England had almost doubled in the past seven years, with the majority coming from state secondary schools, as published figures showed. He stated that the number retiring had increased from 5,580 in 1998-99 to 10,270 in 2006. Whereas an elected and planned early retirement can constitute a satisfying and fulfilling life experience, an enforced early retirement can provoke financial hardship, bitterness and a clear perception of a reduction in life's quality. Age Concern (2006), offer a number of factsheets to assist retirees including advice for ongoing activity and mental stimulation plus physical exercise and a healthy diet. As an antidote to inactivity, positive steps are being taken and many organisations are forming, to harness the skills and vigour of retired people to mutually beneficent aims. Perhaps one of the most rapidly growing and successful of these groups is the University of the Third Age (U3A), which celebrated its 25th anniversary in 2007. Whilst local U3A groups retain autonomy, there is now overall management provided by The Third Age Trust whose Annual Report recorded that in March 2006 there were 582 U3A's in the U.K. with 164,443 members (U3A Annual Report, Year ended 31 March 2006). These statistics indicated considerable recent growth from the figures of 2003 when 500 local U3As were recorded with a membership of over 123,000 men and women. The web-site (http://www.u3a.org.uk, accessed 14.11.07) gives full details of opportunities suggesting that the U3As are "self-help, self-managed lifelong learning co-operatives for older people no longer in full time work, providing opportunities for their members to share learning experiences in such fields as art, languages, music, history, life sciences, philosophy, computing, crafts, photography and walking".

In this chapter we have traced the origins and development of links between health and occupational engagement and looked at research that associates quality of life with personal health and physically and mentally stimulating activities. In Chapter 3 we take a closer look at successful ageing and combating vulnerability.

## CHAPTER 3  SUCCESSFUL AGEING

As we grow older we probably all entertain the same wish, that we can do what is necessary to remain healthy and active: we all want to age successfully. In terms of an elderly person's acknowledged need to remain active, there has been a relatively recent change in theoretical emphasis. Early images of elderly people comfortably settled under rugs in rocking chairs, dozing away the hours, have been largely replaced by action shots of the same aged people on golf courses, mountain climbs or enmeshed deep in healthy green houses. Disengagement theory (Cumming and Henry, 1961) advocated that seniors adjusted by gradually losing interest in activities in preparation for death, but there is now increasing evidence that older people prefer continuing engagement in both occupational and educational pursuits. More recent studies indicate that some form of purposeful occupation, remains important to elderly people in all life phases (Lawton 1985, Lamb *et al.* 1988, Glass *et al.* 1999, Lansdown 1994, Farquhar 1995, Rudman *et al.*, 1997). Senior lobbyist groups also support this concept. For example, the Older and Bolder Project Advisory Group (NIACE 1998) produced a powerful response to the British government Green Paper, 'The Learning Age: A Renaissance for a New Britain'. (Command number 3790), concerning access to education. In the response NIACE gave a detailed rationale for ongoing educational support to elderly people. Also cited are examples of the input of seniors into educational projects such as inter-generational learning experiences. Freeman (1997) graphically highlighted her work with seniors and their use of the Internet, quoting one enthusiastic user:

> *I know for a fact SeniorNet and this computer community have*
> *helped many people find a new and better life. For those who*
> *were isolated because of illness or disabilities, it's been a way*
> *to break out of the confinement into a whole new world. We*
> *have been able to fly- and I don't mean in a plane- I mean fly*
> *FREE, without constraints. Being deaf or crippled or blind (yes*
> *even blind- computers can read to the blind what they can't see*
> *on line)- it doesn't matter. We are FREE.*
>
> *(Freeman 1997:44)*

## Successful Ageing

1999 was the International Year of Older Persons and a world-wide message served to inform all that:

> *Ageing is a natural process of life. Older persons are a valuable resource. They are the repositories of tradition, culture, knowledge and skills. These attributes are essential in maintaining intergenerational links.*
>
> *International Federation on Ageing. IFA: Montreal Declaration. 1999*[1]

Natural though the process of ageing may be, declining health can hinder or even prohibit engagement in previously satisfying occupations, so preventative strategies focussed on the retention of current functioning levels become very important.

Although there are frequently expressed connections between "vulnerability" and "old age", suggesting that chronological age influences activity involvement, the association here is neither straightforward nor consistent. We do well to remember research reports such as that of Carlson *et al.* below:

> *In areas such as musical performance, political leadership, and sports, men and women 100 years of age or more have scaled heights, both literally and figuratively... Such stunning degrees of competence and achievement in later life expose the mythological nature of the stereotype of the elderly as being sick, sedentary, sexless and impoverished*
>
> *(Carlson et al.1998:108)*

Spirduso and Gilliam-MacRae (1991) described something of the range of capacity in old age, with the following comment: "Individuals who live to their seventh, eighth, and ninth decade range from those who are in an excellent state of health to those who are in a state of morbidity" (p.233) and Carlson (1998) continued to report "champions" in their field who had been recognised in their ninth or tenth decade. In 1985, Otto Bucher from Switzerland, aged 99 years, became a hole-in-one golfer at 130 yards; and in 1994 a Japanese man, Ichijirou Araya, aged 100 years, climbed to the 12,388 feet summit of Mount Fuji (Carlson *et al.* 1998).

---

[1] IFA: The Montreal Declaration was released September 8, 1999 at the close of the IFA Fourth Global Conference on Ageing in Montreal, Canada, after final consultation with 1200 participants from 68 countries

Bowling and Dieppe (2005) indicated that finding one failsafe approach to defining successful ageing is unrealistic and they offer a succinct overview of the existing models of successful ageing from social, psychological and medical sciences. They also stress the importance of lay views in testing their validity and establishing their relevance to the populations they are applied to. Following their in-depth assessment of models of successful ageing (Bowling and Iliffe, 2006) they present further evidence for a multi-dimensional lay-based model. They suggest this broader perspective has a greater chance of being relevant to elderly people themselves, with the results supporting a generalist approach to health maintenance rather than a narrow focus on medical, social or psychological fields.

Ageing successfully implies the avoidance of succumbing to vulnerabilities. Whilst eligibility to draw old age pensions in most European countries is normally reached by a 65th birthday, a person becomes neither "old" nor "vulnerable" at this time. A complex process, ageing "reflects the interaction between our genetic inheritance and environmental and lifestyle factors" (Khaw 1997). It is known that adaptive responses to stress are lost as bodily functions progressively decline. At this point there is a growing risk of chronic disease and we become increasingly likely to die. Grimley Evans (2002) commented on the ongoing lack of productive research on the mechanisms of ageing and on age-associated disease and disability in the United Kingdom. He suggested that services are "still driven more by theory than certainty" (p.93). Life expectancy is one of the ways in which the ageing process is monitored. Cunningham and Brookbank (1988) reported maximum lifespans for species; 13 years for a rabbit and 113 years for a human, asserting that this maximum human lifespan has remained constant for the past 30,000 years. More recently however, Kirkwood (2001) proposed new evidence that the human lifespan has increased, when he reported Jean Calman's death at a reliably documented age of 122 years 5 months.

A number of researchers suggest that whilst maximum lifespan is probably genetically determined, judicious adjustment to lifestyle and environment can prevent, or at least postpone, a substantial number of age-related chronic diseases and the accompanying escalating vulnerability. There are now many illustrations of this point. For instance in just ten years the USA experienced a fall of 33% in stroke and a 24% decrease in coronary heart disease (Khaw 1997). In examining changing patterns of life-threatening conditions, we can learn much from studies of immigrant populations. There is a suggestion here that environmental factors are more important than genetic factors. To return to Khaw's (1997) discussion; she cited two examples. Members of the Luo tribe of rural Kenya only showed rising blood pressure with age if they moved to the city of Nairobi. Secondly, Japanese people living in Japan generally have low blood cholesterol levels, whereas any Japanese members in the US army, consuming an American diet, had high cholesterol levels that resembled European army recruits. Because nutrition is now known to play a large part in promoting health, the European Investigation into Cancer and Nutrition (EPIC study) (Riboli and Kaaks, 1997) is examining complex links between diet and health. Researchers from nine European countries are monitoring the long-term health and lifestyle of 400,000 healthy middle-aged men and women volunteers. There is ongoing publication of results for example Pischon *et al.* (2006) who reported strong associations between waist circumference and waist-to-hip ratio (WHR), both indicators of obesity, with colon cancer risk. Boeing *et al.* (2006) conducted research in response to epidemiologic studies suggesting that a high intake of fruits and vegetables is associated with decreased risk of certain cancers. They studied data from 345,904 subjects recruited in seven European countries, who had completed a dietary questionnaire in 1992-1998 and concluded that dietary recommendations should consider the potential benefit of increasing fruits and vegetables consumption for reducing the risk of cancers of the upper aero-digestive tract.

Looking again at environmental influences, Tout (1992) reported other accounts of retained capabilities into advanced old age. Although the exact details of ages may not be as extreme as originally reported, and lifestyles have changed with the increase in tourism, it is still accepted that in South America's Vilcabamba, the valley where "the golden tablets of cholesterol wisdom" were discovered, people tend to live a long time. Honigsbaum (2003) reported a more recent investigative visit when he talked with the locals and found many who were active, fit and mentally acute, well into their eighth and ninth decades, attesting that healthy vegetable diets and ongoing opportunities for work such as tending vegetable patches, were important influences. Tout contrasted this environmental influence with that of the nearby South American city of Potosi where life is "cheap and brief". Here the locus of control has experienced a shift from internal choice to external demand (Baltes and Baltes 1986). In Potosi where male mine workers live in barren blizzard-swept deserts at 15,000 feet, Tout reported malnutrition and multiple industrial diseases were common and by forty years of age, the mine workers were likely to present as "burned out cases", physiologically aged and unable to continue with their daily tasks.

Supportive environments are now widely recognized for their positive contributions to successful ageing. For many older people the ability to remain "at home", with or without support, is a personal ambition; it indicates an ongoing independence and well-being. (Green, Sixsmith J, Ivanoff, Sixsmith A , 2005). There has also been considerable recent interest, both in Europe and in America, in developing specialist environments for retirees. One such scheme reported: "Residents not only lived longer than expected, but achieved a quality of life far exceeding that experienced by residents in traditional homes" (Extracare Charitable Trust 1997). Further environmental studies (Bultena and

Wood 1969, Lucksinger 1994, Kingston *et al.* 2001) support the stance of retirement communities, where there is peer support, safety, stimulation to retain healthy lifestyles and as Kingston *et al.* suggest: "autonomy with inclusion" (p.228). A UK government publication in 2008 is rising to the challenge of meeting an increasing market for housing which meets the needs and interests of older people and has published the Lifetime Homes, Lifetime Neighbourhoods: A National Strategy for Housing in an Ageing Society (2008). This is a bold 176 page document, with the Prime Minister's introduction stating (page 8) "I want to see all new housing built to Lifetime Homes Standards by 2013 – accessible and adaptable homes in thriving neighbourhoods".

Turning to a psychological perspective; age-related vulnerability is again unpredictable. Traditionally, Erikson (1950) had proposed that in the eighth and final life stage, there was a struggle for integrity over despair. His last published work (Erikson *et al.* 1986), reflected his increasing sensitivity to the plight of contemporary elders in industrialised nations, where society tended to marginalise them. He also strongly supported interdependency amongst age-groups, particularly between elders and children. However, there are recent researchers who suggest that Erikson's work, with its neo-Freudian basis, is limited, because human will is not addressed. Erikson never questioned that people were born with an *a priori* set of instinctual concerns. Human struggles were predetermined and took place within a cultural context, but were not provoked by social or cultural factors. Abell (1998) suggested that Erikson's work does little to address the plight of an elderly person who has "fallen into despair and disgust, and who must live in our present culture, bereft of a social milieu that is sensitive to his or her developmental needs" (p.88). Abell put forward the work of Kohut (1977) as a supplement, that in its support of transferential needs, offered a more positive guide to professionals who are working to foster the emotional well-being of their elderly clients. By way of illustration, Abell recounted the case of an elderly retired professor of anthropology who presented with a "clear case of Eriksonian disgust". He had multiple medical problems, compounded by a long-standing frustration that his earlier anthropological research findings had never been fully recognised. During more than a year's individual psychotherapy counselling, a rapport developed in which a young male therapist displayed interest and, himself an academic, a genuine empathy with his client's struggles. Noticeable improvement in both physical and mental health was recorded. Abbell concluded that by integrating central ideas from both Erikson and Kohut, gerontologists are supplied with "a useful model of how to assist the elderly individual in crisis" (p.96).

Psychological theories about later life have given rise to diverse applications in work being conducted with elderly people. On an informal level, it is recognised that social isolation, with consequent loneliness and lowering of mood, occurs commonly as old friends die and new friendships become difficult to cultivate.

Recognising how important it is to prevent social isolation, many projects such as lunch clubs have been initiated. The benefits of mixed ages meeting together are also recognised and inter-generational projects are successfully being implemented in many countries. One rapidly expanding organisation which hosts a number of pioneering intergenerational initiatives is 'On Lok Senior Health Services', based in San Francisco's Chinatown. Their newsletters contain regular accounts of the benefits of intergenerational exchange, as for example (*On Lok News*, 1999) which described the powerful two-way benefits to a group of kindergarten children and a frail older On Lok participant, that were realised over a six year period until and after the death of the participant. On good days they shared ice cream parlour trips, and at other times the children paid hospital visits to take flowers, sing songs and generally convey a sense of caring and friendship.

In addition to inter-generational projects, and on a more formal level, the use of resolution and validation therapy has appeared to be a beneficial approach in working with frail elderly people (Feil 1993). Validation therapy is based on the recognition of the need for individuals in later life to move on beyond feelings of frustration, or perhaps missed opportunities, and to achieve personal acceptance and contentment with a life well-lived. Feil (1993) gives case study examples which indicate how validation therapy is helpful in reaching patients with dementia, and how it is calming and can dramatically improve wandering, agitation and withdrawal. There is however, minimal published research on validation therapy beyond the work of Feil. Cochrane Review (2001) was only able to examine two studies, from which they deduced: "There is insufficient evidence from randomised trials to make any conclusions about the efficacy of validation therapy for people with dementia or cognitive impairment, although observational studies suggest there may be some positive effects".

Reality orientation (RO) was popular as an intervention strategy for people with dementia, during the 1960's and 1970's, being used in an effort to combat or slow cognitive decline. However, by the late 1980's RO had become unpopular (Dietch *et al.* 1989), and was seen as counter-productive. With its potential for misuse it could become a demeaning and confrontational experience. More recently RO has made a comeback with results such as those described by Zanetti *et al.* (2002). They reported from their study of 38 mild to moderately-demented out-patients, that there was some evidence that RO has benefits on both cognition and behaviour in people with Alzheimer's Disease. Woods (2002) however reserved some scepticism in relation to the title of RO, because of previous connotations, and suggested that a new name such as cognitive stimulation may now be preferable.

Although vulnerability arising from cognitive decline in old age, is unpredictable in its onset, it is estimated that the prevalence of dementia increases with age and that it reaches 20% in people aged over 85 years (Gray and Fenn 1993).

Dementia UK (2007) suggested that at this time the number of people with dementia totalled 683,597 in the UK alone, of which only 15,034 were aged under 65 years. It is generally accepted too that with early diagnosis of dementia being uncommon, these numbers may be fairly conservative estimates, although the new National Dementia Strategy: *Living well with dementia* (D.O.H.2009) proposes to redress this. This strategy addresses three key themes - raising awareness, early diagnosis and intervention and improving the quality of care. This new strategy, together with a general heightened emphasis on methods which support mental health throughout the lifespan (Ilott 2008) bode well for future generations.

Whilst successful ageing with ongoing activity involvement is supported for all people in later life and enjoyed by many, the likelihood of "vulnerability" clearly does increase with advanced old age. This is an issue both for the individual and for any services aiming to meet the needs of elderly clients. In America we hear that people over 75 years of age tend to consume "disproportionate amounts of health and long term care services"(US Bureau of the Census 1999), whilst in the United Kingdom we read of increased dependency and escalating health-related costs for the over 75's (National Statistics 2001b). People in their eighth and ninth decade experience a marked increase in degenerative diseases such as arthritis, plus declining eyesight (cataract) and heart conditions. Whilst management and treatment techniques continue to develop to alleviate such conditions, resources and availability are finite. Should older people require hospitalisation, then as Carpenter *et al.* (2002) comment, older patients are at high risk of hospital-acquired deterioration, then when they need extended hospital stays they are stigmatised as "bed blockers, as they play havoc with length of stay figures" (p.97). Consequently some very elderly people feel marginalised as they struggle to cope and endure lengthy periods on health service waiting lists. Lawton *et al.*'s (1990) multi-dimensional study of the last year of life is informative in its presentation of how vulnerability becomes life-threatening frailty. In Philadelphia the researchers conducted interviews with 200 surviving relatives of recently deceased older people, in an aim to reconstruct a picture of the quality for a group who spent most of their final year in the community, rather than in an institution. Although quality of life decreased with increasing vulnerability and the onset of frailty, a stimulating, known community environment, enabled interest and hope to be sustained.

In the previous chapter we reviewed literature which highlights how occupational engagement can contribute to successful ageing. It is worth remembering that occupation can also be used as a means to regain lost skills, and as it were regain a foothold on the ladder of ageing well. Link (1996) for example described her work with elderly people with neuromuscular dysfunction. She outlined an interim phase of treatment that involved range of motion exercises using imagery. For example, whilst doing bilateral exercises a group of patients may be asked to imagine they are casting fishing lines or stirring a cooking pot. When one patient was asked what she was stirring, her response was: "a big bowl of chilli and boy is it thick!" Link noted the many added values of such group sessions, including reminiscence, cognitive stimulation, healthy competition overriding boredom with repetitive exercises ("if she can do it, so can I") and the pure enjoyment in occupationally related tasks.

As we have seen in this chapter, there is no accurate way of determining how to age successfully, nor of depicting when vulnerability becomes life-threatening, or quality of life is diminished to unacceptable levels. We have seen though that there are measures which can be taken to increase the likelihood of the most positive outcomes. Health can be positively encouraged through diet and exercise, and we have evidence that physical and mental stimulation promotes ongoing cognitive well-being. Occupations that involve an element of socialising, perhaps within mixed age groups, are recognised as beneficial, as are supportive environments.

Having reported what we do know about successful ageing and links with occupational engagement, much still remains unknown. Moss and Lawton's (1982) publication described an earlier attempt to shed light on how a group of 535 urban elders spent their days. Using the yesterday interview, the study attempted to explore "meaningfulness" of activities, but found this concept was poorly understood and resorted to the use of "liking" instead. Of the four environmental groups that comprised the sample, the independent living groups expressed liking for a greater range of activities, whilst the more novel activities were equally enjoyed by the individuals in supported environmental groups. The study however gives no detail of the actual activities beyond a simple classification of obligatory and discretionary activities such as social interaction and recreation. Some time later Horgas, Wilms and Baltes (1998) suggested that our knowledge on the topic of how elderly people spend their time remained scant. Their study in Berlin described activity profiles of 516 subjects with a mean age of 84.9 years. In days that averaged 16 hours, basic personal maintenance tasks occurred the most frequently, and most time (17%) was spent watching television. Resting time generally increased with age and with residential home occupancy, whilst couples were found to spend less time in resting and to spend more time in leisure pursuits such as television watching. Whilst this study presented facts about elders and time use, it made no attempt to penetrate the range of occupations engaged in, nor the level of satisfaction that arose from participation. Similarly, these details are again lacking in a more recent study. Bennett (2002), studying social engagement, reported that a low level of social involvement was directly related to mortality. Although detailed measurements were taken over a four year period with the elderly subjects, there was no report of what constituted 'satisfactory social engagement' for the subjects.

At this point then it is time to move forward. The next chapter gives details of the measures used to expand our body of research on the topic of how occupational engagement may contribute to quality in later life.

## CHAPTER 4  USING SCIENTIFIC METHODS TO FIND OUT MORE

*We saw in Chapter 3 that research into successful ageing and its links with occupation and a retained quality of life remains limited. This final chapter of Part 1 therefore now introduces the methods that were recently successfully used to explore the subject in greater depth and reports the results that were obtained. The chapter concludes by showing how the various sources of information were drawn together to provide a full picture as illustrated in the case studies of Part 2.*

## Taking a phenomenological approach

### *What is this and why is it necessary?*

As we have seen in the previous chapter quantitative research approaches have already been used successfully to gather lists of activities and amounts of time on task in relation to elderly peoples' daily lives, but if we want to investigate more deeply and to study the underlying meaning of selected occupations for older community-dwellers, a **qualitative approach** is necessary. Another factor guiding the choice of research approach is the important inclusion of **participant experience.** Although there are several qualitative methodologies that place the subject central-stage and as Denzin and Lincoln (1994) go on to discuss, "qualitative research, as a set of interpretive practices, privileges no single methodology over any other"(p.3) a phenomenological approach is particularly useful here because it offers specific opportunities to study the experiences of daily occupation. Phenomenology holds no intent to search for a single truth, nor does it aim to formulate new theory; rather as each subject is placed centre-stage, multiple realities are recognised and all ensuing findings, however deviant, are valued. At the same time Phenomenological theory also highlights the central role of the epoche (Creswell 1998, p.54). Here the researcher must bracket his/her own ideas about the phenomenon, setting them aside in order to reach understanding through the voices of the subjects.

In critiquing the phenomenological approach and its relevance to health care professionals, and to occupational therapists in particular, attention is drawn to an increased interest over the past two decades. One of the first reported studies, involving occupational therapists was conducted by Mattingly and Fleming (1994). It highlighted that occupational therapists generally used a phenomenological way of thinking in an attempt to understand their clients' aspirations, frequently using both empathy and improvisation as they pictured clients at various points in time. A further study which explored the development of clinical reasoning also highlighted the relevance of a phenomenological approach. The study by McKay and Ryan (1995) described the difference in thinking between a novice and an expert practitioner. They used story telling to explore accounts and revealed that the novice tended to be rule-bound and focussed on an immediate solution, whilst the expert was more able to form a total picture of the client whilst making a more rapid and accurate assessment. A similar approach has proved helpful in probing other complex areas of practice and client meaning. Kirsh (1996) addressed spirituality in her paper using a case study of a 29 year old man with a 10 year history of involvement with the mental health system. She demonstrated how a narrative approach enabled the client to regain understanding of meaning and purpose in his life. Kirsh reminded us of some general issues that promote a research affinity between phenomenology and occupational therapy, namely that occupational therapists are generally highly skilled in eliciting historical and contextual information about a person's life; that facilitating the client to narrate his/her own story places the client in a central position and empowers personal control. Such an approach then is consistent with the core professional beliefs in holism and client-centred practice, and it naturally includes the wider issues concerning interaction of the person with the environment. As Sixsmith and Sixsmith (1987) suggest: "within phenomenology, it is invalid to pursue the traditional subject-object dualism which separates the 'external' physical world from the 'internal' mental world (p.315). Co-constitution of the objective and subjective world is present.

A further study merits attention. Halling, Kunz and Rowe (1994) wrote of their development of the use of reflective conversation as a means of conducting phenomenological research with their psychology students at Seattle University. Student feedback over seven years indicated the success of this method with suggestions that as was intended, the programme is humanistic. Through in-depth reflection, it deepened the appreciation for the human condition. It was existential-phenomenological because it developed openness rather than a pre-judgemental attitude towards psychological realities, and it was therapeutic in its focus on psychological conditions which helped people deal with life's difficulties. They described the approach as a meditative one, involving patience and deep contemplation; consequently the phenomenological researcher is one who is in "no great hurry". In abandoning preconceptions too and in an attempt to enter a client's world the researcher aims:

> *not to deny truth but to understand it with a fresh approach. It*
> *calls us to pay attention to our experience in an attitude of*
> *wonder*

> *Halling, Kunz and Rowe 1994: 116.*

### *Phenomenological method: how to do it*

In implementing a phenomenological approach, the process is lengthy and cannot be hurried or simplified. Finlay (1999) discussed some of the strengths and problems in conducting phenomenological research. An occupational therapist herself, she outlined the importance of conducting research which is compatible with the profession's organismic and humanistic philosophy, hence the popularity of a phenomenological approach. She then moved on to the area of confusion that surrounds implementation and suggested that health care researchers were embracing the phenomenological methodology without sufficient familiarity, then implementing it in several contradictory ways. She cited the five year history of vociferous debates in nursing journals, as a case in point. Some of the initial difficulty, Finlay suggested, was that the early phenomenologists were largely theorists and philosophers who provided little practical advice about how to apply the weighty philosophical ideas. To assist, Finlay provided some guidance in the form of three principles, plus ten individual then eight general phases for the conduct of phenomenological method. They are reported in detail here because the same steps guided the information gathering process which yielded the case studies in chapters 5 to 7.

The three principles are discovery orientation, with methods arising from, and being responsive to the data, and the need for continuous reflexive analysis. The first stage of analysis is focussed on the individual and Finlay adapted her points from those published by Wertz in 1983. Initially the researcher aims to empathise, through immersion in the data. Units or phrases of meaning are discovered and these are studied over time, but no attempt is made to move into premature analysis. The experiential data receive intense scrutiny and probing, particularly where sections appear to hold significant meaning. The researcher then steps back, reflects on the experiences and begins to make links between the various topics as raised in the stories, studying the context and the subject's feelings at the time. Reflection and deep probing continues as existential dimensions such as identity, spatiality and temporality are explored. It is only at this stage that the individual analysis is put into words; names are put to themes and phrases as the researcher uses own words to capture the life world of the subject. Testing and reformulating is necessary with constant return being made to original descriptions to try to stay true to the phenomenon (subject). Themes are modified accordingly, neat packaging is avoided and instead incomplete or contradictory data are prized.

Once all the data have been analysed in terms of the individuals, the researcher turns to study the narratives from all the subjects and to make comparisons across the board. Finlay again adapts her points from the earlier work of Wertz in the following manner. A search is made for general insights: critical consideration is given to the features of individual analyses that might give rise to a general truth. The individual analyses are compared to establish commonalities and differences. The researcher challenges the claims of universality, and begins to establish a hierarchy of individual versus general themes. As essential themes are established, both general truths and individual differences are put into words. Testing and reformulating occurs and themes are modified as necessary. In the final stage the researcher aims to express the findings by using language which brings to life the "flavour of the phenomenological experience" (Finlay 1999:304).

In her account of the process, Finlay clearly outlined that phenomenological analysis demands a systematic but creative approach and like Halling, Kunz and Rowe (1994) she again stressed that deep reflection needs time, and that in the absence of this rigour, the resulting analysis may be superficial and may simply contain the researcher's own predetermined categories.

Bearing in mind the complexity of implementing a phenomenological approach, the use of multiple data collection strategies, as advocated by Massey (1995), is helpful. Next follows a selection of research methods, each designed to give information about the meaning of occupational engagement. Together, they present a full tool-kit, enabling any investigator to gain a full picture of all major relevant issues. As you read through them you will understand the part each method plays in creating a "whole" composite picture of a complex phenomenon.

## Method 1:   The Yesterday Interview

It was Moss and Lawton (1982) who suggested that in asking for immediate recall, a researcher is likely to acquire accuracy in terms of recent events; this is how the Yesterday Interview was born.

Moss and Lawton (1982) reported their use of a detailed record, given by a sample group of 535 urban elderly people, each person outlining the exact detail of activities undertaken during the previous day. This study yielded a meticulous record of exactly how much time had been spent in participating in one of a range of activities, also the amount of liking for each activity and quantitative outcomes were obtained. However as mentioned previously, Moss and Lawton's study gives little detail of the actual activities beyond a simple classification of obligatory and discretionary activities such as social interaction and recreation.

For the purpose of the collecting the case studies reported in Part 2, the practice of recalling yesterday's activities was used, but instead of asking for amounts of time spent on tasks, the respondents were encouraged to describe their "yesterday" from start to finish, to recall their feelings in undertaking specific activities, and to relay details of the experiences, together with the context in which they were undertaken. In this way it was possible to probe the meaning of occupational engagement to each individual, with accuracy facilitated by the immediacy of the recall. In retrospect it was the yesterday interview which yielded the major amount of data for phenomenological analysis of occupational meaning to the people involved.

## Method 2: The Nottingham Longitudinal Study of Activity and Ageing (NLSAA) Instrument

In most studies it is necessary to collect some basic background information. There is nothing worse than having a set of beautifully transcribed tapes, full of dense information about a set of participants, and discovering you omitted to ask the ages or other essential information about some of them!

In this case it was clear that it was necessary to gather a small set of general biographical information for each subject. The Nottingham Longitudinal Study of Activity and Ageing (NLSAA) (Morgan, 1998) was a large scale study of 1042 subjects with reported reliability of the data collection instruments. The subject population in Morgan's study was comparable in age with the intended sample for the current proposed study. Therefore for standardisation purposes, at the opening of the initial interview, basic demographic and mobility data headings was used as per the NLSAA.

## Method 3:    The Short Form Health Survey (SF-36) to examine health status

We realise that occupational potential may be limited, but not always as we shall see later, by the physical and mental health of an individual. Therefore in any study of occupational involvement it is necessary to ask for some basic details about overall health. A standardised and time-efficient method here is the use of the SF-36. The full title is The Moss 36-item short-form health survey (SF-36).

The SF36 survey (Ware and Sherbourne 1992; Jenkinson et al. 1996) was investigated for its relevance to the study in hand, in particular to act as a standardised health measure which would support the completely open data to be obtained from the yesterday interview above. It was anticipated that the SF36 might act as a screening device to assess initial similarities between subjects and to address issues such as age range, emotional limitations, vulnerability or physical frailty levels. Additionally, as health and perceived quality of life are so frequently linked, it was anticipated that the completed SF 36 would facilitate a deeper study of issues linking health and occupational engagement.

Even when a seemingly appropriate research method has been located, it is always necessary to assess its suitability for the current client group and present circumstances. Here, although there was recent debate concerning the suitability of the SF 36 in assessing health status in some elderly populations (Hayes et al. 1995; Mahony et al. 1998; Parker et al. 1998), it was found suitable in use with elderly clients and to be at its most reliable when interviewer administered and when used with ambulant non in-patients. The justification for using the SF36 in this instance was:

- The SF-36 has undergone evaluation and validation in a variety of populations. It is a recognised and standardised assessment.
- The SF36 will be used in circumstances that have previously yielded reliable data.
- It will act as a reliable screening measure and will facilitate comparison of objective feelings of health and wellness with subjective accounts of occupational engagement.

Permission to use the SF36 standardised assessment for the purposes of the current study must be sought and granted[2]. Intending researchers need to bear in mind that this is an essential ethical requisite, and they must allow time for any request to be processed.

## Method 4:    Use of the Multiple sorting task (MST)

The MST has been found to be a useful methodological tool amongst social scientists working in the area of empirical phenomenology. Sixsmith and Sixsmith (1987) provide full details of this method, and then illustrate how the "inner perceptions" of phenomenology can be harnessed via the MST to provide an objective and empirical result. They suggest such "hardening" of the phenomenological approach renders it scientifically more rigorous. They remind us too that earlier philosophers indicated a need for this; for instance Husserl (1950) suggested that the phenomenological method should be both empirical and scientific and generalisable across situations. The MST therefore suggests itself as an appropriate additional tool in investigating the current topic as it may facilitate a structured exploration of the described occupations.

---

[2] SF36 permission to use for the purpose of this study; obtained from the Medical Outcomes Trust, 20 Park Plaza, Suite 1014, Boston, MA 02116-4314. June 2000.

In practice the MST was used as follows:

- Occupational categories were identified from the original interview data, then listed on individual cards and returned to the people concerned for the purpose of member checking and for the individual's involvement in sorting and developing the categories to enhance individual meaning.
- Individuals were able to choose their own criteria for sorting purposes, with "preferences" and "frequency" being held as researcher suggestions, to be used when the subject asked for help with criteria selection.
- It was the intention that the process could be beneficial to both researcher and subject, as the latter could reflect on action as a precursor to making positive change, for example when a preferred occupation was no longer enjoyed due to current poor health.

## Method 5:    Using Visual Analogue Scales (VAS)

Researchers have noted how difficult it is to obtain data about abstract qualities such as quality of life. Moss and Lawton (1982) recorded that their research team had to compromise; part of their study attempted to explore "meaningfulness" of activities, but they found this concept was poorly understood and they resorted to the use of "liking" instead. Tiplady et al. 1998 reported that VAS were valid in assessing subjective states like these, with young and older subjects. In particular Tiplady's study discovered that educational duration and qualification did not affect the outcome and VAS scoring; this was seen as relevant to the current study where it was known that the oldest subjects may well have left formal education at the age of fourteen years. VAS have previously been used by me (Green 1998) and they were found manageable and acceptable to elderly people as a means of recording the abstract concept of quality of life. This time the VAS were designed to be interviewer administered in order to collect each interviewee's perception of current quality of life status, and the personal amount of satisfaction with the present level of occupation. So two visual analogue scales formed a subsection of each respondent's data.

## Method 6:    Taking account of potential economic influences

Although there is no direct relationship between an older person's wealth and their activity patterns, it is accepted that absolute extremes generally hold true. So, the scope and potential for wide-ranging occupational pursuits is much easier when funds are plentiful; alternatively, when money is short, a great deal of ingenuity may be needed in order to establish a varied programme of occupational pursuits.

In exploring this area, the use of Geodemographic typology (GT) can be helpful. GT recognizes that an additional major determinant as to how elders may choose to spend their time may well rest in the broad field of the individual's socio-economic past and present. Geodemography, and in particular the construct of super-profiles. (Batey and Brown, 1995. Brown et al. 1998). Batey and Brown (1995) describe the field of geodemographics as having a background in urban research where urban planners have used small area classification systems to check on main sources of social and economic variation within cities, with a prime aim of developing a consistent and systematic approach to resource allocation. By the late 1980s, in the U.K. a complex system of super-profiles had been developed into a recognised and accepted general-purpose classification system. Work has progressed and a recent version of the Super Profiles typology is based upon information derived from the 1991 Census. It has thus become possible to link all postal codes within the UK with a defined typology. The typology features three levels of description for each postal area. Firstly there is a very detailed 160 Super Profile cluster level, then an intermediate 40 Target Market level, then a much broader level of description at which 10 lifestyles are distinguished (Brown et al. 1998). The use of the ten super profile lifestyles has assisted planning teams, including those of the NHS, in various parts of the U.K. Local databases exist and with the use of these it is possible to identify lifestyle profiles for participants in U.K. studies where accurate post codes are available. Giving a brief flavour of these profiles, the descriptors below represent the people of the case studies to follow in chapters 4 and 5.

**Lifestyle descriptors** (Super Profile Lifestyle Pen Pictures, CDMS Limited 1994)

**Lifestyle A-** Affluent Achievers: high income families with a lifestyle to match. Sophisticated tastes and aspirations.

**Lifestyle B-** Thriving Greys: older than affluent achievers, possibly taken early retirement. Prosperity is retained, there is money for luxuries.

**Lifestyle C-** Settled Suburbans: well established, white collar and middle management, fairly affluent lifestyles.

**Lifestyle D-** Nest Builders: middle management, white collar workers, little money for luxury purposes, tend to socialise at home.

**Life style G-** Senior Citizens: elderly group, living in small, possibly sheltered accommodation. High proportion of lone single female pensioners. Prefer to shop at convenience stores in own neighbourhoods, passive recreations such as television.

**Lifestyle J-** "Have Nots": cramped flats, underprivileged, low qualifications, on income support, television is a major recreation, with high take up of satellite and cable TV, betting is popular.

Readers will note that these are very "broad" pen pictures, and may immediately feel accuracy is limited in these circumstances. However, such a tool remains a valuable additional instrument when exploring complex topics with multiple cause and effect constituents.

## Recording the findings

Now we shall look at the data that were recorded, using above methods 2,3,5 and 6. (methods 1 and 4 lead directly into the case study findings reported later). The participants who took part in the study are introduced, each is provided with a pseudonym and background information is presented, to portray the characteristics of the group. Purposive sampling (Coyne 1997) was used and inclusion criteria for the study established that all the participants lived alone and in the community; that one third should be active in the community, one third in need of some community support and that one third should be mainly or entirely homebound. The standardised test results from above methods provide an accurate picture of each individual's level of functioning which in turn is helpful when studying the major factors that may influence the achievement of a satisfying occupational day.

### Table 1.1  The study participants

| Pseudonym | Age/ years | Sex | Marital status | Present living environment |
|---|---|---|---|---|
| Ann | 75 | F. | widow | house |
| Beatrice | 90 | F. | widow | house |
| Cath | 77 | F. | widow | house |
| Doris | 76 | F. | single | house |
| Edith | 88 | F. | widow | bungalow |
| Fay | 83 | F. | widow | house |
| Gladys | 83 | F. | widow | house |
| Horace | 77 | M. | widower | house |
| Ian | 85 | M. | widower | house |
| Joyce | 98 | F. | widow | bungalow |
| Karl | 91 | M. | widower | house |
| Lucy | 85 | F. | widow | apartment |

**Ann** is an active member of her community, but two recent falls have caused her to question whether she can continue her regular sporting commitments and membership of the ramblers club.

**Beatrice** has lived in the same house for 45 years. She is independent but now rarely goes out and she is bothered by her increasing forgetfulness.

**Cath** likes her active pursuits and walks and visits a local gym regularly. Recent knee surgery reminded her that she may not always be able to be as active as her current activities dictate.

**Doris** continues to enjoy her once a week voluntary work. In-between times she attests to be lonely and restless. She would like to do more walking but does not like group excursions and is afraid to walk in the countryside alone.

**Edith** is a very creative woman, for whom there are never enough hours in the day. Fiercely independent; she gardens, cooks, paints and sews. Knowing that others do not share her creative passions, she worries about what will happen to her many artefacts when she dies.

**Fay** is profoundly deaf and has a lot of pain from arthritis. She cannot walk far, but thoroughly enjoys her weekly swim with the local disabled group.

**Gladys** has pain and health problems and is limited in what she can do. She lives on the ground floor of her large house and enjoys the support and companionship of local Age Concern activities.

**Horace** has lived alone since his wife died ten years ago. He rides his bike to the shops and enjoys helping with a local youth group. Just recently he has tired very quickly and has been hospitalised for investigations

**Ian** was his wife's carer until she died a year ago; he misses her a great deal. Ian has much pain and stiffness in many of his joints due to arthritis. He goes out briefly twice a week, otherwise he watches television.

**Joyce** is housebound but has many visitors. Her sight is very poor and her balance is not good. She enjoys singing and being a raconteur.

**Karl** has always been an active man, with many local interests. Just recently his balance has become precarious and he now feels unable to leave the house alone.

**Lucy** is trying to come to terms with deteriorating eyesight. She is now unable to read or pursue any of her former handicraft hobbies. She has chosen shortly to leave her own home and move into residential accommodation.

## Results: Nottingham longitudinal study of activity and ageing Instrument (NLSAA)

In addition to facts portrayed in **Table 1.1,** the following additional information was gleaned. The average period of living after the death of a spouse was twelve years, with three people having outlived their spouse by periods in excess of twenty years. In keeping with a normal gender disparity, females were noted to have the four longest periods of widow-hood. Females also registered the higher mean period of widow-hood, of thirteen years compared with a mean of eight years for the males.

In exploring the family compositions, as no participants had surviving parents, immediate relatives were taken to include children plus brothers and sisters. Within these parameters the participants recorded a range of family members from 0 to 4. Three participants had no living immediate relatives. The geographic distribution of relatives was wide, with four people reporting relatives who lived in Canada or the USA, and three participants with relatives in the UK but in excess of 100 miles away. Seven people had relatives living within ten miles; of these seven, four reported that they saw at least one family member at least once per week.

The NLSAA Instrument also records basic personal mobility levels. Of the twelve participants, **five** reported themselves as fully ambulant. Of these five people one took a regular 6-7 mile ramble most weeks, three walked 2-3 miles most days and one walked up to half a mile several times a week. None of these five people used any walking aids, although one said she had a stick for use on uneven ground. There were two car owners and drivers within the fully ambulant group plus one person who regularly rode a bike. **Four** participants reported themselves as slowly ambulant. All of this group used a stick out of doors, walking was limited to between 25 and 100 yards, and most of these people used taxis or a local special bus for independent transport to shops. **Three** participants reported themselves as mobile only within their own homes. Two of the three were able to make short trips out of doors if they used a stick and were escorted by one person. One of the people used a zimmer walking frame and was housebound. She stated that she had last been out three months previously when a therapist had collected her in a specially adapted bus.

In terms of housing, ten participants had lived in their present house for more than twenty years, including three people who had occupied their present house for more than forty years. The maximum period of residence was 59 years. The houses occupied by the participant group comprised both twentieth century semi-detached and terraced residences and large older Victorian style properties, plus two bungalows. Of the two people who had made more recent moves, one had moved eleven years before into a council-owned bungalow with a warden in the neighbourhood, and one person moved 9 years before into a ground floor Housing Association apartment with a warden.

As part of the NLSAA data collection process, occupations of the participants were requested. Eleven people had been fully retired for periods of time between fifteen and thirty-seven years. One person continued to work one or two days per month in an office. Of the three male participants, two were retired from manual work, brick-laying and polishing at a shipyard, and the third was a retired insurance agent and magistrate. Of the nine female participants, eight had worked both before and during their marriages, the ninth reported brief periods of work before she became the 'hands' for her husband as he was disabled. The female occupations included: in-service, waitress and cook (2), wages clerk and comptometer operator, a member of the Women's land army, a maths teacher and the manager of boarding kennels.

## Results:    Short Form Health Survey (SF36)

This second standardised test yielded a complete set of health-related data for each of the twelve participants. In **Table 1.2**, with headings as per the standardised test, a score of 100 equates with maximum health in any particular field.

### Table 1.2 SF36 results for study participants

| Pseudonym | Physical Function | Social function | Mental health | Energy /vitality | Pain | Physical limitations | Emotional limitations |
|-----------|-------------------|-----------------|---------------|------------------|------|----------------------|-----------------------|
| Ann      | 95 | 100  | 88 | 80 | 77.8 | 100 | 100  |
| Beatrice | 75 | 100  | 48 | 55 | 77.8 | 50  | 66.7 |
| Cath     | 70 | 100  | 60 | 25 | 77.8 | 100 | 100  |
| Doris    | 80 | 100  | 44 | 50 | 33.3 | 100 | 100  |
| Edith    | 85 | 88.9 | 92 | 70 | 55.6 | 75  | 100  |
| Fay      | 20 | 55.5 | 64 | 45 | 22.2 | 25  | 33.3 |
| Gladys   | 45 | 100  | 88 | 40 | 33.3 | 25  | 66.7 |
| Horace   | 95 | 100  | 64 | 75 | 88.8 | 50  | 66.7 |
| Ian      | 10 | 44.4 | 52 | 30 | 22.2 | 50  | 0    |
| Joyce    | 0  | 33.3 | 90 | 30 | 55.6 | 50  | 100  |
| Karl     | 20 | 55.6 | 88 | 70 | 100  | 75  | 100  |
| Lucy     | 10 | 11.1 | 36 | 30 | 55.6 | 25  | 0    |

As may be expected from the research selection criteria, none of the participants was completely healthy in all domains. All participants to a greater or lesser extent had a degree of physical incapacity, although three people did not feel that this limited their selected activity roles. All participants also had a degree of mental incapacity, although this was only below the 50% level for one person who had been subject to clinical depression for many years. Interestingly, six participants still managed to score 100% (i.e. no emotional limitations) for their capacity to cope emotionally, despite the degree of mental and physical impairment.

In further examining the above scores, there is great diversity in all areas. It is of particular interest to note that despite some considerable degrees of physical or mental incapacity, half of the participants scored full marks for social functioning. The category with a uniformly lower level of scores was that of energy levels and vitality, the highest score here being 80% and this was reported by Ann, who at 75years of age, was the group's youngest study participant. The nonagenarians Beatrice, Joyce and Karl, did not however exhibit a commensurate very low level of vitality. Pain is clearly a predictor of limitations, as is expected, with Fay and Ian both recording a high level of day to day pain and both reporting low levels of physical functioning, although it is of interest that Ian had appeared to compensate to a level where he could fulfil an acceptable proportion (50%) of his day-to-day physical roles. The eldest participant, Joyce, with 0% for physical function, scored highly in the area of mental health and the SF36 recorded her as having no emotional limitations.

## Results:     Visual analogue scales (VAS)

As detailed in the above methods, at the close of the first interview each participant, was asked to mark two visual analogue scales, recording the level of their feelings "today". In the Table below, the first numerical column gives the score for quality of life, which ranged from 0 (very poor) to 10 (excellent). The second numerical column rates satisfaction with level of activity, ranging from 0 (very dissatisfied) to 10 (completely satisfied; as busy as I want to be)

It can be seen from **Table 1.3** that perceptions related to quality of life ranged from Fay who rated herself at 0.9, commenting that her current high level of pain in her ankle drastically reduced her quality of life, to Edith who rated her current quality of life as 9.7 because each day was so exciting with lovely things to do.

The range of reported satisfaction with level of activity was equally great. Again Fay recorded the lowest score of 1.7 because she had had to reduce her activities a great deal recently, due to increasing limitations imposed by her arthritis. Ann reported the highest level of satisfaction with amount of activity. She thoroughly enjoyed her wide-ranging activities, but was mindful that "this level cannot go on for ever".

In six of the study participants there appears to be a fairly close correlation between the two scores, to within two points. So that Ann, Beatrice, Cath and Gladys all have a more than average level of satisfaction with both their quality of life and their activity levels and at the other end of the scale, Fay and Ian indicate a correlation between their dissatisfaction with both quality of life and activity level. Of the four people who reported greater variance between the two scores, Doris said she was very active but usually anxious about most things,

Edith held such high aspirations for what she wanted to achieve each day, that invariably her activity level failed to live up to expectations, Horace expressed similar frustrations when his tiredness prevented him from completing all his chosen activities. Karl by way of contrast regarded that for his age, he was pleased with what he was able to do each day, even though his overall quality of life was only mediocre compared with the past.

## Table 1.3 Visual analogue scales

| Pseudonym | Age/ years | | Quality of life | Level of activity |
|---|---|---|---|---|
| Ann | 75 | F. | 8.5 | 9.8 |
| Beatrice | 90 | F. | 9.0 | 9.0 |
| Cath | 77 | F. | 7.6 | 9.1 |
| Doris | 76 | F. | 2.9 | 6.3 |
| Edith | 88 | F. | 9.7 | 6.1 |
| Fay | 83 | F. | 0.9 | 1.7 |
| Gladys | 83 | F. | 5.9 | 6.1 |
| Horace | 77 | M. | 8.5 | 3.1 |
| Ian | 85 | M. | 4.0 | 5.4 |
| Joyce | 98 | F. | 6.0 | 3.0 |
| Karl | 91 | M. | 5.0 | 9.0 |
| Lucy | 85 | F. | 4.8 | 2.0 |

It is of interest to note that chronological age within the participant sample appears to have little effect on either perceived quality of life or satisfaction with activity level. Beatrice, a nonagenarian achieves one of the highest combined scores, whilst Joyce, another nonagenarian, achieves a low combined score. Equally amongst the septuagenarians there is Ann with one of the highest combined scores and Horace with one of the lowest combined scores.

Rokeach (1973) and other later researchers, suggested that there was always close correlation between physical health and quality of life. This is evident in the current study, and again is unconnected to chronological age. Four out of five participants who scored highly for physical health status/ function on the SF36, namely Ann, Horace, Edith and Beatrice, scored the highest results also in the VAS, all with results at 8.5 or above.

A final comment regarding the visual analogue scale results, looks at gender. The mean male score for quality of life is 5.83, and the mean female score is 6.21. For activity level satisfaction the mean male score is 5.83 and the mean female score is 5.9. As the range is great throughout it is also helpful to note the median scores here. For male participants the median quality of life measurement is 5.0 and 6.0 for female subjects. The satisfaction with activity level mean is 5.4 for males and 6.1 for female participants. Although numerically any differences are small, it is interesting to note that in all measures, the trend of perceived life quality and satisfaction with activity levels is marginally higher for the female study participants.

## Results:      Geodemographic typology

With the use of the local database, it was possible to identify lifestyle profiles for nine of the participants in the study with the following results, (the remaining three did not have full post-codes available).

---

### Table1.4:  Super Profile Lifestyles for study participants

Lifestyle profile  A        one person
Lifestyle profile  B        two people
Lifestyle profile  C        one person
Lifestyle profile  D        one person
Lifestyle profile  G        two people
Lifestyle profile  J         two people

---

It is seen from the preceding **Table1.4**, and the outlined general descriptors given earlier in this chapter, that the nine participants come from a relatively wide range of social backgrounds.

## Summarising what has been learnt so far

The background data revealed results for the participant group aged between 75 and 98 years. The twelve people live singly in the community as the study's inclusion criterion specified. All three men are widowers whilst one woman is single, and eight women are widowed. SF36 and NLSA results revealed wide diversity in mental and physical fitness plus general mobility levels. There are interesting correlations and non-correlations between dysfunction and limitations, in that low physical function appears to impose minimal limitations on two of the people, suggesting that other factors, either personal or environmental, may exert greater impact here. Poor mental health however appears to hold a stronger correlation with physical and emotional limitations. The person with the lowest mental health score also presented with the lowest VAS score for activity level satisfaction. Such findings merit further exploration in the detail of the individual case studies and discussion to follow.

The strongest correlation, as has been reported elsewhere, is between physical health and perceived quality of life. The four study participants with the highest scores in VAS for perceived quality of life, are the same four people who presented with four out of the five top scores for physical health and function in the SF36.

In terms of chronological age, it is interesting to note the two extreme boundary points. Test results revealed that the youngest study participant is clearly the most active, whilst twenty-three years her senior, the eldest person is clearly the least active of the group. However, within these boundary points any correlation is less clear, with long-term conditions such as arthritis imposing activity limitations on three subjects in their mid-eighties, whilst another ninety year old remains active in her local community.

Geodemographic typology confirmed that the study participants come from a wide range of social backgrounds. Most of them have lived in their current houses and environments for more than twenty years, suggesting that the local environment could strongly influence day-to-day contacts and occupations. With remaining relatives widespread, most participants saw no family members on a regular basis. In view of this trend, alternative support mechanisms and relationships merit further study.

Despite personal hardships in terms of pain, restricted mobility and declining abilities, the visual analogue scales revealed a group, relatively satisfied with both their quality of life and their current levels of activity. There was little indication of complacency, more an intent to find methods of compensation. Further investigations are reported in the detail of the twelve case studies, presented in Part 2, to follow.

# OCCUPATION AND QUALITY IN LATER LIFE

## PART 2   TWELVE CASE STUDIES

**Synopsis**:    *The previous chapter explored methods that have been successfully used to study occupation in later life. Such strategies guide therapists to use all relevant tools in assessing and assisting their clients to attain maximum occupational satisfaction, commensurate with health status and personal interests and ambitions. Now the results from the use of the major data collection tool of the Yesterday Interview, have been taped and transcribed and analysis begun and they yield the detailed case study material presented here in chapters 5-7. Results from the multiple sorting task (MST) are also included.*

- *See Tables 1.1 and 1.2 of the previous chapter for ready reference to the study participants and their health status.*
- *These detailed cases and personal quotations (pseudonyms used throughout) will enable therapists to identify familiar and unfamiliar traits and to support positive action in their clients. They stimulate discussion around important issues such as fostering new friendships in old age, productivity and creativity when health is impaired and environmental impact upon activity choices.*
- *The themes arising in these case studies are grouped for discussion in Part 3.*

**Note:** *In re-telling these stories, whilst retaining the present tense of their telling, there is a real attempt to enter each person's world, and to penetrate personal concepts of meaning and value associated with a satisfying occupational day. From a research point of view it is important that care has been taken with people's words. Kirsh (1996) reminded us that when the client is allowed to narrate his/her own story, the client is placed in a central position of control. This is consistent with client-centred practice and empathetic to the study of people in the context of their environment. The yesterday interview, selected as the major data collection tool, yielded much rich data at an individual level. Following in-depth analysis of each transcript it was possible to elicit individual themes that exerted an influence over the day: these are presented below and supported by direct quotations. Each case study is introduced with a vignette derived from the initial interview situation and the background test results obtained at that time.*

## CHAPTER 5  ANN, BEATRICE, CATH AND DORIS

## Ann

**Introduction**        Ann is 75 years old and currently enjoying good physical and mental health. She has a positive outlook and values her sporting activities such as badminton, yoga and rambling. Having been widowed for seventeen years, she has established many social contacts whom she sees on a regular basis; usually when she takes part in one of the organised activities, which form a structured part of her weekly programme. She takes care of her own large semi-detached house, and although she has family within 10 miles, she does not see them every week and is content with this arrangement.

Ann describes a day in March. She indicates that yesterday began like the great majority of her other days: "I get up in the morning, I have a paper delivered, have my breakfast and read the paper and try to do the small crossword (laughs) and that is before I get myself ready to go out". Describing a Thursday, there follows a yoga class, then a badminton game, followed by a light lunch before an afternoon shopping trip. Evening dinner, grilled chicken and two vegetables, was cooked before Ann hopped back into her car to go to one of her twice-weekly Scottish Country Dance groups. Ann suggested that yesterday was fairly typical for her. She tends to be out most days at one or two of the many activities that she enjoys. However when at home, she asserts that she is content, with the radio's music in the background for company, providing she has something to do.

## Ann's Activities

Ann revealed a wide-ranging list of activities with an emphasis on physical activities such as badminton, yoga and walking. She clearly expressed a greater level of enjoyment in some of her activities as follows:

| | |
|---|---|
| **of high enjoyment:** | badminton, crosswords, having a cup of tea, dining out, driving the car, holidays, reading the newspaper, walking and yoga. |
| **of medium enjoyment:** | housework, sewing- most enjoyed when it is creative, seeing the children- not highly enjoyed because there "is usually something wrong with them", telephone chats- "I'm not a great lover of lengthy phone gossips". |

**of low enjoyment:** cooking- "it takes too long, uses a lot of effort and is all gone in under an hour"!

Ann mentions few mundane day-to-day chores, such as taking care of herself or her household needs. A well-groomed lady and an attractively kept house perhaps indicate that Ann's automatic mode comes into play when she tackles such issues, and she discounts them as "activities". It is also perhaps an indication of her current good state of health in that personal care and domestic issues are easily dealt with. In the interview she makes only one mention of housework "I don't mind doing the hovering; there is a result there". She is aware of a need to be focussed and to "accomplish some clearing out", but is reluctant to embark on this:

> *I can't get the impetus to do that until the move actually comes*
> *on and I think well why clear out bits when its all got to go*
> *010:2*

## Ann's personal characteristics that influence her occupational day

Ann's interview suggested that she likes ***routine and structure***. As indicated in the Introduction, Ann has a consistent early morning breakfast routine, then she suggests in regard to her chosen activities that "most things are organised because there are times when you can do these things and times when you can't". Perhaps it is the need for a well-developed underlying infrastructure that is important to Ann; her networks of friends and social contacts:

> *I belong to different groups, because I go to N…….. on a*
> *Wednesday morning playing badminton and they are a different*
> *crowd altogether.*          *010:3*

and in relation to her different circles of friends:

> *I am going out for a meal on Saturday night to that new Italian*
> *restaurant in N………..Each week someone tries to choose a*
> *different place to eat every so often, and they said why not try*
> *there.*          *010:3*

This helps to answer the question of a slight ambiguity when early in the interview, Ann smilingly offers: "Well I am generally just quite happy doing what comes along in the day". For with her infrastructure of group memberships and contacts already well-established, Ann can enjoy a flexible approach to scheduling her current daily activities as she is secure in the knowledge that there will always be something interesting to do.

A second personal characteristic of apparent influence is Ann's ongoing interest in ***being busy***. She suggested that from an early age she always enjoyed having something to do.

> *Yes I have always been busy in that way. I have always done*
> *keep fit of some sort over the years. Even when we were in*
> *business in the pub, I mean I was up in the morning to see the*
> *family out, cleaners in and the catering went on all day...*
>
> *010:3*

and going back further Ann indicates her earlier interests:

> *Well I have always liked activity and I am lucky enough to be*
> *able to do it...I mean any inclination, I played tennis when I*
> *was younger as we did as a family*        *010:4*

Ann also recognises a link between ***health and activity.*** She referred to this on several occasions during interview and during the MST she chose to rate her activities in relation to their impact on her health as follows:

| **Activities with high influence over health** | badminton, yoga, Scottish country dancing, walking, driving the car "because it facilitates other activities", and crosswords "for the mind" |
|---|---|
| **Activities with medium influence over health** | newspapers because "they have health tips" and the radio, for the same reason |

An additional theme appears to be Ann's interest in ***maintaining the status quo.*** In talking about her yoga class she describes, somewhat regretfully:

> *it started as a 50+ group, and that was sixteen years ago, but*
> *there are only two of us now who are founder members, you*
> *know people have died, people have moved on or got too*
> *old...there used to be thirty to forty of us joining in. We had a*
> *small committee and outings...but that is all gone.*
>
> *010:1-2*

Ann places great emphasis on still being "lucky enough to do it all". Badminton remains Ann's favourite activity; she plays at least four times each week. Her husband died of a coronary, sixteen years ago during their game of badminton, at the same leisure centre where Ann still plays. Ann does not consider that her health will deteriorate, (see SF36 results in Part 1), and she considers sheltered housing as unnecessary for herself.

## The occupational influences of Ann's home environment

Although Ann likes to be out, she expresses feelings of safety and comfort in her home with phrases like:

> *if I have anything to do, I am quite happy staying in....I can*
> *quite happily stay in by myself and not worry about other*
> *people.*                    *010:1*

Seemingly neither the home's interior plus garden, nor the immediate neighbourhood are of prime importance to Ann because she in now looking for "something smaller with a view". She talks of a move to an apartment within the locality, but says exact position is not important. This is perhaps explained by Ann's widespread social and sporting networks and facilitated by her car ownership. She suggests that "having a car makes a great difference" and in response to the researcher's question: "Do you use your car most days?", she remarked:

> *yes, oh yes. I certainly wouldn't go out at night as much if I*
> *didn't have the car.*                    *010:2*

Ann asserts that her friends think she should move quickly, but her retort is: "I am in no hurry".

## Conclusion

During the time between interviewing Ann for a first and second time, she had stumbled over an uneven paving stone on a summer's evening walk. She had strained both her back and her right wrist at the time. Unable to play any of her usual sports, she went to stay with her daughter for a week and needed to lie flat until her back healed. Although Ann made a full recovery, this episode very much upset her and Ann used the second interview as a positive time of reflection. She considered what she would or could do when her more active pursuits are no longer possible and was pleased to realise that she had a number of more sedentary pastimes held in reserve, such as needlework.

For Ann occupation currently means physical action; each day equates with one or more planned activities. Being active is habitual and she aims to maintain a status quo. As her SF36 results record, she does not consider that her health will deteriorate. Ann works to preserve her health, through both her aerobic exercise and her healthy diet. It would seem that lack of occupational involvement would be not just lack of quality living for Ann, it would be denial *of existence*.

## Beatrice

**Introduction**        Beatrice aged 90 years enjoys her large old Victorian semi-detached house. She moved here forty-five years ago because at the time she was in service and her employer, a local land-owner, offered it to her. Beatrice thought the house a little too big at this time, but was keen to get away from the sooty atmosphere of a nearby suburb. She has now lived alone in the house since the death of her husband six years ago. Her only son and his third wife live in Canada. Beatrice has a positive outlook concerning her capabilities. She is well-known to neighbours and has younger relatives of relatives who pop in most weeks. Having been an active person, she has had two recent severe chest infections which have left her somewhat breathless and tired. On sunny days she still walks down to the village; at other times, relatives and neighbours shop for her. Recently too she has reluctantly accepted her son's advice that she must have someone to clean her house for her. She enjoys tending her many pot plants but finds some of the days are long and is frequently happy to close the television programmes for the night, with the comment "another day over". She comments wryly but without rancour that "days are no longer exciting". Beatrice has a sharp sense of humour and takes much pleasure from telling life stories and humorous anecdotes to visitors. Over the past couple of years her short-term memory has become less reliable, as reflected in her SF36 mental health score (see previous chapter) and she now needs to use many memory aids to prompt her. Her son recently visited for her ninetieth birthday and left her a small book into which most visitors write a brief entry as a reminder of recent events. This book is in daily use and is an additional source of pleasure to Beatrice. She occasionally talks warily about what she will do when she can no longer cope. She has two sisters still living, one of whom is in a nursing home; Beatrice does not want to "end up like her" but neither does she want to move to a sheltered housing complex; her current home and environment are very important to her and she values the fact that she can take care of herself and her own needs.

The first interview was conducted on a sunny June afternoon. Initially Beatrice was unsure about how useful her story would be: "Well I'm just a miserable old xxx who never goes anywhere, doesn't like bingo and clubs...". When the purpose of the research was repeated however, and the need for "all types of elderly person's typical days" was stressed, Beatrice relaxed and readily participated. The interview was conducted in Beatrice's front room, with scent from her freshly cut garden roses coming from the nearby coffee table. The interview was interjected with Beatrice's humour and the researcher had some difficulty in confining the subject to the occupations of yesterday; there were many stories to tell. Beatrice said yesterday had been typical, they were mostly alike; a morning routine, walk down to the village, sitting in the garden and

46

always a cooked dinner with several vegetables. In the evening there was the television until it was dark, and then 10pm bedtime. Beatrice's story arises from two interviews, three month's apart, and from field notes completed by the researcher.

## Beatrice's activities

Beatrice viewed her occupational day as being guided by how she felt each morning:

> *then I say to myself 'what shall I do today'. Sometimes I'll say*
> *'I'll just do that little job'- I never kill myself by going like mad*
> *all day, doing too much. I just ration myself, to a certain point.*
> *011:1*

She described yesterday as beginning in the usual manner with her rising about 8am. Then followed her normal routine; coming "down in dressing gown and nightie, making my porridge and having breakfast". She then proceeded to describe twenty discrete occupations, which during the MST Beatrice later sorted as follows:

**high frequency**
**(every day)** television- "it is company", closing the curtains, reading or reciting poetry, cooking, sitting in the garden- "whenever I can" having a cup of tea, planning, sitting and thinking, reading Friendship Book saying prayers- "I do this every day now, I only started about a year ago"

**medium frequency**
**(once/ twice a week)** reading the newspaper, sorting out, people-watching- "well I don't do it all the time, but I do sometimes watch through the window" sorting out, tending cut flowers, spending time with children- "I see the little girl next door; I just bought her a bar of chocolate, I said I would then I didn't see her, so I ate it. I shall have to go and buy another one now!" going to the village- "I don't go as often as I used to", housework- "I do tidy around regularly, talking on the phone- "this is too expensive to do every day".

**low frequency
(occasional)**      supermarket shopping "I only need to go once or twice a month", reminiscing/ sharing memories- "I don't get many opportunities", playing cards- "there is no-one to play with these days", seeing her son, just once per year because he lives in Canada.

Beatrice next rated the enjoyment that she gained from her daily activities:

**high enjoyment**      spending time with children " I always have time for them", television "for the company",
having a cup of tea, reading the *Friendship Book*, going to the village "I'm always glad when I get there", planning "deciding what I am going to do", sitting in the garden "I love this",
poetry, sharing memories, tending cut flowers, playing cards "I love this, but they [friends] have all gone now, well most of them",
people watching "especially in N....!"
(a favourite sea-side resort).

**medium enjoyment:**      supermarket shopping "I have never really enjoyed this", saying prayers "I feel I *ought* to do this", reading the paper "it is so often depressing", cooking "I am fed up with this, I do it every day, you know a piece of cauliflower, a carrot.....but I have to make myself do it", housework, sorting out, sitting and thinking "I have no choice, I do plenty of this".

**low enjoyment:**      closing the curtains "I always do this, but I don't like it; it is shutting out the light".

In talking of the various activities that Beatrice had undertaken yesterday, she was quite clear about activities which were completed because they brought pleasure and equally clear about the "duty" tasks, undertaken due to necessity. This latter category included cooking the daily dinner. During the interview Beatrice talked graphically of formative earlier experiences that had convinced her of the necessity of this activity:

> *I always make sure I have a dinner...and make sure I eat. I*
> *have seen so many old people starving themselves. I used to go*
> *and see friends...going back a bit..., when I was young and they*

> *were old. When I said "what did you have to eat today", she*
> *said nothing, just a cup of tea. She ended up and her skin and*
> *everything went*                                                011:1

In considering the activities which brought pleasure there were a number now, which had become infrequent due to lack of opportunities, and in particular lack of old friends with whom they could be shared. These are highlighted in the way Beatrice sorted the activities above, particularly with regard to pastimes such as reminiscing and playing cards.

## Beatrice's personal characteristics influencing her occupational day

A recurring feature of Beatrice's interview was evidence of her *positive outlook*. She said she got "fed up with people who moan" for "nobody wants you when you moan, do they?" attesting her personal philosophy to "make the best of each day". Although able to describe earlier frightening experiences and deprivation during the war years, Beatrice was still able to say:

> *you know I have been lucky in life- meeting lovely people, no*
> *but I have, I have been very lucky*                             011:2

and she went on to illustrate this with an incident which had occurred some years previously. She had fallen from a ladder whilst cleaning windows, leaving her leg pinned between the ladder's rungs. A trip to the hospital followed, then fourteen stitches without anaesthetic, and six weeks of outpatient appointments for dressings. However, the end result was that "I got my rest that I had been wanting", because she had a six-week break from her job, at a time when she felt "totally worn out".

A close ally to the positive outlook is Beatrice's **sense of humour**. The yesterday interview was punctuated by regular periods of laughter. At times the realism was almost macabre:

> *not that when you get to this age there's much to look forward*
> *to except a nice box with handles on!*                          011:1

Beatrice used her humour both as an ice-breaker into more difficult subject areas, such as above, and also as a natural and ready adjunct to many topics of conversation. In relation to going to the village, and the mention of a liking for fish, the researcher casually asked if Beatrice got her fish from the village. The ready retort here was: "No, from the freezer!" In keeping with Beatrice's positive outlook is an **avoidance of depressing stimuli**. This is particularly noticeable in her avoidance of daily newspapers because they: "are all doom and gloom" and "murder, moan, moan". A further personal characteristic which appears to influence Beatrice's daily occupations is the theme of **spirituality** . Under this theme there is mention of several activities. Beatrice spoke of a return to prayer:

> *I say my prayers, thank you for a nice day, and then I try to go*
> *to sleep..."*                                            011:4

She added that she always knew there was a God, but for years "had no direct communication". She now feels grateful to be back in touch. She does not go to church, because she feels the vicar will wonder why she has not been before. Beatrice finds support too in her daily readings from the *Friendship Book*, which a friend sends each Christmas. Kept on the breakfast room table, it is ready for each morning's passage to be read. Also in support of this theme is Beatrice's liking of poetry, and particularly inspirational verses such as Kipling's *If,* which she can recite right through. An area which continues to enrich day-to-day life is Beatrice's longstanding **liking of children**. She talks with regret that she had only one son, whilst she came from a family of nine children. She looks out for the little girl next door and takes every opportunity to foster and develop relationships with children and young people.

A major influence on Beatrice's occupational day is a group of activities and responses which can perhaps best be grouped under the theme of a **flexible concept of time.** This theme encompasses the 'looking back in time activities', the reminiscing and sharing of memories, which is greatly enjoyed. This is coupled with a strong awareness of the past and learning from past experiences in order to influence current practice (e.g. dietary intake, described above). 'Time' structures both the week: "*The Mail* on Saturday helps me plan the week's {television} programmes" and the day too, in that when the television programmes are closed it is "another day, or week gone", and bed-time is governed by the onset of night, as:

> *with the light nights coming, I am staying {up} longer because I*
> *like to close the curtains around the house and I don't like to*
> *close them up when it is light*                          011:4

There is also the barely expressed concept of 'time hanging heavily'. This is revealed in such comments as "I don't say that I am very, very bored" and:

> *I am not a reader, if I read I am sure the time would go .... You*
> *know when sometimes you think time is going a bit slow, I do*
> *pick up a book and I think oh that has seen that hour off*
>                                                            011:4

Under this theme too, is the reinforcement of past or present times, because "there is not much to look forward to". As short-term memory is becoming more of a problem for Beatrice, she possibly feels more secure in past time; she does however show strong personal resourcefulness in combating her memory problems. An example of this is recorded in the researcher's field-notes on the occasion of the second interview:

> 15th October I organised last week that B would come to my house around 3pm to have a further research discussion – and tea and cakes. She had not arrived by 3.50 and I was unsure whether poor memory, illness or reluctance to come, was preventing her arrival. I called on her to find her behind the front door "just going out". Assuming unhappily that she had forgotten our rendezvous I enquired where she was off to. Thankfully her reply was "to you and come and see why". At this point I was led back into her house, to an ornamental dagger hanging above the mantelpiece. To this was pinned the message: "Sharon 4pm Friday". I need not have worried, after all what is an hour when you are 90!
>
> *Field notes: 011:3*

## Beatrice's occupational influences of the home environment

Beatrice's home environment appears to facilitate some of her ongoing occupations, whilst doing little to support other enjoyed pastimes. Having lived in the same house for 45 years, the strongest positive influence lies here; the neighbours are supportive and village shops are known, and personally accessible during the summer months when Beatrice "feels like going out". During the winter months:

> *someone is always there to go for me if I need it. N is very*
> *good, he has been getting my paper every Saturday...I think it is*
> *very handy here for the village and the people there are all very*
> *nice, there is no-one I wouldn't go to.*          011:3

On the other hand Beatrice indirectly expresses periods of loneliness. She misses having someone to "share memories with" and regrets that she now rarely has the opportunity to play cards. A sheltered housing environment could provide Beatrice with some of the companionship she lacks, but this has never been a serious consideration for Beatrice, she asserts that she remains lucky that she can "do for herself". She recognises that the house is big for her, but she has help now with the housework once per fortnight; her son insisted here, although Beatrice remarks that she is perfectly capable of doing it herself. She has thought of the future, and even if housebound, she feels she has room to exercise within her own home. The garden, tended regularly by a gardener, is also enjoyed in the summer, and Beatrice takes pleasure in always having cut garden roses indoors.

## Conclusion

Beatrice's interviews revealed a lady, content in her home environment. To those who do not know her well, it may appear that a change to a more supportive living arrangement may lessen her loneliness and enhance a general quality of life through the security that such systems bring. However, the exploration of her activities reveals many ongoing pastimes that can still be pursued. These are generally passive, such as people watching and television and reading the Friendship Book, and they can be ongoing and neither limited by advanced age nor increasing frailty. The familiarity of the home and its surroundings provides reinforcement of happy past memories, and a place for the various mementoes and photographs which also provide ongoing pleasure, and a known base for former friends and their children, to return to for visits, when opportunity permits.

Examination of the phenomenon of occupation reveals that after an active, often exhausting working life, Beatrice has settled into a routine that permits her time to reflect and reminisce. She is aware that she never had time or opportunity to develop hobbies that may help her to pass the time now, but without rancour she accepts that "some days are long" and holds a resolve that she should "read more" because that would help to pass the time. A surprising revelation in Beatrice's case is that a large Victorian semi-detached house with six bedrooms can actually be a supportive environment. It raises the issues of the powerful positive influence over occupation that longevity within a neighbourhood can bring. She has intergenerational visitors who always know where to find her, and she is well-known to neighbours and shop keepers. Beatrice has not neglected to consider the frequently proffered alternatives that she should perhaps move to a sheltered environment, but has weighed up the factors and concluded that even if housebound she has room to exercise within her home. As many of her pastimes are sedentary, such as reading her *Friendship Book* or reminiscing with the aid of old photographs and artefacts and enjoyment from sitting in the garden, or savouring the scent of newly-cut roses, it appears that Beatrice has adapted well to her advancing years. Quality of life includes occupational satisfaction and Beatrice generally achieves this in her current environment. This case study may exemplify the case of seniors who after long working hours at a younger age, have few interests to revisit in older age. Social pursuits such as playing cards are not possible when the requisite group is no longer there and the prospect of fostering new pastimes is not relished.

## Cath

**Introduction**          Cath aged 77 years, is fully mobile and walks and visits a gym several times each week. Her SF36 scores reveal no current physical limitations, although with a score of 25% for energy levels, she says that some times she has to "battle". After twenty years of caring for her husband following his cerebral haemorrhage, Cath found it very difficult to be alone when her husband died four years ago. She takes care of the home they developed together, enjoying its spotless appearance and she also appreciates her ongoing car ownership which facilitates her twice weekly trips to the shops. During a recent period of discomfort in her knee her mobility was restricted and she needed support from a stick when out-doors. However a cartilage operation followed and Cath is now pleased that she has re-gained her ability to "take a decent walk most days of the week", describing local walks each of around two miles. She now no longer needs the support of a walking stick. One of Cath's closest relatives is her sister who lives in Connecticut; a recent trip to the USA for a visit was greatly enjoyed. Cath is concerned about what she should do with the many books that her husband owned, for purposes of study and reference. She would like them to be of use to someone else.

Cath was interviewed on a warm summer afternoon, sitting comfortably in her neat lounge. Recently returned from a six-week trip to visit her sister in the USA, Cath talked about her liking for travel and her interest in remaining active. She described her last four years as having been difficult, following the death of her husband. Prior to his death Cath had nursed him ("a brilliant, shy man") for twenty years after his cerebral haemorrhage. She described how she had "been his hands"; he issuing instructions and Cath carrying out projects, from re-wiring circuits in the home, to car maintenance. When her husband died, Cath realised she needed an absorbing, regular occupation to help her overcome her loss. It was at this time that she discovered and joined a local gym, and she looks back on this discovery as a "lifeline" to her. During the interview, Cath sat poised, apparently ready for action, hands occupied with a handkerchief when the cup of tea was finished.

## Cath's activities

During the interview, Cath revealed and repeated that she liked to be active all the day. Recently having regained full, mostly painfree movement in her knee, following a successful cartilage operation, meant that she could now be as active as she wanted to be. Sitting "doing nothing" was not a comfortable state. Cath described an organised day that included the following discrete occupations:

> Cooking, housework,
> walking, going to the gym,

car driving and maintenance,
planning, sorting out

In terms of preferred occupations, Cath suggested that her two mile walk to the gym made her "feel good", and as always she enjoyed the ongoing exercise on the equipment, once she arrived. She mentioned cooking as a somewhat neutral task:

> *I do all my own cooking. I cook a main meal every other day...I*
> *eat healthily, lots of fruit and vegetables. I eat chicken and fish,*
> *but not so much meat.*         *012:1*

as was car driving. She remarked that she only used the car for the more major shopping trips, usually about twice per week. Yesterday Cath had "steeled" herself to do some sorting out. She has a huge collection of her husband's specialist books, and worries about how to dispose of these.

## Cath's personal characteristics influencing her occupational day

Cath has a strong need to **be busy.** She expressed this frequently throughout the interview, with such phrases as: "I don't let myself just sit". She rated being calm and relaxed, as an undesirable state, and one that she did not usually permit, although she does have a few "quiet moments" in each day. During the evenings she likes to have a needlework project "on the go". Cath acknowledges that she is perhaps quite unusual in that she has **a wide spectrum of practical skills.** Because her husband was skilled in electronics and all aspects of home maintenance, yet was physically unable to carry out practical tasks in the home, Cath learnt the many intricacies of wiring, decorating etc. under her husband's instruction. She points out several features such as cocktail cabinet lighting, with the comment that she "was the hands" for completing all such projects. She is also able to carry out a number of car maintenance tasks.

A further theme which recurs during Cath's interview is an emphasis on **planning.** She mentions that although she feels tired on most days, because she plans the daily activities well, she is able to avoid becoming over tired. She knows that she cannot carry heavy goods, so organises her week to shop for heavy items only once or twice per week, when she will take the car. She feels that her planning ability also helps her avoid pain:

> *I don't ever let myself get worn out, because I plan my*
> *activities, and I plan the time for activities too, so that I wont*
> *push myself and cause pain in my knees*         *012:2*

With a brother in Reading and a sister in Connecticut, Cath has more recently resumed **an interest in travel.** She remarks that this gives her a great deal. She looks out for travel programmes on the television, and enjoys both the anticipation and the actuality of her fairly regular American trips.

## Occupational Influences of Cath's home environment

Cath takes an enormous pride in both the internal and external appearance of her home. Because she and her husband have worked as a team to effect home improvements over a twenty-five year period, it means a great deal to her. Her brother tends the garden for her, and she suggests that all is planned for easy maintenance; "it always has been". The situation of the house, within a short car ride of most shops and within a one to two mile walk of leisure pursuits, remains acceptable to Cath. No mention was made of any links with the immediate neighbourhood.

## Conclusion

Cath appears content with her occupational day as it is. Her careful planning ensures that she can accomplish her daily goals without undue stress. Due to recent knee surgery, her walking capabilities have increased, to enable her to walk two to three miles out of doors, now without the need for a stick. Because the design, decoration and content of the home hold so many memories for Cath, she would not contemplate a move.

For Cath occupational involvement appears to represent an essential component for all of each waking day. Although she tires quickly, her need to have something to do at all times, perhaps represents the "blanket" that activity can present, shielding an individual from moments of inactivity when feelings surface, and distracting the mind from unwelcome thoughts. To reinforce this position, Cath had asserted during the SF36 assessment that "feeling quiet and calm" was undesirable. Whatever the reason for compulsive occupational engagement, Cath stresses that she would be very unhappy were she to find herself idle. Cath has a very physical reminder of *being*, as her environment is a constant reminder of a major life role which was to support her husband, "a brilliant and shy man", and then for many years to "be his hands" after he became profoundly disabled. To a large extent Cath's existence today is founded in her past, in her home environment, because this is a constant memory of her husband, and she has a need to perpetuate occupation and ongoing activity as a reminder of this time.

## Doris

**Introduction**      Doris aged 76 years, has been contemplating a move from her rented terraced house for a number of years and has recently looked at two sheltered schemes, both of which seem expensive to her, and she hopes instead that her land-lord will eventually carry out the promised modernisations to her current house. Testing revealed that Doris currently rates her quality of life as 2.9 out of a maximum of 10; the low score being partly justified by her home circumstances which she finds cold and noisy. Doris's SF36 scores indicate high physical functioning with no limitations and she says she has always been an active but somewhat restless person. She used to enjoy long solitary walks but has now been advised that this is not safe practice; in fact she admits to having been threatened on one occasion. Instead of the solitary walks, Doris now uses the treadmill at the gym. Doris is a weight watcher, takes a keen interest in her diet and has maintained a slim, seven and a half stone weight for many years. Recently she has had a number of "fainting attacks" when out, but says the doctor can find nothing wrong. She feels happier now when going on an organised trip, because she knows someone is on hand to help if anything untoward happens. She has no close relatives in this country and has lost contact with relatives who went out to Australia some years ago. She usually has a fortnightly visit from a nephew, and she spends time each week helping a younger friend who has difficulties in coping with her own small children.

Doris was interviewed in her front room on a summer afternoon. She has back-ache much of the time, so tended to shift her position regularly as we talked. Doris was keen to tell me something of her background, when she lived in a nearby, now demolished street. So this was how the interview started, giving Doris time to relax. She described a "difficult" childhood; her mother had died early and her father had a succession of young housekeepers who were themselves at school. Consequently Doris spent much of her pre-school time alone, standing on a chair in the hall, trying to open the front door. She has lived in her current rented house for over 20 years, originally with her two sisters who both died some time ago.

### Doris's activities
Doris described a day that involved a number of "comings and goings". In studying the text, the discrete activities she described were as follows:

> walking, going to the gym, preparing meals,
> shopping, window shopping, light housework and tidying,
> checking the house and windows, going to the launderette,

visiting a friend with children, Weight-watchers,
having coffee, television,

Doris suggested that she did not have a structured morning routine: "I don't always get up at the same time", but her breakfast routine normally concluded with either the 9am or the 10am news on the radio, then she prepared for the first shopping trip of the day. She shops daily for food, walks miles each day and visits the gym at least four times per week. Doris asserted that two things she did daily were to "tidy round" and to "check the windows", each time before she goes out. When the daily trips are over Doris normally spends the evenings watching television; she would like to read more but:

> *I can't concentrate. There's so much traffic in this busy little*
> *street, and the people next door have two children. She has one*
> *that cries regularly 'cos they're only young*      *013:5*

## Personal characteristics influencing Doris's occupational day

At several times during the interview, Doris referred to her ***interest in weight control.*** She asserts that:

> *I know I must stay 7 stone 12; I mean I am only small, I'm five*
> *foot one and a half and 7.12 is my weight*      *013:4*

She begins her day with a weight-watcher's breakfast of fruit and cereal, saying: "I do believe in what the weight watchers say, it takes three meals a day". This theme is closely linked to her ***interest in healthy eating***, so that she has a low fat diet, plenty of vegetables, bought fresh every day, and fish or chicken. Her rigour in this area does however cause her anxiety, particularly at Christmas or the time of her birthday:

> *if I've had a birthday, which I have, they bring me things, my*
> *relatives. I eat them and then its sort of stimulated my appetite*
> *for sweet things and I think, oh, I'm indulging again*
> *013:4*

This is noticeable again when Doris talks of a young relative who calls on her every couple of weeks and stays for a cup of tea:

> *then I tell him he must bring his own cake because I'm a*
> *weight-watcher. Because if I buy biscuits, I wont eat one I'll eat*
> *the packet. No will power!*      *013:3*

A further related theme emerging from Doris's day, is her **need to be active**. She described herself as a somewhat restless person, and talks of her delight in discovering the local gym. Prior to joining the gym she was used to taking long solitary walks, often along a fairly un-populated stretch of coast-line. However, friends and her dentist advised her that this was unsafe, and on one occasion she was subject to a minor incident that convinced her that she should look for a safer pastime. She now attends the local gym at least four times a week, and talks enthusiastically of her activities there:

> *the classes usually 2 to 2.30 and I do aerobics, step or simple*
> *exercises, then I might go in the gym half an hour and I go on*
> *the treadmill and I go on the cycle, just these simple things*
> *013:2*

Then during the summer months, when the "nights are light", Doris returns to the gym in the evenings to "do one and a half hours" including a stretch and relax class, before walking the mile and a half back home.

Although not spoken of directly, Doris's occupational choices appear to be influenced by her nature of **being solitary.** Her walks, shopping trips etc. are all undertaken as solitary pursuits. She remarked early in the interview that this arose because:

> *Most of my friends are dead. They all died young in their*
> *thirties and forties, some in their twenties. That was why I*
> *travelled. I am not rich enough to go back and see anybody so I*
> *just forgot them over the years, they faded...*    *013:6*

Now Doris's choice of television programmes is influenced by these early experiences, and she enjoys the travel programmes because they enable her to re-live past memories:

> *Years and years ago I emigrated to Canada, so I've been a part*
> *of Canada and had a few vacations there, so when I see them*
> *on the television, I think 'oh I've been there'*    *013:4*

Doris refers to her solitary lifestyle again in talking about the lottery, suggesting that a win would enable her to travel to look up old friends and places, and in terms of her chances of winning: "oh I think there is something in the pipeline for me somewhere, sometime". She goes on to suggest that she has "a knowing mind", but does not find herself in the right place to buy her tickets at the right time, also:

*and with me not having anybody to talk to, I don't discuss*
*anything you see*                                    *013:7*

Doris remarked that she used to like ballroom dancing, but she sees some heavy ladies at the gym, and knows that afternoon dances now entail "slower movement, cups of tea and cake", so it is not for her. Likewise, she used to attend church regularly, but "now it has all changed" and Doris feels:

*now we are only there for marrying or funerals, and I don't like*
*the way they talk to you any more and I don't like some of the*
*people who go there, I don't know, their attitude to life. Its none*
*of my business whether you are married or single or what you*
*chose to do, because sometimes you try to be married and it*
*doesn't work out*                                    *013:8*

A regular solitary occupation, which brings Doris into contact with others, is her visit to the launderette.

*I go twice a week if I can and that's like half a day out...about a*
*fifteen minute walk but I don't mind, it's a pleasant walk*
                                                      *013:3,4*

and as she described during interview, she has a young friend who has problems with depression. Doris takes pleasure and pride in being able to help her out with childcare and household chores on a fairly regular basis:

*sometimes they'll phone me of a week-end and we'll go the*
*park. I'll play with them and help her do the dishes, which have*
*usually accumulated a day or two you know, because she is*
*depressed*                                           *013:3*

## Occupational influences of Doris's home environment

Doris's home environment appears to influence her occupational choices a great deal. She talks graphically and repeatedly of a secondary reason for going to the gym. She appreciates the shower facilities there, because her own bathroom is unheated:

*when I go to the toilet here, I put a hat on and I have an extra*
*woolly, I do. I go around with more on, than when I go out*
                                                      *013:6*

Consequently, Doris was delighted to discover the facilities at the gym:

*When I saw the shower room, all the individual showers and the sauna, I thought oh I will come here all winter, I wont be cold in that bathroom*          *013:6*

Although her current environment is conveniently situated for bus routes and shops, her house itself with the noisy street and lack of garden ("to keep a little herbaceous border weeded and hoed and to have a few perennials, would be much better" [than a yard]) causes her a diminished quality of life. She worries too about burglaries and carefully checks each window is locked every time she is about to leave the house. Doris acknowledges the need to look for somewhere else to live and has been to visit two sheltered housing complexes, but thought them very expensive, particularly as "they don't do anything for you" and "there is only a little electric heater in the corner of the bathroom, no radiator to keep your towel warm and dry".

## Conclusion

Doris's yesterday interview revealed how she creates an active lifestyle and a structure to her day. Some environmental features appear to mitigate against her and cause her reduced occupational opportunities. Doris says that she has now accepted that she must move from her current house. However when she was seen again on an informal basis twelve months later, her comment was: "I think I can manage another twelve months there, then I will need to move on".

For Doris the concept of occupation appears closely allied with being active, but there is little clear link with purposeful activity, apart from the concept of being a weight-watcher. Physical activity, normally undertaken on a solitary basis, fills the daylight hours and the evenings are always occupied in watching the television. Doris reported a low score for quality of life which possibly reflects something of her low involvement in purposeful activity. Friends have mostly died and even the stimulation of ongoing periodic work duties is due to finish soon when an old company closes down. Doris's most animated conversation centred around recent day trips undertaken by coach; she expressed pleasure in new places seen, shopping centres visited and in the availability of different food products. Should similar focussed daily activities be fostered and encouraged, Doris may well experience greater overall satisfaction with her days. A major bar to this however is her loneliness and as she expressed, "there is no-one to discuss things with". The therapeutic nature of purposeful activity is indicated in Doris's case and it suggests a role for supportive client-centred practice in the area, in order to promote positive change. Doris expresses little contentment in *being* in her current state, but has no definite plans to make a change.

## CHAPTER 6  EDITH, FAY, GLADYS AND HORACE

## Edith

**Introduction**    Edith aged 88 years, is absorbed in each day. When her husband died twenty years ago she made a determined effort to find fulfilling occupations to fill the void. She has lived in her bungalow for forty-eight years and takes daily pleasure from its garden which she tends enthusiastically. She grows abundant soft fruits and vegetables in addition to year round flowers and shrub displays. Her one concession to advancing age is that this year she had her small lawn replaced by paving stones so that she does not have to cut the grass. Indoors, Edith's environment is equally treasured and colourful. Her rooms are full of her own creative endeavours from water colour paintings to an extensive collection of shell sculptures. The latter are of such a high standard that she has exhibited them locally on more than one occasion. Edith is acutely aware of the numbers of hours in each day because she always has much she would like to accomplish. She consequently presented a VAS activity level score of 6.1, although she rated her overall quality of life at 9.7. She sees her daughter only infrequently as she lives with her family some 80 miles away. Locally Edith has cultivated friendships amongst like-minded creative people and although alone she says she is not lonely. She is aware however that she has a distinct tendency to "hold on to willing visitors" because she so enjoys talking to them. Fully independent she cooks her own mostly fish and vegetable meals and entertains her sister to lunch most weeks. Two recent bouts of polmyalgia rheumatica have caused her pain and periods of limited mobility and function. These periods caused her a great deal of worry; the feeling that she was suddenly "done for" was devastating. However, with carefully self- administered medication, she has made a good recovery and continues to enjoy her many activities. One ongoing cause for concern is what she should do with her many household possessions, in particular the shells which are many and have been collected from around the world and are currently stored carefully, for example a drawer of tiny New Zealand pink corals for the cheeks of fairy sculptures. She has two friends who share an interest and enthusiasm for shell sculpturing and she is contemplating approaching them with a view to "taking over" her supplies.

I met Edith for an initial interview, as revealed in the field-notes:

---

*26th July. This afternoon E was in the front garden loading clippings into her wheelie bin. She welcomed me into her 'spider's web' of a house…. First a lighted display cabinet full of exquisite sculptures; all turned out to be made entirely of natural and exotic shells, down to coral for the lips, and witches and fairies in moving poses were accompanied by poems, all made by E. since 1959 when took up a self-made challenge that she could do better than a purchased creation. Watercolours hung in every room, they and the half-made, altered pure silk suit on the dining room table, were also E's own work. A small, lively lady, E suggested we sit in the garden (also all E's own handiwork) to talk. It was an oasis of colour; butterflies and relaxed-looking blackbirds sipping from the birdbath. Person-high yellow, red and white lilies by the back door, next pots of violas and hundreds of hardy cyclamen and a most colourful backdrop of roses, bushes and fruit trees beyond, as we sat side by side on the lawn seat. A natural, outgoing person, E. chatted on for three hours, stopping only to get us both a sun hat and umbrella, then eventually to prepare tea and scotch pancakes with strawberry jam.*

*Field notes 014:1*

---

## Edith's activities

Edith spoke of a Saturday to describe a day's activities and revealed a wide range of occupations that she had undertaken. Towards the end of the interview she spoke also of her other occupations, about which she is "passionate". She said that Saturdays were always a "bit different" because she had *The Times* and began the crossword with her three morning cups of tea. Examination of the interview content revealed a wide range of activities that was later subjected to two sorts, firstly for frequency:

|  |  |
|---|---|
| **very frequent:** | visiting charity shops, gardening, water colour painting, classical FM radio (not as a background), crosswords, and cryptic puzzles, cup of tea, cooking, picking soft fruit, garden design, creative sewing |
| **once/ twice per week:** | composing verses, reading newspaper, housework, TV, sorting out, having relative to a meal, the T-Pot bus (Age Concern) |

| **occasionally:** | knitting, crochet, shelling, embroidery, buying fish, jam making, hat making. |
|---|---|

The second sort was for the enjoyment, with Edith choosing the two categories:

| **high enjoyment:** | seeing friends, charity shops, creative embroidery, hat-making, the T-Pot bus, having relative to a meal, having a cup of tea, crochet, writing verses, gardening, shelling, garden design, picking fruit and any edibles, crosswords, painting (mainly water colour). |
|---|---|
| **tedious, done only because of the end product:** | knitting (although the design phase is of high enjoyment), jam-making, sorting out, housework, reading the newspaper, cooking, sewing (needed in order to make her clothes fit), buying fish. |

On the given Saturday, Edith began her morning by picking her garden's Tay berries raspberries, loganberries, and blackberries and sugaring them ready for her sister who was visiting for lunch the following day. There then followed an organised day which included planting out the recently purchased alpines in a neighbour's rockery, the latter having been designed and built by Edith earlier in the summer, and culminating in a cooked evening dinner and a session to finish the crossword.

## Edith's Personal Characteristics influencing the Occupational Day

The interest and pleasure derived from ***creative occupations*** is evident in every page of Edith's yesterday interview and supported by the sorted results above. One of Edith's more unusual occupations is shelling or the making of intricate shell sculptures. She talks of the intensity of her involvement here:

> *...you wouldn't get them {shells} out unless you had absolute free time ahead for at least a fortnight, and if D... came for a meal she would have to have it on her knee in the front room. I wouldn't clear the table...It is intensive, takes precedence over everything. I can put the painting away, aside, and have a rest from it, say garden again, but if I am shelling that is a different story...I can lose myself and forget everything*      014:4

The theme of enjoyment in creative pursuits is mirrored in her other preferred occupations too. Talking of a hat she had recently made, she displayed it with the remark: "It is my own design, hasn't it worked well? I love it you know!"

Incorporated in the creativity theme are two sub-themes, the first being an **appreciation of colour and beauty.** Edith refers to this on many occasions, in relation to her frequent visits to charity shops she says: "I find beautiful colours and beautiful materials and bring them home to remodel". This is also reflected in her love of gardening which is reported in the researcher field-notes above and again when Edith talks of her afternoon spent helping her neighbour establish a rockery:

> *then I went next door…and started to place the beautiful*
> *collection of alpines we had bought, deciding exactly which was*
> *the best little pocket,…knowing which needed the ericaceous*
> *soil and which needed good drainage, which could be put at*
> *ground level to make a nice cascade with something else…*
> *014:1*

The above quotation leads into the second theme related to creativity, that is an **interest in producing the best.** This is not expressed with any sense of competitiveness, but more in relation to **knowing** and **improving one's art.** Edith dismisses much of the television programming, including garden programmes, because: "I learn little if anything from them"; she took up shelling as a personal challenge to improve on a crude shell sculpture made elsewhere, and she plays no musical instruments because:

> *I did play the piano, but I didn't excel so my heart wasn't in it*
> *014:8*

A second major theme which clearly facilitates Edith's creative expression and productivity, is her interest in **always having something to do.** She has no problem in achieving this aim when in her own home, because "I always have several projects on the go", however when she goes to visit her daughter, she plans carefully:

> *I have been sorting out some knitting to take away with me so*
> *that I have something to do on those moments when you are left*
> *with nothing to do. I can't be left with nothing to do, I must*
> *have something…. Then you see when I have been there a few*
> *days, I can pluck up courage and ask if I can weed the front*
> *garden!* *014:4,5*

Edith is focussed in her occupations, without compulsion, but with the realisation that she has much she still wants to accomplish. In order to do this she regards crossword completion as a treat for a Saturday or the end of a day, and she is aware that the more mundane tasks take second place in her order of things: "I am a bit upset that my house isn't as spick and span as it ought to be….". She maximises her time-involvement in the regular chores which she must do, for instance in her daily meal cookery:

> *Well I cook perhaps every other day but I eat a cooked meal*
> *every day because I cook enough for two days and put it in the*
> *microwave, just saving time. I don't waste anything, don't*
> *waste anything. I save as much as I can. I often cook the*
> *potatoes in advance like that but I prefer the greens to be*
> *freshly cooked.*        *014:2,3*

Edith gives several more examples of how she makes the most, not just of time, but of resources too. During interview she shows a small watercolour she is just finishing, with the comment: "well if it doesn't turn out well, I shall use the back for something else". This theme is also echoed in her judicious use of all the fabric she acquires from charity shop clothes, and is highlighted again in a related theme that could be described as ***perpetuity.*** On several occasions Edith spoke of her desire to "carry things on". She has no religious beliefs, but she has a strong sense of perpetuating what is of value. She spoke nostalgically of some beautiful embroidery, rescued from her deceased sister's dressing gown, and she showed how she had been able to incorporate this into an attractive hat decoration. Edith then wore her finished hat at a grandson's wedding, then: "something of K {sister} was at the wedding".

Not only does Edith recognise the value of an absorbing occupation for herself, but she shows a clear understanding of the deprivation which others have experienced when no longer able to indulge. She described a tortuous route she thought out each week for a weekly outing, when her husband first became ill and could no longer play cricket, in order that he would not have: "to hear the sound of willow on wood", because "it tugged at his heart strings so much". For herself, she reflected that she had always enjoyed many activities, and had little problem in finding a new hobby, because "there is no such thing as a vacuum…there is always something to take its {tennis} place".

A final theme emerging in this category is that of ***healthy eating.*** Edith stresses that this is a subsidiary theme, pursued only because she wants to live a long time in order to accomplish as much as possible. Into this subject arena came Edith's love of fish; the story about today's fresh fish, bought from a shop counter, was preceded by a past account of Edith and her husband taking regular trips to a local shoreline, armed with "a set of lay fishing lines each with a hundred hooks and a whole load of copper stair rods to affix the lines". These were laid a mile from shore and a few hours later after the next tide, their lugworm bait used to result in: "dabs, as sweet as honey, a few plaice, but best of all was the bass". Today Edith had acquired her fish by a more conventional method and she stressed that:

> *I have a very healthy diet, lots of fruit and lots and lots of*
> *vegetables and chicken predominantly. I do love meat and I*
> *have it every now and then. I am not a vegetarian by any*
> *means.*                                                     *014:2*

Edith grows many of her own vegetables, in addition to her plentiful fruit and she tries to ensure that down to the last windfall apple, all will be put to good use. She suggested that her wartime upbringing had given her these deeply rooted principles. She remembered her father, a schoolteacher, working hard on his allotment to provide plentiful vegetables for the family.

## Occupational influences of Edith's home environment

The yesterday interview clearly revealed the importance of the home environment to Edith. On a visual level, both the house and its creative contents and the garden packed with colour and edible items, provided a strong indication that Edith's immediate environment facilitates her occupational endeavours. At the close of the interview, Edith was happy to speak on this topic too:

> *I am surrounded by lovely things, and I have so much to do....*
> *However it could be managed, I would wish to stay here, that*
> *would be my aim, to stay here until I am no longer*
> *anywhere...and whatever it took to make that possible, that*
> *would be my desire...and I would still hope to do all the things*
> *that I...I always hope to do, more painting, more shelling, keep*
> *the garden better, but I know a lot of that is wishful thinking.*
>                                                              *014:6*

Edith is realistic about the few things that she cannot manage. She does not saw down any large trees in her garden and she does no plumbing; most other tasks are within her repertoire. Beyond the house and garden, Edith values the immediate neighbourhood:

> *I love living where I do, in a cul de sac position, everybody*
> *knows everybody; its all Christian names*        *014:6*

A little further afield too, there is a regular bus route, now with a specially adapted bus. It accommodates wheelchair users and is also helpful to Edith and others with laden shopping trolleys. Although taking a "roundabout route", the bus goes to the town's small shopping centre. This is also where the weekly Age Concern "T Pot Bus" makes its regular stops, and Edith values the friendships fostered here.

One downside to Edith's home, is that having occupied the same bungalow for many years, she has accumulated many items, both of her own and from deceased relatives, this causes her some stress:

> *I am trying very hard to sort things out a little, but I have had*
> *so many things dumped on me when people have*
> *died...everybody got landed with boxes of this and that to go*
> *through.... I don't know I seem to get a lot more clutter than I*
> *really want, and I've got clutter of my own, absolutely essential*
> *clutter because I need so many shells, I've got them*
> *everywhere. But it will all go in a skip when I go because*
> *nobody will want to use it...*            *014:7*

Edith suggests though that she is making an effort to sort things out, and sometimes she thinks she is winning. Her current project is to get her clothes sorted out, "having something nice to wear whenever I might want it". It was at this point that Edith fetched her newly completed hat, to demonstrate her point.

## Conclusion

Edith's two interviews revealed a lady contented with her quality of life and her opportunities to make the most of her creative talents. She remains ambitious to make the most out of every day, to share her hobbies and skills with those who are interested, and to continue to accomplish as much as possible. Her occupational interests are supported by her long-standing residence in a bungalow with a self-landscaped garden, and with interior light and space to display Edith's completed work. Just after the second interview Edith had the first of three bouts of polymialgia rheumatica (PMR). In addition to intense pain and weakness, Edith was psychologically distraught during the first episode of the illness, describing it as: "I felt I was done for...". However with medication and support from her GP, and from friends who made Internet checks for information about the condition, Edith has weathered these crises, and is able with controlled medication, to continue as before. She is also pleased to have located two creative acquaintances who may be able to take over her shell collections.

Purposeful occupation means a great deal to Edith and her days are centred around how much she can accomplish. She describes the pleasure in "ticking off her progress" mentally each night, when she recognises her achievements both large and small. In her occupational account Edith describes something of the high sense of value that she places on both being productive and in producing the best. These standards are long-standing and she recognises that *time* is a precious commodity: luxuries such as crossword completion are reserved for once a week or late evening enjoyment. Interestingly Edith indicates that "there is never a void"; she never lacks a new creative project to undertake as another venture finishes. One great concern is that ill-health may at some point prevent her from continuing her current independent lifestyle and creative occupations. In existential terms, Edith is *making of life what she will*. She recognises the finality of death, but hopes fervently that she may be "shelling at the time".

## Fay

**Introduction** Fay revealed in both her SF36 scores and her VAS scores, that she has some severe physical limitations, which result in a degree of social isolation and consequent loneliness. She is profoundly deaf, deriving some benefit from a hearing aid, but is reliant mainly on lip reading for comprehension of conversation. Paget's disease and associated arthritic changes affects her hips and now her right ankle. This causes her much pain and limits her activity considerably. She is awaiting surgery for a new ankle joint but has concerns that immediately post-operatively she may be even more limited, and perhaps unable to go up stairs at all. She walks with the help of a stick for brief distances only. Her husband died twenty-four years ago and she is unable to see her daughter or son on a regular basis. Her daughter lives in London and her son in North Wales. Two of Fay's sisters have died and the remaining sister is in a coma in a local hospital. Despite her limitations Fay copes with her own housework in her semi-detached house where she has lived for over thirty years. She has tried to get help in both her house and back garden, but has not yet found anyone satisfactory. With her increasing immobility Fay has recently joined schemes which now provide her with a degree of security and assistance. A local "dial-a-ride" scheme helps her with outdoor transport, a day centre provides company and a hot meal on two days per week and a local female contact takes her shopping on a regular basis.

Fay had alerted the researcher, before interview, to the fact that she is deaf. However, at the time of interview, with front lighting, she lip-read fairly accurately. She has Paget's Disease, and was clearly in pain at the moment. The interview was conducted in a rear living room where two of Fay's watercolours were hanging and a large album of certificates for preserving and swimming rested on the coffee table. Due mainly to Fay's deafness, it was sometimes difficult to confine the interview to the specific topic of yesterday's activities, however Fay was very happy to talk about her many current occupations.

## Fay's Activities

Fay described the occupations she currently enjoyed, and pointed out that unless she has a specific reason for going out, to a Day Centre, or shopping with a friend, she is mainly housebound at the moment. She hopes very much that her forthcoming ankle-replacement will bring her restored mobility. The activities described were:

> Monday Day Centre, having a cup of tea,
> using a Dial a ride bus or a taxi, scrabble, sailing,
> going shopping with a friend, swimming, cooking,
> preserving, growing vegetables and flowers,
> flower-pressing, painting, tidying the house.

Fay spoke very animatedly about her newest hobby, swimming. She attends a disabled swimming club on Friday afternoons and has been to Stoke Mandeville with the club members. Due to her deafness and joint problems she says she would not be able to go to an ordinary swimming club, she comments: "I can only swim on my back, and get scared when people swim under me". Fay described having a focal point to most days, so that Monday she goes to a lunch club, Tuesdays a friend takes her shopping, another day it is an Age Concern painting class and Sundays she liked to go sailing with a disabled group, but could not do this every week as the £10 taxi fare is a deterrent here. In fact now that Fay cannot manage to travel on a regular bus, and is also very limited in her walking ability, she is finding transport something of a problem, and regular taxi use is prohibitively expensive. Fay also outlined that even simple tasks such as tidying around the house takes so much longer at the moment because of her immobility. She has tried to minimise cleaning, has floors that she can mop over because she cannot manage a Hoover, and tries to leave "things handy" so that she does not have to "traipse from room to room".

## Fay's Personal Characteristics influencing her Occupational Day

Perhaps the major theme here is that of *stoicism.* Fay spoke at some length about a hip replacement that had not worked:

> *after 3 years it gave up...and quite recently I was in agony*
> *because it was loose. I remember going shopping in the village;*
> *it was alright going there, but coming back it was agony.... It*
> *used to lock and I used to pray it wouldn't happen when I was*
> *crossing the road.*                        *015:2*

then a broken pelvis resulting from a fall when mowing the front lawn, and cracked ribs when she fell through her son's window during a "dizzy spell". However, she appears to have battled her way through all the trauma and periods of immobility, mostly with very little help and support. She describes how she reacts when offered help:

> *I was at the lip-reading class and a lady said to me "Do you*
> *need any help" and I said "oh no I am fine", I am always very*
> *independent. But I said "I know a lady in her nineties who does*
> *need help". They said we're not interested in her, we are*
> *interested in you!*                                          015:4

Having recently discovered the Monday lunch club, she struggled to get there on a bus, for a trial run, but could not walk the 100 yards from the bus stop, so she took a taxi for her first proper visit the next day. She was worried about the £5 fare, but would not have mentioned this, except when pressed to disclose the cost, and was then delighted to be told of "a scheme whereby you pay £5 per week which covers your lunch and a taxi". Although not dwelling on the problems of deafness, coping here clearly demands much perseverance. She remarked that she had been "ripped off" by supposed gardeners or house-cleaners, and that her handbag was stolen in a local supermarket, probably because she had not heard someone approaching and delving into her basket.

One of Fay's coping strategies is her ***sense of humour.*** She mentioned this on a number of occasions, from everyday situations to more critical instances where an ability to laugh at her own misfortunes clearly assists her. On the occasion when she broke her pelvis, she was unaware of this, thought it was her hip "playing up again", and her son took her back to his house to "recuperate". She remarked that the only way she could get to the table for tea, was on her son's builder's trolley and "the two grandchildren were awestruck at gran being pushed!". The following day she was admitted to hospital and remained flat out for a month. Fay then went on to describe her shopping trip of yesterday, suggesting that as always this was one of the highlights of every week. A deaf friend drives her:

> *she is a wonderful driver and we laugh all the way. They have*
> *threatened to throw us out of Sainsbury's, we are such a riot!"*
>                                          *015:4*

A related theme, possibly deriving from Fay's understanding of what life is like when you are coping with one or more disabilities in an able-bodied world, is her ***empathy.*** She describes a visit this week of the Lord and Lady Mayoress to her lunch club. Fay had taken along a photograph of her new grandchild and one of the girls asked if the mayor could read the inscription:

> *but I didn't know the poor man was short- sighted. he had thick*
> *lenses, took them off and tried to read it but he couldn't. I felt*
> *so sorry for him and would have read it to them had I known*
>                                          *015:1*

Fay demonstrates this again when talking of some of the other people who attend the club, talking of a lively lady who has had both her legs amputated. When Fay was "fooling around" and said "I feel ninety this week", this lady "piped up well I am ninety-two".

Fay indicates ***an enjoyment of a varied activity routine.*** She participates as fully as possible in active sports, such as sailing and swimming and says the thing that she misses the most is "being able to take a brisk walk". She also has an interest in creative hobbies such as water colour painting and flower-pressing. Fay indicates an understanding of the therapeutic value of occupation too:

> *yes I used to make bread until recently too, it is very good for*
> *you, the dough, if you are feeling bad tempered!* 015:6

Fay shows pride in her accomplishments over the years, as demonstrated in her collection of certificates, many for jam-making and preserving (she made 50 jars of marmalade for the swimming club this year), and the most recent ones for swimming. She comments about her collection and hints at a sense of ***perpetuity*** too when she says:

> *I thought my grand-daughter might be glad of it, I don't want a*
> *lot of it thrown away* 015:6,7

Fay also refers to ***an interest in diet*** when she talks of cooking a main meal each day for herself, going on to say:

> *I have fish about twice a week, I don't eat much red meat,*
> *mostly white meat, I think it is better for me. I do get a bit*
> *scared with this BSE and I found that if I saw raw meat, it puts*
> *me off, so I eat a lot of vegs. I grow a few peas and beans and*
> *potatoes, about my limit now, but you almost have a meal with*
> *just those* 015:6

## Occupational Influences of Fay's Home Environment

Fay has lived alone in her house for the past 24 years, since her husband died. With a daughter in London and a son in North Wales, she does not see her family very frequently, nor does she make any mention of her immediate neighbours, or of any neighbourhood facilities she uses. Since mobility has become an increased problem she tends to be driven to activities that take place some distance away. Fay speaks with mixed feelings about her house and garden, clearly the stairs are difficult and she has problems in finding suitable help with cleaning:

> *I had a lady for 2 hours for £10, but she just did the bathroom*
> *and half the stairs, not like P.., who did everywhere in 2 hours*
> *and I used to say "stop!"* 015:7

Similarly Fay has difficulty in coping with the garden, she talks of "big long rows of sweet peas" which she used to grow, but now she is unable "to dig deep" for planting and she is looking for some reliable help in the garden. Fay's strongest positive comment about her environment concerns her store of memories. She says:

> *We were expecting J... and my husband came home with four*
> *roses he had bought in Woolworths, so I put one in each corner*
> *of the garden, there was nothing in it at the time but mint and*
> *weeds. One lived, it produced one flower in 30+ years. The*
> *year he died- 70 roses and it has been like this ever since. It is*
> *that one there and it is the first to come out in May- all those*
> *years!* 015:6

Indoors too, Fay has indications of her hobbies all around her. She has planned her house so that "things are left handy", although she indicates she has to do a lot of work whenever her daughter comes to visit because she invariably comments: "mother your house is like a pig-sty!"

## Conclusion

Fay presented as a lady who clearly has to struggle through each day. Nevertheless, within the limits imposed by pain and profound deafness, she has sought out a number of occupations that she continues to enjoy on a day-to-day basis. Although her home is now difficult for her to care for, Fay made no mention of looking for any alternative.

In Fay's case personal resources and traits such as stoicism and use of humour, have enabled her to maintain an active involvement in a wide range of pursuits. Her physical and sensory limitations are considerable, but these have not impeded her varied programme of interests. She has shown adaptation skills in taking on new ventures, such as her recent membership of a disabled swimming club, when other activities such as gym sessions, became too difficult. Fay did not refer directly to her need for occupation, but she made clear reference to her planning which incorporated one activity per day. Other evidence of the value of activities to Fay was provided when she displayed her collection of certificates in recognition of previous hobbies such as jam and chutney making. She suggested too that she would like to pass this collection on to her new grand-daughter in the future. This suggests that Fay places a high value on occupational success; it is worth struggling for against the odds and the records are worth preserving for future generations. An existential interpretation could be that such records provide evidence of *being*. As personalised and individualised documents, they serve as proof of Fay's authentic existence.


## Gladys

**Introduction**    Gladys has been widowed for two and a half years and still misses her husband a great deal. She now lives alone in the ground floor of her large six-bedroomed house. The house used to be an old people's home before she and her husband bought it twenty years ago. As the VAS scores reveal, Gladys suggested that both her quality of life and her satisfaction with personal activity levels are limited by her physical limitations. She has angina and severe pain and limited movement in her right hip; she had a left hip replacement some ten years ago and now uses a walking stick whenever she leaves the house. Her back also causes her pain since she slipped from her rocking chair six months ago. Despite her many problems, Gladys has organised her lifestyle so that she can cope; this is reflected in her SF36 score of 100% for social functioning. She takes a local bus and uses a trolley for shopping. She uses ready meals, has help with heavy housework and wears loose clothes that she can handle herself, declaring "I haven't worn socks or stockings since N (her husband) died". With a strong religious faith Gladys has derived much support from her local church; in return she helps out at a number of their afternoon activities, especially the ladies group and mother and toddler sessions. With a smile too she declares that this gives her chance to reduce her collection of books; she takes a few per week to sell to support church group funds. She has also, in recent past enjoyed Arthritis Care meetings, but when her local council withdrew transport to these events, she felt their replacement service of a low level bus charging £3.50 per trip, was too expensive. Gladys says her main support comes from good friends and neighbours, she sees little of her family. She has a daughter in Canada and one in poor health living in York and a son who lives ten miles away, but he is very busy and does a lot of line dancing. Gladys feels that she will not always be able to cope in her current environment, but she knows of a local residential home, which she has visited and she feels she could be quite happy here when the time comes.


Gladys was interviewed in the front lounge of her large Victorian house. A large pink hydrangea in the front garden filled the sunny bay window, and Gladys proved a bright conversationalist. Her right hip is now limited to 90% of flexion, and getting her small frame in and out of the armchair was a laborious process. Gladys was happy to talk about her yesterday. She led into the subject with a little information about her earlier jobs and occupational activities.

## Gladys's Daily Activities

Gladys spoke of a typical day, which normally involved rising at half past seven, having a light breakfast before dressing, then being ready to go shopping by 9.30 am. In this way she could be sure of buying fresh milk before supplies ran low. The afternoon was occupied by a mother and toddler group where Gladys helps out on a weekly basis, she commented: "whilst the kids are fighting, we have a good old natter". Gladys prepared her evening meal, a pre-packed chicken drumstick and vegetable dish, then settled down to an evening of reading. The MST completed some three months later, was able to explore Gladys's current occupations in greater depth. The first sort was for frequency:

| | |
|---|---|
| **Every day/ most days:** | cooking, shopping, reading, cups of tea, seeing friends, radio. |
| **Once a week:** | "T-pot bus", church, time with children, re-selling books, ladies group, television, Salvation Army teas, having a wander, sorting out, seeing her grandchildren. |
| **Occasionally:** | outings- has been on five this year. |

Gladys mentioned that with ten grandchildren and four great grandchildren, she sees at least one of them each week. She sees a lot less of her children.

Gladys then sorted the occupations for enjoyment:

| | |
|---|---|
| **Very much enjoyed:** | seeing friends, reading books, reading *The Echo* to "keep in touch", outings, time with children, having a wander and meeting people, "T-pot bus", ladies group, radio, cup of tea, selling books- as a money-raiser for charity. |
| **Done because they are a necessity:** | cooking- "not much fun for one", going shopping- "recently this has become a chore, I have to take my trolley just for a pint of milk now; it is something to hold on to", TV- only a few programmes enjoyed, eg. UK travel and archaeology. sorting out. |

Gladys places great emphasis on seeing her friends. She has both newer friends, made mainly via her local church activities, and a group of friends from many years ago. She referred frequently to the fact that "my friends are very important in my life". The long-standing group of friends began when the members were all teenagers together, in a local girl guide patrol. Eight to ten members of this group continue to meet once or twice per year at a nearby city church where they can "get a good meal". Gladys also has long-term friends from her night-school days.

## Personal Characteristics influencing Gladys's Occupational Day

Gladys returned several times during interview to a theme of ***meeting people.*** Her week is planned so that four days of each week include a scheduled meeting with people. Her church, ladies group, mother and toddler group and Age Concern T-pot bus are all features of a normal week. In between times Gladys spoke of liking to be out early in her local shopping centre:

> *I check my list, then get out. I've got a pass I can use any time, I*
> *don't have to wait for half nine.... So I go and have a wander*
> *around there. Its funny because nearly every time you meet*
> *somebody you know.*                                          *016:3*

Gladys has been a keen night school attendee for many years and has studied subjects from cookery to radio construction and Egyptology. She retains her membership of a local photographic club, although she is not able to get to many of the meetings. Gladys remains friends with people she met many years previously during her active participation in societies and classes.

Gladys clearly has an ongoing ***interest in the church.*** Many of her friendships are fostered here and she has found great support here when in times of difficulty. She described her first visit to the Salvation Army after her husband died:

> *the major who was there then, she couldn't have been kinder,*
> *she didn't say anything, she just put her arms around me and*
> *led me to a chair and sat me down....*                       *016:6*

This is a longstanding theme in Gladys's life; she had wanted to become a missionary doctor when she left school, but her father did not support her in this.

Gladys shows an ability to ***occupy time*** in ways that are meaningful to her and she enjoys ***continuing to learn.*** Not a great television addict, she responded to the researcher's question on the topic with:

> *Enjoy television....corr! I mean it is either violence, sex or bad*
> *language, or a mixture of the three. I might watch once or twice*
> *per week. Now last night I did watch; the programme about*

> *King Arthur about 1500 years ago when the whole sky went*
> *black….*                                                                 *016:5*

In the evening Gladys described "losing herself" in one of her books, with the comment that she did a lot of reading and often the children bought her books for Christmas. This theme led directly into her concern that she **has too many books.** Gladys commented that:

> *I have not hundreds but thousands. The small room upstairs,*
> *the walls are bookcases and well there's none in the bathroom*
> *but every other room has books, so I have started selling them*
> *at Arthritis Care once a month. Because people there cant get*
> *out much, so they probably do more reading than the average.*
> *They're probably like me, fed up to the back teeth with*
> *television*                                                              *016:5*

Gladys is doubly concerned about her large book collection because her son does not share her interest in books:

> *But I know what I… will do if anything happens to me. He'll get*
> *one of those big things and just bung everything in and they'll*
> *all finish on B…tip! If I know I…. I don't think he ever reads;*
> *well he is busy with line dancing now.*                                   *016:6*

Much of Gladys's account of yesterday was punctuated with **humorous anecdotes**. There was a wonderful fruit cake she produced in a cookery class and delivered to the children's tea table:

> *then I very proudly brought in this cake, expecting them to do*
> *the usual "oh isn't it lovely". There was dead silence from the*
> *two girls and I… pipes up "oh you haven't iced it". I could*
> *have hit him over the head with it!*                                      *016:4*

At the end of the interview, in response to the researcher's closure question soliciting anything Gladys would like if we could wave a magic wand, she giggled and responded:

> *I would straighten this road out. I have a nasty feeling it is*
> *sinking at the bottom and rising at the top, so that each time I*
> *come up, it seems a little bit steeper!*                                  *016:6*

Although said with humour, this remark suggests that Gladys's angina troubles her and some features of her immediate environment cause her increased difficulties in day-to-day living.

## Occupational Influences of Gladys's Home Environment

As Gladys had hinted during the first interview that she had some difficulties in coping with her hilly street, it seemed important to explore the environmental theme more fully as part of the MST. A third sort at this time was undertaken on the topic of environmental influence on occupational choices:

| | |
|---|---|
| **Activities dependent upon current house/ environment:** | selling books; there may not be outlets elsewhere. |
| **Activities not dependent upon current house and environment:** | all other activities. Gladys examined all her listed activities and stressed that she could and would make an active attempt to carry them out if in a new environment, finding a new church as a hub if necessary. |

The researcher followed this sorting activity with a question soliciting whether Gladys saw herself staying on in her current house. The response was: "as long as I can manage; there is a Methodist Home on the corner if I need it". Some years ago Gladys was a regular visitor to this Home when she collected for an Insurance Agency.

An additional feature that exacerbates environmental problems is *lack of suitable transport.* Gladys spoke of having to give up her car some years earlier because she had been in hospital four times with heart trouble which could "come on so soon. One minute I am sitting like this, the next out for the count". Since this time she has been able to use a bus for shopping, but has had to give up membership of some of the societies she enjoyed, for example the local archaeological society:

> *I don't go now because they moved down to...Park for the meetings. Of course the bus would be very handy but it doesn't run in the evenings, only in the day.*    016:3

## Conclusion

Gladys presented as a lively lady who despite quite severe health problems, continues to pursue social interactions and meaningful pastimes. She is sustained by friendships both new and old. She enjoys the company of her grandchildren but acknowledges that her children are not normally seen as part of a regular schedule. Her immediate environment and neighbourhood is of less importance to Gladys than her contacts and friends, and it appears that she will readily accept a move to a local Home which is known, when more help is needed.

The social element of occupational engagement figured high on Gladys' agenda. She spoke of her pleasure in meeting people and she participates in a number of social group events that are held in the afternoons. Quick to sense a chance for social encounter, Gladys comments on her daily shopping trips: "you nearly always meet someone you know". The same trips also appear to help Gladys structure her day: the occupational routine, beginning with early morning shopping for milk, acts as a timed starting point to most week-days. Gladys' faith and religious beliefs provide her with a strong *raison d'etre* and link closely with her personal ambitions to use time in a meaningful way. The church-orientated activities also enable Gladys to reciprocate and "give something back". Having received support from the church at the time of her husband's death, Gladys is now pleased to return this support by helping out and selling her books to boost church funds. In considering her future too, Gladys finds reassurance in knowing a Methodist Home nearby as "being there if I need it".

## Horace

**Introduction**      Horace aged 77years, cycles to the shops and to activities such as the local youth club where he helps out on a regular basis, and his health assessment (SF36) reveals high scores for both physical and social functioning. Horace asserts that he has to be strict with himself, in order to get through all the necessary jobs in a day. He has lived in his large semi-detached house for thirty-eight years and continues to take care of all his own housework. Although he considers his health is very good, he is frustrated that he has to struggle each day to get through the chores, sometimes even setting an alarm to wake him, should he fall asleep during the day. Horace has one stepson whom he sees infrequently, also a sister and niece fifteen miles away. Normally one member of his family will visit him about every six weeks. One of his hobbies is dancing, which he enjoys on a weekly basis with a new lady friend. Horace scores highly in both the SF36 function tests and in his quality of life rating. His frustration in fighting to "keep up" or "do more" each day, causes him mental discomfort and tension and a low self score of 3.1 out of 10 for his level of satisfaction with activities. He does not see that his health will get any worse and does not foresee that his environment will need to change.

Horace was interviewed on a hot July afternoon. The researcher was greeted on the doorstep of the large Edwardian semi. with "would you like a can of coke or a cup of tea?". On opting for the latter, this determined the place of interview, in the back room near the kitchen and whistling kettle. Horace opened a new packet of custard creams and we settled for the interview. He was a willing subject with much to say and was both tense and eager to stick to the remit for the interview. Before we began, he remarked that he had to work every day to "keep the house up". Since his wife's death ten years earlier, Horace has tried very hard to emulate her standards. As yesterday was a Sunday and therefore not a "usual sort of day", Horace opted to talk about last Thursday to describe his daily occupations.

## Horace's Daily Activities

Horace's day began at 7am, as did all his days except Sunday, when he permits a lie-in until 7.30 am. He then described a day that began with a cooked breakfast, then a bike ride to the local shops where purchases were dictated by a weekly shopping list that has been in use for many years. The Age Concern's "T-Pot" bus provided a mug of hot chocolate and a friendly chat, then Horace returned home about 2.30 pm. Later in the day he went to a monthly union meeting, then had "a few pints with the fellas", before returning home for supper. Horace remarked that he usually had his supper standing up, because if he sat down he fell asleep in front of the gas fire. He may not then wake for several hours, to find he has "been paying for the gas when the bedclothes should be doing the job". Horace spoke also of several other occupations that he enjoyed on a weekly basis. His list of activities comprised:

> having a cup of tea or chocolate, cooking breakfast,
> checking shopping list, housework, shopping,
> Age Concern's "T-Pot bus", riding a bike,
> Union meeting and a pint afterwards, cooking dinner,
> Friday youth club, table tennis, keyboard playing,
> dancing and music, seeing friends, church and communion.

An important part of each week is Horace's role in helping with a local youth club. He plays table tennis with the eight to eleven year old boys who attend.

## Personal characteristics influencing Horace's occupational day

An underlying group of themes appears to exert a strong influence over Horace's occupational day. He is quite a strict *disciplinarian*, who is very conscious of *the pressure of time*. In examining these themes together we can understand something of Horace's restless nature, which was evident throughout the interview and began with his account of getting up in the morning:

> *I get up at seven o'clock every morning except Sunday when its*
> *half past seven. I used to get up at half seven on Saturday and*
> *Sunday but I now find that's too much, I can't permit that, so I*
> *get up at half seven just on Sunday*         017:1

These themes are evident at the other end of the day too with Horace asserting that when he stayed in during the evenings, a "priority would be housework", because he does everything himself. He remarked that he bought himself a keyboard but hasn't been able to play it recently because:

> *the amount of work I have to do, it just stays there. There was a*
> *time when the washing was piled high, almost to the ceiling and*
> *I thought something has to be done...*        017:3

and at the end of each day too Horace is strict with himself again:

> *so the answer to that one is that I don't sit down for my supper*
> *then I can't fall asleep. I have it standing up, its usually just a*
> *few biscuits and cocoa as per the dietician's orders*
>                                        017:2

Horace has been worried about his increasing tiredness and sets an alarm for himself if he sits down in the afternoon, so that he will not fall asleep and waste time. On one occasion he went to visit a friend in hospital and fell asleep in the hospital corridor. He found himself admitted for investigations, but was released after a few days when they could find nothing wrong with him. In keeping with the theme of not wasting time, Horace has chosen to have no telephone and no television. He asserts that his bike and his radio are his "pals". He is able to adhere to advice too; when he was found to be a little anaemic a dietician recommended liquorice and chocolate, and liking both, Horace was happy "to comply". He is strict about having two cooked meals per day, breakfast and an evening dinner, and he remarks:

> *yes, I cook every day, a good sized dinner. I mean anything like*
> *meals on wheels would be an anathema to me, it really would. I*
> *sit down to a really good meal*           017:2

Enjoying a daily cooked breakfast too:

*bacon and I liked fried potatoes a lot- potatoes that I've boiled the day before, and I keep one back {laughs}. I delude myself its not kept over but I'm always glad to see it has been left over!*

*017:2*

A second group of themes occurring in Horace's interview embraces ***continuity and perpetuity*** that is linked to Horace's expression of ***spiritual direction*** and ***social conscience.*** Horace talked about his late wife and the shopping list she compiled :

*you will be horrified at the state of this I know. My wife made it ten years ago, before she died, and I keep to it. I do everything that my wife did. I regard my wife as a fellow runner in an Olympic race, and she dropped the baton when she died and I picked it up and carried on running, and part of the baton is this shopping list!*

*017:1*

So on the Thursday in question, as part of Horace's yesterday, he had bought the joint for the week-end, along with rice pudding, peas and beans, just as his wife had listed.

Horace spoke much during the interview about his involvement with a local youth club, suggesting that he did this because he needed to "pay something back". Horace mentioned attendance at church and communion early during the interview and the researcher pursued this with a question about spiritual direction, did this influence his decision to work with the young people for instance? Horace gave a full reply here, beginning with his belief about a life hereafter. On being asked his belief on this topic by an elderly friend, Horace's response was:

*I do {believe} to be quite honest I do. ....I read once an article by a priest and he put it this way, to imagine a chocolate factory. Into one end goes the cocoa, sugar, milk, all the ingredients necessary to make the sweets. They were processed and came out the other end, but what if they just went into a fire and got burned?- Too ridiculous for words; that we live our lives, strive for this and that, only to reach the end and get burned.*

*017:5*

This led Horace into revealing his justification for working so hard with the young youth club attendees. He spoke about the war and the fact that he "had a good time in the war, as long as he could get to the dances and the booze". He later felt that his actions were totally irresponsible because "others were having their guts gouged out for the likes of me". He then spoke directly of the youth club:

> *I've been there fourteen years... The children are those of those*
> *who did have their guts gouged out and I feel a certain*
> *responsibility to do something....Now I feel as though I am*
> *putting something in. So there's a spiritual action, I feel as*
> *though I have got to do something back*          *017:5*

A final theme emerging in this category is that of *valuing activity as a passport to friendships.* Horace mentioned this in relation to a number of activities and events. Visits to the "T-pot bus" were seen as enjoyable because "I am very friendly with the man there and vice versa", and the Union meetings were seen as an opportunity to "socialise with the fellas". In discussing gardening, Horace commented:

> *I don't dislike gardening, in so far as I used to work for the W...*
> *Council of Voluntary Service. That was about eight years ago.*
> *So although I was never one with green fingers I got into it just*
> *the same and could then join in the gardening conversation*
> *017:4*

Horace places much value too on an early friendship when he learnt to play table tennis during the nineteen thirties:

> *but I little thought 50 years hence that table tennis was going to*
> *be my salvation because I can lick practically all the kids at the*
> *youth club.*          *017:3*

## Occupational influences of Horace's home environment

Horace is very much aware that his current house is too big for his needs. However he feels he cannot move on and away from the family house at the moment until some family disagreements are settled. He is estranged from his step-son and feels he must sort out matters here, before he can dispose of contents from the family home. Having lived in his present house for thirty-nine years, Horace is familiar with his neighbourhood, although many of his activities take place either a bike ride or a bus ride away. He made only one mention of a friendship with a neighbour, this is a 91 year old gentleman whom Horace is currently visiting in hospital. Horace has a garden but has little time for it at present. Beyond the house and immediate neighbourhood, Horace places great emphasis on friendships and support networks. A regular Sunday morning communicant, Horace described how he met his current lady friend, some six years ago. At an early morning communion service Horace had a chat to the priest, also a friend and newly discharged from hospital, before the service began. They agreed that Horace would finish the communion wine as regulations dictate, as the priest's health forbade this. However just as the service began, a lady communicant arrived, and Horace had to engineer the process in order to remain the last communicant. He felt the need to explain this to the lady after the service and a new friendship began here. Now activities such as dancing, music and joint holidays are once again possible.

## Conclusion

Horace is working hard to fit the tasks into each day. He has many friends and support systems that are readily accessible to him within five miles of his home. He is able to cycle to many regular venues, but occasionally uses a bus. He does not like to use a bus to go to the youth club though, because:

> *they seem to expect me on the bike. They would regard me as*
> *beginning to crumble, to crack up if I didn't go on my bike*
> *{laughs}*            *017:2*

Horace has some plans to try to organise a family get-together within the near future, in the hopes that some long-standing disagreements may be resolved. If this should happen, he may be able to move to smaller accommodation that would entail less work for him. He has no lack of occupations, but is frustrated by his lack of time in which to pursue them.

For Horace, occupation has come to mean pressure, for he struggles each day to accomplish the tasks that he feels should be done, then finds himself tired and having no time or energy for hobbies he would like to do. The meaning of occupation for Horace appears steeped in legacy in that he feels strong needs to repay debts of the past and to carry on traditions that his wife introduced several decades ago. He has religious beliefs that support his personal philosophy of reaping what one sows, and it is possibly such beliefs that force him to drive himself so hard. This does not bring contentment as his VAS scores show. Occupation fails to reflect Horace's current *being;* rather it reflects characters and occurrences from his past.

# CHAPTER 7  IAN, JOYCE, KARL AND LUCY

## Ian

**Introduction**        Ian is still experiencing bereavement and acute periods of overwhelming sadness. After 58 years of marriage, his wife died fifteen months ago. For the final three years of her life Ian had been her full-time carer and their home was re-adjusted with downstairs bedroom etc. to facilitate this. Some fifteen years before this time, Ian had taken early retirement in order to help his wife when she first became ill. Ian has lived in the same terraced house for over fifty-nine years, being moved here when his parental home was bombed and his mother was killed at the same time. Ian is not in good health himself and rheumatoid arthritis causes him considerable pain. He uses two sticks out of doors and his walking capability is limited to one short block. His hands are also affected which means that all tasks involving grip are difficult. As a retired craftsman, much of his home furniture is self-made and French polished and his current level of disability causes increased sadness. Ian has other health problems too and is "on a daily cocktail of pills". He is mostly housebound, going out once per week to his local church for half an hour. As the standardised tests reveal, scores on the SF36 are low in particular for physical function and emotional status and the self-charted VAS scores reveal a low to moderate quality of life score. Ian has a niece who visits most weeks, his two brothers and an elder sister have all died and he has no children.

For the interview, the researcher was welcomed into a comfortable back lounge, furnished with tables, shelves, fire surround and cabinet that were all Ian's own handiwork. During his working life Ian was a French polisher at a local shipyard for over thirty years and he still keeps a full set of his carpentry tools, although due to multiple joint arthritic involvement, he can no longer use or even hold the tools. He is in pain for much of the time, and has a reactive depression following the death of his wife fifteen months ago. Ian had been her constant carer for the three-year period prior to her death and he misses her a great deal. Before starting the interview, Ian moved a large emptied margarine box, full of his assorted daily medications, to make space for the researcher on the sofa. Ian described himself as, like people of the time, those who grew up in the war, very independent, having very little but then those next door had very little either, so you made the best, got on with it, and asked for nothing because nobody had anything to give.

## *Ian, Joyce, Karl and Lucy*

## Ian's Daily Activities

Ian described his yesterday, although he said that "all the days are pretty much the same". He indicated that the only exceptions would be Thursdays when he "went down for his pension" and was usually out about half an hour and Saturday evenings when he crossed the road to his local church and was again out for half an hour. Ian said that he slept poorly and was up several times each night to visit the toilet because of his prostate problems for which he is awaiting potential surgery later this month. He is always awake from 3.30 am onwards, and dozes after this time. About getting up he says:

> *Round about 8 o'clock if I want to get up I can't be bothered. I*
> *just lie there, might lie until 9 o'clock, then come downstairs,*
> *feeling neither one thing nor the other.*           *018:1*

Ian then went on to describe a day that involved some household tasks, interspersed with lengthy periods of "just sitting". During the course of interview he talked of the following occupations that he still undertakes:

Cooking, weekly attendance at church, sitting,
sport on television, visits from his niece,
going to the post office, old time discs or tapes,
reminiscing, sitting in the garden, tidying around.

## Personal Characteristics influencing Ian's Occupational Day

Although Ian clearly attempts to find a positive outlook, he is greatly inhibited by both ***physical pain and immobility*** and ***constant depression***. He struggles not to dwell on his problems with the outlook that:

> *but I think I am lucky; I've got a lot of problems but who*
> *hasn't?...and I think if you dwell on your own problems you*
> *can make yourself more ill than what you are, and not only that*
> *but you depress everyone else don't you?*           *018:3*

However he clearly finds this difficult to do and describes how the depression can overwhelm him when he gets up:

> *occasionally I have come down{stairs} and felt exceptionally*
> *great, and I've thought: "oh this is smashing", no headache,*
> *feeling really good and it lasts about an hour. Then it is almost*
> *like a weight that comes on me, like a headache this type of*
> *depression comes on me...*           *018:1*

He returns to this theme later in the interview as he thinks about retiring for the night, when again he is trying not to think of his problems and not to "become a martyr" to himself. He talks to himself:

> *oh for God's sake, shake yourself out of it, there's a million*
> *people worse off than what you are…doesn't make my case any*
> *easier, but that's not the point. The point is as you get older like*
> *me you must not start having any doubts in your mind. Although*
> *I still admit when night- time comes around, its nearly always*
> *worrying especially if you are feeling a bit off colour….*
>
> *018:2*

Although Ian is worried about his health, an accompanying theme is **stoicism** or as he himself describes it: "pig-headedness". The researcher asked did he have anyone he could call on if he felt unwell or worried in the evenings and his response was: "its just the way I have been brought up, I don't think I would". Then he added that he did not want to bother anybody, despite the fact that two neighbours and his niece have encouraged him to ring at any time if he needs help, so he has decided if he needs help because of feeling ill, he will just ring the hospital.

One theme which brought instant animation was Ian's **recall of past events.** He mentioned this on a number of occasions, and these were clearly times when he enjoyed a great deal of sport. Earlier as a child, he regularly played football in the local park:

> *we lived right by the park, so we used to mainly go there, play*
> *football you know and finish up with a score like 99, 96!*
>
> *018:4*

and he currently enjoys listening to old discs and tapes:

> *…talking about the women and when they went to the washing*
> *places over the river and when they were on the dole, and the*
> *overhead railway and all the liners and all that.*  *018:2*

He enjoys his niece's regular visits too, because "she is interesting", she "laughs a lot" and she also likes to ask about the past with questions like: "when you and my dad were young, what did you used to do?" He also enjoys these visits because he can clearly become involved, he collects coupons for school computers, because his niece is a supply teacher and always in need of equipment and resources.

Frequently during the yesterday interview, Ian referred to the theme of ***just sitting.*** When he had finished his breakfast and tidied the papers, he would "go to the door to get some fresh air, then just generally sit around". After lunch he did not take a rest, he may watch the television if it was sport or travel "but generally I just sit", and in the evening of yesterday he commented:

> *I just er...let the world go by. Its just a case of sitting around*
> *and letting the evening pass.*                    *018:2*

On the theme of ***cooking*** Ian was quite positive with:

> *oh I never go hungry, never go hungry. I'll have cornflakes and*
> *fruit juice of a morning and dinner hour as I say I can cook,*
> *beans, fish..., sausage and mash, so I have no problem at all*
> *with my food, a bit of a problem with opening things but I get*
> *round it.*                              *018:2*

## Occupational Influences of Ian's Home Environment

Ian is surrounded on a daily basis with reminders of how difficult life has become. He still has a downstairs bedroom that he does not use, but it was converted for his wife during her illness. A small corner table in the lounge with a large photograph of his late wife and constant fresh flowers, is also a reminder of his loss. Ian's love of carpentry and marquetry is also in evidence in items of hand-crafted lounge furniture, and he is particularly sad that he can no longer manage such hobbies. Ian enjoys sitting in his garden even though he can manage little of the manual work necessary to maintain it: he has paid help here and can manage a little light work outside. Beyond the immediate environment Ian speaks of knowing few people in the street, although two middle aged neighbours have offered to help him if he is in need. It is helpful that both his local church and a local post-office are within short walking distance as these provide focal points for short weekly excursions. Ian did not talk of a move away from his family home, even though he is clearly concerned if he has to go to bed at night knowing that he feels unwell.

## Conclusion

Ian reported a day, in fact most days, which brought him little satisfaction, although he clearly tried hard not to dwell on this topic. On a final note as the interview finished, Ian mentioned two occupations that he could still manage although he did not feel sufficiently stimulated to sit and concentrate very often; these activities were ***poetry composition and painting.*** It appeared that with further encouragement he may find satisfaction in such activities in the future.

The researcher was given a copy of two of Ian's poems as the interview drew to a close. The poems were entitled "The old tramp steamer" and "Mother".

The meaning of occupation for Ian is complex to untangle. Surrounded by his own hand-made furniture whose construction he can no longer contemplate due to arthritic deformities in his hands, and faced daily by memories of his deceased wife and her long-term illness, in that the dining room still remains as her converted bedroom, Ian struggles with what today's occupational role constitutes. His environment provides strong, constant memories of *past occupation*s and Ian is able to recall this period of his life with a mixture of pleasure and regret that this productive time is over. He reflects on the many years he spent upstairs working on his marquetry, totally absorbed and only roused when "my wife used to call me down for my meals". Today's occupational role is however nebulous and made further indistinct due to pain and multiple health problems that cloud any future ambitions. Watercolour painting and poetry composition are potential occupations that are brought to mind as possible future occupations, but they are not for today, Ian will wait until he feels better enough to tackle them.

## Joyce

**Introduction**        Joyce lives alone in a council bungalow, supported by a team of three carers who are employed on a rota basis to provide three daily visits, morning, lunch-time and evening. The bungalows also have a warden scheme, providing a warden who calls round each day. Additionally Joyce has a weekly visit from a nurse to assist with bathing. Joyce moved to her bungalow eleven years ago, from older property in the area. She is housebound, stating that the last time she went out was approximately three months ago, by special minibus. Within her home she uses a walking frame and can move from room to room independently. With very limited sight, Joyce is highly dependent on familiar surroundings, describing how difficult life can become if she has a new carer who inadvertently places her prepared ham sandwich tea in the wrong place in the refrigerator, meaning that Joyce will not be able to locate it when tea-time comes. Joyce is also moderately deaf, but living alone she only uses her hearing aid infrequently. In examining standardised test results, the SF36 reveals a zero score for her physical function, and the NLSA records that Joyce has no living relatives in this country, just one niece in Canada. Her husband died thirty years ago and their only son had died at aged eighteen months from meningitis. In addition her seven younger siblings have all died. Despite such negative findings, Joyce scores above average on the quality of life VAS and a full 100% on the SF36 with regard to emotional limitations. She has a positive outlook, backed by a religious faith, and over the past few years she has actively cultivated new friendships. She is an excellent raconteur, a powerful singer and barely a day goes by without a visitor. She sleeps only fitfully at nights, but sings along to the radio when she is awake. She says "I love my little bungalow" and she hopes to be there to receive her 100th birthday telegram from the Queen.

Joyce's interview took place in her own home. Researcher field notes record the occasion:

> *I was let in via an intercom buzzer, from the bedroom.*
> *Joyce was seated on the edge of her bed, with rollator and walker in front of her. After introductions we went into the front room where Joyce had put the heater on earlier. We had a magical two plus hours with amazing glimpses into over ninety years of her life. Due to profound deafness and very poor eye-sight, the interview had to take a non-standard approach and was at times difficult to conduct. Joyce was however a willing conversationalist and clearly loved singing.*
>
> Field notes: 019:1

Joyce has lived in her bungalow, with minimal support from a warden-scheme, for the past eleven years. A professed "no pills" lady she exudes warmth and a strong interest in others and in her surroundings. She mentioned on questioning that she had last been out about three months ago when taken in a specially adapted van, to a Valentine's Day dinner.

## Joyce's Daily Activities

Joyce followed the researcher's advice in attempting to describe her yesterday. However there were many sidetracks taken into relevant and associated areas, some connected with the past and others associated with coping with a double sensory deprivation problem. The whole interview provided a clear picture of a lady who is content in her surroundings, and is supported by a team of three carers who come in for three brief periods in the day, at 9 am to assist with dressing and preparation of breakfast, at midday for preparation of a light lunch and at 7.45 pm to assist Joyce with retiring for the night. The radio provides a strong occupational element to both the day and the night.

## Personal Characteristics influencing Joyce's Occupational Day

Throughout the interview Joyce's *positive outlook* was apparent. This was a natural manifestation, not enforced. There was no sense or mention of "looking on the bright side", and despite many hardships which were apparent to the researcher there was no mention of life being difficult. Joyce appears to have accepted her many losses which included death of an only son from meningitis when he was aged 18 months, all relatives including seven siblings who have died, and the loss too of much of her own sight and hearing, without rancour. She remembers in particular the "goodness" of her mother in the days when she made ointments for horses' hooves to sell at the local market and cooked for the large family, frequently preparing fish:

> *she was very, very clever my mother. She could make ointments, standbuck...and my brothers used to go fishing, they had a licence to go fishing in the Shropshire Union {Canal}.... We had a great big aquarium at home in the back yard and they used to fetch trout and eels home....She used to cook the eels, but she skinned them like that and she dried the skins for sprained wrists.* 019:5

and again, she saw her mother as an admirable figure:

> *she was very good my mother, she used to go and scrub the church hall for nothing, aye and there was no carpets in them days, you made your rag mats.* 019:8

In the same vein too, Joyce talks of her current carers, describing them as "a good bunch of girls". She stresses too the importance to her of having her regular carers because she quickly has problems if a new carer comes along and replaces anything (from tea towel, to sandwich tea) in the wrong place, Joyce would not be able to find it. On dull days her sight is so poor that she sees very little. Joyce's positive outlook is evident in her ambition, "to be here in my own home to get my telegram from the Queen"; this is looking two years hence.

Linked to the first theme is Joyce's sense of *valuing friendships.* She has made conscious attempts to cultivate friendships and now one friend whom she met in a pub some twenty years ago, is "almost like a son" to her. He and his wife visit every week and keep her company. On the researcher's second visit, the friend was there and he and Joyce were sharing their usual Friday afternoon can of Guinness. Joyce comments too that she always values her carers too and makes sure they make themselves a cup of tea as well as providing for her. She goes on to say:

> *all the girls that come here, they like coming and I speak for*
> *them…. They all like me; well you may as well make a friend*
> *010:3*

She talks proudly too of her friendly rapport with her doctor. Although she professes never to take medications, she rings her doctor regularly to talk over any problems she is encountering. Through her friendships Joyce remains outward looking and retains an interest in those around her and her community, even though she is rarely able to leave her house. Joyce has a good **sense of humour** too and this shows as she describes feeling happy when she "meets old friends too":

> *do you know, when you go to sleep at night, I think you're dead,*
> *because it is nearly always them who have gone before that you*
> *dream about. Its funny isn't it!* *010:7*

A further theme also relates to Joyce's positive outlook, this is **faith**. Joyce holds strong Christian beliefs and has a vast repertoire of inspirational hymns that she knows off by heart, and sings to herself. As she finished singing one of her favourite hymns she replied almost indignantly to the researcher's question about the relevance of God in her life, with:

> *oh he's never out of it, oh no. How do you think I manage here?*
> *I'll tell you what comes in here: (sings) "Following Jesus, ever*
> *day by day nothing can harm me when he leads the way…"*
> *010:7*

As regards **diet** Joyce mentions several times that she has always been very fond of fish, it is "brain food". Nowadays, every Friday her friends bring her a piece of haddock from the market for her tea. She tried meals on wheels, but had to stop them some time ago, they were much too big:

> *I couldn't eat them, I was giving them to the cat and the birds*
> *and the pigeons at the back* *010:2*

As part of her daily diet too, Joyce is a firm believer in a tot of whisky every night. She attests that she had an early diagnosis of hardening of the arteries, but now feels that her daily whisky helps this problem. She says she should have a regular pint of Guinness also, but cannot now pour it without it "going all over the place", so she only has her afternoon Guinness when her friend comes to open the can.

The single **occupational entertainment** which Joyce enjoys daily is her **radio** and tape player. She has a radio in her living room and one in her bedroom as she sleeps fitfully at nights, so frequently has the radio on during the night hours. She likes old songs and hymns in particular. Joyce has an excellent memory for the words of the old songs, and retains a powerful singing voice, so frequently she sings along to the radio or tapes. During interview Joyce talked of the morning she went to school after the Titanic sank:

> *our teachers said there's a boat gone down and there's children*
> *on board so we sang for them {sings} "Nearer my God to thee*
> *nearer to thee...".* 010:7

She comments that she can no longer see to read and although virtually unable to see the television, she keeps a small set because "you see I might have friends that want to see it".

## Occupational Influences of Joyce's Home Environment

Joyce's home environment exerts a strong influence over her capacity to enjoy occupations that are meaningful to her. As her sight has diminished gradually over the past few years, the familiarity of her surroundings enables her to locate both essential items and her treasured possessions. Although unable to see her favourite photographs displayed around her lounge, she knows the images by heart and can point them out to share with visitors and friends. In her own home too, she is able to play her radio sufficiently loudly for her to hear, without fear of disturbing any-one, whether during the day or night. In any less private circumstances, such as sheltered housing or a residential facility, this practice would be regarded as anti-social. An essential factor that bridges home environment and community involvement, is the comprehensive care package that Joyce has. Her team of three carers, plus weekly nurse and regular home visits from a chiropodist, are all essential components in her ability to remain ambulant and continue living in her own home. Joyce commented on how important it is for her regular carers to remain as constant as possible:

> *and then they make me a sandwich for my tea. I can't see in the*
> *fridge you see so they put everything just where I know I can*
> *get it out the fridge* 010:3

Joyce then demonstrated the critical half shelf in the fridge where she knows she will always be able to locate her prepared tea. Any change in carer, can disrupt this finely tuned ability to cope. The warden also helps Joyce to feel involved in her community, Joyce remarked:

> *the warden over there, she comes to see me every day, oh aye I*
> *bought a couple of draw tickets for the horses yesterday. I don't*

*believe in them, don't like horses, but my husband loved them,*
*he always did the races.*                                    *010:2*

Joyce makes visitors welcome in her home, which means that she has many callers. She feels secure with her intercom door entry system, linked to a buzzer, and knows whom she is admitting. Last week an ex-carer visited with her new born baby, and Joyce had greatly enjoyed having "him plonked on my knee".

## Conclusion

Joyce presents as a lady with a strong faith and life-force. She has a positive outlook despite serious sensory deprivation and lack of any living relatives for support. She retains an interest in others and has made active attempts to cultivate friendships. These have become increasingly important as her mobility has declined and she has become housebound. Until recently Joyce has always had a cat to provide companionship, but says with regret that she could no longer care for one. The immediate environment, together with an organised support routine is vital in assisting Joyce to maintain both her independent living and her ongoing participation in occupations that she continues to enjoy.

In exploring the meaning of occupation for Joyce we find a major focus on *times past*. Great value is placed on both people and events of the past and they are subject to regular recall. Singing hymns of her childhood and youth and listening to popular music of the 1940s and 1950s brings Joyce a great deal of current pleasure. Likewise remembering and recounting tales of childhood and her mother's activities, is also a pleasurable experience for Joyce. Although she cannot see many of her old photographs, they are strategically placed in her home, their positions are known well, and in this way Joyce can locate them to point out and share with friends. Today's occupations, although drawing strongly on the past for stimulus material are rooted in today in a *social sense*, for Joyce takes good care to make all visitors and carers feel welcome with the comment that: "well you might as well make a friend". Joyce's approach to today is grounded in a strong religious faith and it is this that sustains her ongoing *existence*.

## Karl

**Introduction**        Karl has lived alone in his own semi-detached house, since his second wife died twelve years ago. He has lived in the same house for over forty years and just recently he had a chairlift fitted on his stairs. His son lives "just ten minutes away". He is disabled himself and walks with two sticks but he is able to collect Karl and take him to his home for Sunday teas. Although Karl reports himself as generally in good health for his age, he has recently had balance problems and a number of falls. He has furniture strategically placed in his home, to provide support should he become unsteady and out of doors he needs a person's arm and a stick. Alternatively he uses a pavement scooter for longer distances. He graphically describes his first need for the scooter some three years ago, after "the awfulness of the doctor taking away the car, when my legs first gave way". Always an active man and something of a public figure in his community, Karl still rates himself in the VAS as being very satisfied with his current level of activity, although frustrated sometimes when activities, even dressing, take a long time to accomplish. He is pleased to be pain free and mentally astute, and scored full marks for health status in these areas. A sociable person Karl enjoys ongoing involvement with local committee work and the social side of being taken to church on a Sunday.

Karl's interview took place in his front lounge. Painters were busily decorating the house exterior and Karl mentioned that until recently he had always done this himself. Karl has been an active member of his community, holding such public offices as magistrate and council member. Today he was an articulate and clear thinking interviewee who clearly found some questions quite thought provoking. For instance one question on the SF36 Form asks how true is the statement: "I expect my health to get worse". Here Karl pondered the truth of the statement versus the expectation and the fact that he does not dwell on it; was this then true or false...? A twice married gentleman, Karl now takes care of all his own needs and is independent within his home.

## Karl's Daily Activities

Karl would have been pleased to describe his actual yesterday, but as it was a most unusual day (a neighbour drove him out into the countryside and they had lunch out), it was a joint decision that Karl would report on an "ordinary" day, so he reflected on the day before yesterday, although he was a little worried that this would "sound awfully dull". His day begins at quarter to eight with breakfast, two cups of tea and usually part of a newspaper. After washing the pots, he sits in the armchair by the fire for half an hour. Then he takes the ewbank to clean around where he eats his meals. At this point he took the stairlift up to the bathroom and toilet, had a wash and shave and came downstairs to put washing in the machine. He then reflected that he could not have tea until the washing was finished because he could not take the water off the supply. So he read a little more of the paper, then sat and thought about what he had read, and so his day progressed. The discrete daily activities mentioned were:

washing and dressing, reading the newspaper,
meal preparation, receiving a letter, watching the television,

listening to the radio news, sitting and reflecting,
having a cup of tea, doing the washing, tidying the house,
looking out of the window, having a snooze.

Karl reported that he reflected on a Thursday, a highlight day of the week as he always received a letter from an old friend in Devon, this is a person who "is almost a son, he was brought up with my son". Retired himself, the friend writes every week, although Karl remarks that he cannot respond so frequently as he has "nothing newsy" to say. Another enjoyed day during the week is a Sunday when a congregation member picks him up by car to go to the local Baptist Church, his neighbour brings him a cooked lunch and he then goes to his son, a 5 minute car drive away, for his tea.

## Personal Characteristics influencing Karl's Occupational Day

A recurring theme that has a strong influence on Karl's day is his capacity as a **thinker and reflector**. His day is interspersed with periods when he sits and thinks. His mid-morning routine includes the period whilst his washing machine is going:

> *then if there is anything left in the newspaper from the day*
> *before, I finish that off, then sit down and think about what I*
> *have read*                                       *020:1*

He uses his skills of reflection frequently throughout his day; this may be to assist his own personal progress such as when he is in the local supermarket and actively examines the shelves with the quest for "something new for tea", and it extends too to his general view of **working to improve oneself**:

> *I have always believed that doing a job today will lead me to do*
> *it better tomorrow and if I go on progressing in that way, I am*
> *then leading the life I want to live.*              *020:3*

He goes on to say that he cannot understand the people who are "always content to do the same job, and never want to improve it", adding that he could never be content if he was not "aiming to get better". Karl returns to the theme of reflection as he plans his late evening, with the comment:

> *I go to bed round about half eleven to twelve, on the premise that*
> *I am not going to sleep more than about six hours anyway. This*
> *is just part of me, and if it's a winter morning I can't find*
> *anything to think about at that time, but if its light there's plenty*
> *to think about.*                                   *020:2*

It interests him that his ability to think creatively is influenced by the level of light and he goes on to ask the researcher: "Now can you sort that one out? I can't!"

Although well able to use his inactive times for creative thinking, there is also a sense that Karl spends a considerable portion of each day ***waiting***. He frequently prepares a "packet lunch", although once a week he always cooks fresh vegetables. Then after his lunch he refers to the period when he "waits for one o'clock", for the radio news. Again, later in the day after his tea he comments: "then I wait for the six o'clock news on the television, a big event of the day". In-between times Karl is aware that the period from 4pm to 5pm is an awkward one:

> *that can be the dull spot of the day... I mean Countdown or*
> *Fifteen to One is good, until you see how limited you are in*
> *relation to the contestants!*                           020:1

Now that Karl is mainly housebound he values a particular ***observation point,*** his lounge window:

> *this window is my window on the world and I very frequently go*
> *to it. The neighbours, I wonder if they think I am nosey? Not*
> *that I particularly care. But I know there are two kinds of*
> *people; those who always look at me and those that never look*
> *{laughs}*                           020:1

Following the observation theme and linking this to Karl's television preferences, he remarks that he used to watch *Coronation Street*, feeling that it was true to life, but he has now become more critical in his observation and comments that "everyone seems to be going round in circles" and that they seem to be leading a very stilted life. Now instead he prefers the spontaneous wit of programmes such as *Have I got News for You*. His newspaper choice for the week is the Saturday *Times* because it has the TV times in it, and "it is voluminous, whereas a tabloid has nothing to it".

A final personal characteristic theme which runs through the day and the week is Karl's ***support from the church.*** He attests that he is "not a religious man", but he has been a regular attender at a local Baptist Church for nearly seventy years. He met both his first and his second wife here, and now a member of the congregation collects him every Sunday to drive him there in her car. Although he readily admits that he has no religious convictions, Karl enjoys the social contact and tomorrow for instance, some church visitors are calling for his help with the books.

## Occupational Influences of Karl's Home Environment

As noted above, Karl enjoys his local neighbourhood in a number of ways, he has a good friend in a next door neighbour, a lady whom he has helped with research in the past, so now it is not difficult for him to accept the regular Sunday lunch which she cooks for him. Although he cannot now walk out unaided, he takes a weekly trip on his pavement scooter to the local park, and indoors he has the recent adaptation of a stair lift. He also has furniture strategically placed around his home, so that should he feel unstable, he always has a solid item to use to grasp and steady himself. He is now unable to tend his own garden, but he has help here and clearly still takes a great deal of pride in the smart appearance of his longstanding home. He values the ways in which he can still contribute towards his community; this he expresses in the reciprocal support with his neighbour, and the tasks, such as book keeping which he undertakes for his local church.

## Conclusion

Karl is clearly keen to remain in his home. He understands and appreciates the community care support he has; he values his window on the world and his independent life-style. He would not want to be in a Home, and queries the compatibility of the residents, suggesting that it could be like being on a perpetual cruise where you could not choose your travelling companions! He is also aware of some Homes that smell. So Karl feels his current environment is very important to him and his being within it helps him structure his day.

In unpicking the meaning of occupation for Karl we see a person who in the past was used to full occupational involvement in his community, now making judicious and reflective use of an expanded time frame in ways that help him satisfy his need to *improve and do better tomorrow*. He plans carefully so that as far as possible time is not wasted. Knowing that he can only use wakeful periods at night for *constructive thinking* when it is daylight, he elects to go to bed later in the winter, because the mornings are darker and therefore of little use to him. He does not like to lie awake if he cannot think. During the day too Karl uses all available stimuli to assist his reflection. Choosing a large, content-laden weekly paper, he reads sections at a time during the week, then considers what he has read. Likewise he prefers television programmes that provide a degree of challenge and provoke independent thought. He evaluates the programmes too, making changes in his viewing habits when any programme fails to stimulate his desire for progress. Although unable to walk out alone, Karl has carefully thought through how he can continue to *be in the community*. He makes use of his large lounge window, using it as a regular observation point and as he describes it his "window on the world". He is not unrealistic about his future, but rather prefers to dwell on the *here and now*, because he has control over his current pattern of existence and intends to make the most of it. To this end he is currently working on his 4-5 pm time slot in each weekday, because at the moment it is "the dull spot of the day".

## Lucy

**Introduction**        Lucy moved to her current sheltered housing association complex nine years ago, just after the death of her second husband. She moved sixty miles to be closer to her stepson, knowing no one in her new locality. Her stepson lives some fifteen miles away and she does not see him very often. As the SF36 scores reveal. Lucy's health is not good. Her mobility is severely restricted since she fell and splintered the head of her right femur, two years ago. She has considerable pain, and can walk about one hundred yards on a "good day", with the help of a stick. She has intermittent problems with falls, most recently she cracked five ribs when she fell in her bathroom. Lucy has just relinquished her bus pass because she is no longer able to get on and off the local busses, and she now relies on the weekly specially adapted van that takes residents to the local supermarket. An added complication for Lucy is caused by her bouts of severe clinical depression. Although on constant medication, she still experiences very black periods, when she is often unable to do anything until mid-day. Her most recently diagnosed health problem is macular degeneration and her eyesight is now severely restricted. In a bright light she can identify objects, but she can no longer read nor do any of her formerly enjoyed handicrafts. The multiple health problems provide explanation for low self-ratings on the VAS scores; Lucy rated her quality of life as below average and her satisfaction with activity level as 2 out of the possible score of 10.

Lucy's sheltered housing unit is tucked behind an arbour with seat and giant climbing yellow rose bush in the open plan garden. Behind her ground floor apartment is a sheltered private patio, a haven for birds and the morning sun. After an entry-phone admission, Lucy welcomed the researcher into her front lounge and a fascinating conversation with a forthright lady followed. Lucy's upright posture, immaculate hairstyle and strong facial structure belied her eighty-five years, also her painful shattered hip and the enormous frustration of decreasing eyesight due to macular degeneration, plus the burden of a twelve year history of clinical depression, when "the gremlins take over at 6am and can stay for four hours at a time". With multiple health problems, Lucy currently does not go out alone, but within her home she copes independently.

## Lucy's Daily Activities

All the following activities were mentioned by Lucy as having taken place yesterday:

sorting out, feeding the birds and squirrels, preparing meals,
knitting, watching television, making long distance phone calls,
tidying the house, sitting around, sitting and looking in the garden,
having a rest after lunch, sitting and dreaming.

During the week too, Lucy mentioned a number of other activities, such as a weekly minibus trip down the road to a local supermarket, having her hair done by the warden's wife, going to a craft class and going out for a meal with friends. She mentioned that she likes to have one activity per day organised, that is quite sufficient and they usually take place in the afternoon.

## Personal Characteristics influencing Lucy's Occupational Day

Lucy works hard to ***manage her ill-health***. On the morning of the interview, the "gremlins" had been, which meant that her day began to be productive at a later time than normal. She has made every effort to learn all she can about clinical depression, so that she is best equipped to live with it:

> *I have been waking at 6 o'clock in the morning- it's the*
> *gremlins you see, and then I just get up, you are worse lying*
> *down you see. So I say to myself: "You must get up, don't lie*
> *there, you must DO something"*          *021:1*

She recently attended a series of twelve group meetings for elderly people with depression. She found that all the other participants had a reactive form of the illness, whereas hers is of unknown origin. After this series, Lucy comments:

> *I have learnt to manage it now. If I wake up with the gremlins, I*
> *just say: "Oh go away, shut up, I don't want you". You see I do*
> *know now that it will all pass. I just need to be patient, and not*
> *get in a state, and not have a panic attack; they are the worst*
> *things.*          *021:1*

Lucy clearly misses the busy life she had and her hobbies such as letter writing:

> *Oh, I loved it {letter writing}, it was one of my hobbies. I could*
> *write anything up to ten pages, but I could relate what I was*
> *doing because I had a busy life.*          *021:3*

She enjoyed all sorts of handicrafts too, but by way of compensation she has actively sought something she can do, so is now knitting squares for international appeals. Lucy describes how a group of four knitters work on the squares, then one member sews them together, a convoy collects the blankets each month and the last consignment went to Romania. Lucy says of this new hobby:

> *it does mean I can just pick it up and I find it, to a certain*
> *extent, really quite soothing, now that I can do something.*
> *021:4*

So Lucy compensates for her increasing incapacities by careful planning and by modifying her lifestyle and activities.

Lucy has a **practical interest in diet**; again this is frequently related to her health. For instance she prepares an evening snack because "my doctor said: 'have something in your stomach, don't leave it empty all those hours, that might help you'". Her store cupboard always contains ready foods such as tinned rice pudding and jelly, and yesterday for lunch she had prepared a frozen fish cutlet with chips and mushy peas "because it was easy". Lucy takes care to start the day well, with a healthy breakfast that always includes an item of fruit.

Lucy clearly **values friendships.** She enjoys the social occasion of eating out with friends on a weekly basis, and appreciates the company of other residents when they gather in the summer, with cups of afternoon tea in the front arbour. On past occasions Lucy has had several periods of respite care at a nearby residential home and she greatly values the friendliness of the carers here:

> *oh they are great fun! When I left last time I said to them "You*
> *know, I do love you girls, you are like my daughters or grand*
> *daughters"*                                  *021:4*

Lucy smiled as she recounted that in this particular home "they always have a laugh and there is a lot of banter between me and the staff!" Lucy recognizes that being with other people is a great help to her particularly when she is feeling low, and she plans accordingly so that most days of the week she sees other people. There are regular coffee mornings and she has a friend in for tea on a regular basis. She speaks of her difficult days too when she has no outside contact:

> *Sunday is always a dull day here.... Saturdays and Sundays are*
> *the difficult days. I find I am very, very lonely on those two days*
> *021:1,2*

Before her retirement Lucy ran kennels, and although she has no pets at the moment, she retains her **liking of animals.** She has a morning routine of feeding the garden birds and a tame squirrel and two pigeons on her patio, whilst she has breakfast in the adjoining room. She comments: "this keeps me going through breakfast, I love my animals".

## Occupational Influences of Lucy's Home Environment

To many people Lucy's environment would appear ideal for her needs. It is physically accessible, supported by a warden and services such as a weekly bus to the supermarket. It is also conducive to hobbies that she currently enjoys, such as the morning routine of feeding the many wild birds on her patio and her lunch-time routine:

> *I like a glass of wine before my lunch, so I sit down about half*
> *past eleven and look in the garden                021:2*

Again later in the day, Lucy mentions her enjoyment in the surroundings:

> *sometimes I sit out here you see, or just walk around. I used to*
> *walk round a lot but I have got lazy on that, it's very bad*
> *because the less I walk, the less I will walk and I've got to pull*
> *myself together on that score                021:3*

There is also much natural light in both the lounge and dining room, so that Lucy has maximum support for her failing eyesight, and she has items strategically placed to meet her needs.

However the one negative aspect for Lucy is that during her severe bouts of depression, or at times when she has fallen, she needs constant help and care. With this in mind she has chosen to go into the residential home which she knows and where she feels valued. The "girls" had recently remarked to her: "Oh ... we love you too, we hope you will come in soon and stay". Lucy describes her reasoning as she came to her decision, beginning with an account of all the many hobbies she used to enjoy before her sight and mobility decreased:

> *and of course that's all taken from me, so I've got to make*
> *something to fill in this. Its taken a lot of thought, so one of*
> *them is to go into this Residential Home because I would never*
> *be alone. If I cant do anything or there is nothing to do, there is*
> *always someone to talk to...someone sitting somewhere and you*
> *can go and sit beside them even if you don't want to talk*
> *021:4*

As Lucy's chosen residential home is not far away, she envisages she will still see and go out with all her current friends. She will not need to make changes here.

## Conclusion

With the knowledge that additional company will help her, and that decreased stress and worries may lessen her depressive bouts, Lucy now waits for a suitable room to become vacant in the Home she has chosen. She hopes this will happen within the next twelve months. She has no close relatives but many supportive friendships and looks forward to these continuing in her new environment. Lucy retains her interest in both "intelligent" conversation and any practical, handicraft tasks she can manage. Increased stimulation on both of these fronts may well enhance Lucy's quality of life once she has settled into her new surroundings.

Examining the meaning of occupation for Lucy, we find her struggling on many fronts. In earlier life Lucy was very active with a busy job and holding down key community roles such as chair of her local Women's Institute group. Any spare time was filled productively with projects such as fine embroidery. Now however Lucy battles to contend with both physical and mental illness and the reality of gradually failing eyesight. Today is not generally a happy place for her but she has not given up. Having made every attempt to understand and manage her long-standing depression, Lucy plans her day to day existence to revolve around one social contact per day and aims to make use of her time by knitting squares that she knows will be of benefit to others. Planning is placed high on Lucy's agenda and in particular *future time* causes her anxieties. She acknowledges her need for company, satisfactorily met at the moment when she is well, but she fears for the future. To this end she has tested and selected a residential home where she feels valued and where even if unable to do anything, she will always be able to sit beside someone. In having plans to combat her deep concerns about *being alone*, Lucy appears to have found a degree of contentment.

In the previous three chapters we have entered the worlds of twelve very different older people, each in their own home environment. Whilst every case study is unique, we shall see in Part 3 how common issues and themes are distilled.

# OCCUPATION AND QUALITY IN LATER LIFE

## PART 3   ACHIEVING QUALITY AND SATISFYING OCCUPATION

*Synopsis:*   *Part 2, in the previous three chapters, told the stories of twelve detailed case studies. Each study is individual, provided by a "real" person identified by a pseudonym, and accurate to the account of each yesterday interview as given.*

*Part 3, based on an in-depth analysis of the above accounts, now draws together the issues raised, discusses and illustrates the major emerging common themes and shows how together they can be balanced to create a satisfying day.*

*Chapter 8 begins with a phenomenological summary of the findings from the twelve cases and the life issues they reveal. From the case stories four common themes are described:*

> ➤ *using time*
> ➤ *socialising*
> ➤ *fulfilling aspirations*
> ➤ *having a range of pastimes within current capabilities*

*Chapter 9 uses every day terms together with figures and illustrations, to show what makes up these themes and examples from our case stories illustrate how the themes interact and when considered together, how they can be balanced to create a satisfying occupational day.*

*Chapter 10 and now it is time for action! We can find out how you, either as a therapist or health professional working together with your client, or as a mature person investigating your own time use patterns, can make practical use of the information presented so far, to assess how you can make positive changes. In this chapter we cover:*

- *Investigating your own concerns that go to make up the themes*
- *Representing these in the form of a model*
- *Filling out the Assessment Tool and goal setting*
- *Monitoring changes through re-evaluation*
- *Creating your own personal records*

*Note: In moving to present the major common themes, it is important to remember that they have been arrived at only after extensive analysis:*

*...analysing qualitative data is not a simple or quick task.*
*Done properly it is systematic and rigorous, and therefore*
*labour intensive for the researcher/s involved and time*
*consuming. Fielding (1993) contends that "good qualitative*
*analysis is able to document its claim to reflect some of the*
*truth of a phenomenon by reference to systematically gathered*
*data", in contrast "poor qualitative analysis is anecdotal,*
*unreflective, descriptive without being focussed on a coherent*
*line of inquiry".*

Pope, Ziebland, Mays 1999, 52.

## CHAPTER 8  WHAT THE RESEARCH HAS TAUGHT US

### Summary of the twelve cases

In-depth examination of the twelve case studies has revealed occupation as being central to all. As physical health declines, factors such as adaptation and compensation, personal ambition and social support all play an interwoven part in creating a day which is experienced as occupationally satisfying. At a superficial level occupation is experienced as a means to *pass the time*, or as a distraction from morbid thoughts or discomfort. At a more profound level, occupation and its products is experienced as self-validating or as veritable proof of *existence*. Although each case is unique in its content, it is possible to study a range of general issues that have been raised.

In phenomenological terms Sartre (1943) would have focussed the debate on *existence* and the role for the human as *being-for-itself,* or in other words the human need to choose what he/she will become through the actions taken, there being no pre-ordained blueprint to which humans must conform. This highlights the central role of occupation, and as Frankl (1984) also suggested, a powerful way to find life's meaning is by *creating a work or doing a deed.* He too recognised that:

> *Man's search for meaning is the primary motivation in his*
> *life.......This meaning is unique and specific in that it must and*
> *can be fulfilled by him alone.*
>
> *Frankl 1984:121.*

The current study in probing this topic, has yielded much rich information; the study participants have spoken of many factors which combine to provide balance and give meaning to their occupational days. But it is the study of the factors themselves which provides some phenomenological answers.

In studying the person as *a being in time,* occupation provides self-validation or even a visible *proof of existence.* There is frequently an end product that lasts beyond the period of activity, and sometimes it can be shared with others. Study participants registered this in several ways, referring to a dislike for cooking: *it takes too long and is gone too soon* and a preference for more rewarding occupations or pastimes with longer-lasting results: *I work on and on until it is as good as it can be {shell sculpture} and then I am satisfied.*

Occupation is also the vehicle for linking the *present* to the *past.* In exploring the relevance of looking to *past-time* we can understand something of the power and pleasure of reminiscence as the subjects revealed. Memories of times that were good and *when I was strong* are powerful antidotes to discomforts and incapacities of the present. For the person who was experiencing bereavement and depression, the occupation of listening to old tapes of the steamers and the trams, brought pleasant release, and stories of long football games in the mud of the local park revoked similar pleasant memories. The ability and stimulus to indulge in such selective and pleasurable reminiscence activities brings *consolation* and helps individuals to deal with the negative things of the present.

Moving to *future time,* this is an area where most study participants did not like to dwell: *well there is only a box with two handles to look forward to,* so the ability to make flexible use of time, shifting from *being in the present* to *being in the past,* provides a powerful way of coping, and when time is filled in these ways there is little space for morbid thoughts of the future. Practical tasks such as *sorting out* are not enjoyed as the MST results revealed, but such preparations for the future can be conducted without undue thought. Retention of ambition and drive *to do more, to do better,* were also strong aspirations which blotted out future reality. Such aspirations, expressed as *hope,* helped the people to cope; they were almost personal secrets, and they were supportive. In terms of occupational influence then, we see statements such as: *I always aim to do more shelling, to keep the garden better, but I know a lot of it is wishful thinking,* and in relation to questions about health: *well I suppose I know it will get worse, but I don't like to think about it.*

An additional way to cope and tackle the negativity of facing *future time* was seen in the examples of *perpetuity.* Edith was quick to point out that this was in no way connected to a future life, such things held no meaning for her. However, she appreciated one of her recent occupations a great deal because in making a hat for a nephew's wedding, she was able to incorporate embroidery that had belonged to a dear and now deceased sister. Knowing that *something of K... was at the wedding,* brought her a great deal of pleasure. It seems then that occupations involving *perpetuity* provide additional reinforcement of *existence;* they can transform the transience of life today into something more permanent.

Other strong proofs of *being* are found in friendships, social contracts and community liaisons with intergenerational links. This area highlights the importance of a supportive environment; it illustrates co-constitution and it reinforces the *transactive* links between the person and the chosen occupations, set in the context of the environment. The *person* perhaps experiences the greatest *sense of being* when his presence is reflected through positive actions, within a given environment. Here we find the much referred to theme of *reciprocity*, which serves almost as a mirror. For in acts of reciprocity, ones own good deeds are reflected back. It seems here that the power in the *social and organisational environment* lies in the opportunities it provides for an individual to enhance the visibility of *who I am.* Social contacts and links with a local community are therefore providing anchor points and evidence of *existence.* Occupations such as helping with the books for the local church or assisting a neighbour with a gardening project, therefore hold great significance for the individual concerned.

Occupations cannot be completed in a vacuum, and it is here that a theme of *using time* emerges. Time is experienced as a container for the occupations of a day; its size governs what can take place and dictates which *proofs of existence* are feasible to tackle; it quantifies and structures the day, providing clues as to what happens next. Further reinforcement of *being in time* is provided when the regular daily occupations are undertaken. Tea is prepared in time for *News at 6.* Curtains are closed *when it is dark;* bedtime occurs later in winter when the individual estimates he may wake before daylight and would thus *lose time* because he knows he cannot think creatively before dawn.

Phenomenologically then we can see that meaningful occupation acts as evidence of *being.* Its place is at the very core of existence, a position that may be particularly important for vulnerable older people because they are seeking resolution and validation that their lives have *been worthwhile* and that they continue to hold meaning.

## The major emerging themes

Above is a summary of life-world concerns, related to the relevance of meaningful occupation in the lives of vulnerable elderly people. The summary gives rise to some newly identified life concerns which provide a fresh viewpoint for further exploration; they suggest that meaningful occupation:

## *What the research has taught us*

- ❖ Reinforces the self and staves off isolation.
- ❖ Provides validation of time experienced as well-spent.
- ❖ Is comforting in the face of loss and blocks out morbid thoughts of the future.
- ❖ Provides a repository for memories and artefacts that will live on: the feeling of life's transience is thereby reduced.
- ❖ Is experienced through socialising which provides external reinforcement.

Moving into a deeper analysis it is now helpful to return to the words of the study participants, and to move beyond individual narratives in pursuit of the common or general themes as we shall call them. In keeping with a concept of *honesty* (Savin-Baden and Fisher 2002), and in line with the recognition that *differences* are valued, as well as *similarities,* the data were re-explored in a search for general insights. A brief summary of individual analyses suggests that various aspects are influential in how the subjects make up their occupational days. (For a list of the subjects and their health status please refer back to Tables 1.1 and 1.2 in Part 1).

**Subject Ann** displays a preference for routine and structure to each day and an interest from early days in "being busy". Enjoying a number of physically active occupations Ann recognises that health and activity are linked, and that she is keen to maintain the status quo as far as her occupations are involved. She acknowledges that providing she has something to do, she can happily stay at home alone; her home environment makes her feel safe and comfortable. Environment influences Ann's occupations :

- *in a physically negative way*; she uses only part only of a large house
- *in a socially neutral way*; her contacts are all a car-drive away
- *in an organisationally neutral way*; it provides safety and comfort but is apparently non-influential to current activities

**Subject Beatrice** asserts that her personal philosophy is to make the most of each day. This positive outlook is linked to her sense of humour and her active avoidance of depressing stimuli such as daily newspaper contents. A recent return to prayer and readings from inspirational books provides spiritual support. A happy day is one when she has contact with children. A strong personal concept of time provides pleasure if current time hangs heavily, because she can readily step back in time to enjoy early reminiscences. Beatrice's environment exerts influence in her day as follows:

- *physically*: negative to neutral; a large 3 storey house, but remains accessible
- *socially*: positive plus; she is well known in a small village community
- *organisationally*: positive plus; necessary help and support is to hand

**Subject Cath** focuses on remaining active. Foreign travel to see relatives is greatly enjoyed, and in the home her range of practical skills facilitates a wide range of occupations. The days are organised so as to avoid "sitting doing nothing". Home is a very important place as it holds memories of pre-widowhood times. As Cath's late husband was severely disabled for many years, she herself effected much of the home decoration that still surrounds her. Her environment holds the following influences:

- *physically*: positive; suitable to current needs
- *socially*: positive with ongoing regular contacts in walking distance
- *organisationally*: positive; supporting past memories and current planning

**Subject Doris** has a constant need to be active and describes herself as a somewhat restless person. She makes frequent solitary trips to and from her home each day. Having been advised that she was not always safe in taking long solitary walks, she opted to join a local gym instead. She enjoys all the facilities and classes at the gym, is an active weight-watcher and has a general interest in healthy eating. Although she recognises that her current home is both noisy and cold in winter, she has not yet found a suitable alternative. Doris's environment has considerable impact which is:

- *physically*: negative; cold and noisy
- *socially*: negative; no local contacts
- *organisationally*: positive; habitual routines are well-established

**Subject Edith** has a strong interest in many creative pastimes. She appreciates colour and beauty all around her, and has a deep desire to continue improving, so that it is always the best that is produced. She likes to have something to do at all times and enjoys her home because of this. At home she is always surrounded by "several projects on the go". Her creativity enables her to perpetuate what is good, for example an old piece of embroidery, added to a new hat for a forthcoming wedding. Edith's environment holds considerable influence:

- *physically*: positive plus; bungalow in cul de sac on bus route
- *socially*: positive; neighbours all well-known, friends visit
- *organisationally*: positive plus; facilitates and houses many ongoing occupational interests

**Subject Fay** has a number of health and mobility problems and a stoical attitude towards coping with them. With a strong sense of humour, coupled with described empathy for others in trouble, she endeavours to plan a varied weekly programme of activities, with something happening each day. An enjoyment in certain creative activities leads her to reflect on perpetuity and she hopes to pass on some of her collections to her grand daughter. Although her house with stairs and garden is now difficult to manage, things are strategically placed in handy positions and no alternative living arrangement is currently sought. Her environment exerts the following influences:

- *physically*: negative; stairs, care of house and garden are problematic
- *socially*: negative; all contacts are a car trip or an expensive taxi-ride away
- *organisationally*: neutral with the positive influence of strategically placed items in regular use

**Subject Gladys** speaks many times of her interest in meeting people. This is achieved inadvertently when she shops, and intentionally when she attends one of several church groups. Reciprocity means that she had support from her church when her husband died and now she returns the assistance by helping at some of the afternoon meetings. Preferring her time to be occupied in ways that are meaningful, the television is rarely watched, but evenings are spent "lost" in one of her several thousand books. The large book collection causes her to worry about their eventual disposal. With a fund of humorous anecdotes, a serious side is shown in future planning and it is anticipated that a local Methodist home, already visited by Gladys, "will be there when I need it". She currently finds that her road "gets steeper each time I come home". Environmentally the influences can be summarised as:

- *physically*: negative; large house, only ground floor accessible, hilly street
- *socially*: neutral; has friends, immaterial to current environment
- *organisationally*: positive; just able to wander to shops and reach church meetings

**Subject Horace** is conscious of the pressure of time each day, and has to be very disciplined in order to accomplish all the daily chores. The intent is that the house will be kept and provisioned just as it was when his wife was alive. With a strong social conscience and sense of spiritual direction, he feels a need to provide regular support to a local youth group, as a way of giving something back to the community. Activities are seen as "passports" to potential friendships. Horace's environment exerts the following influences:

- *physically*: negative; house too large with time-consuming work
- *socially*: neutral; contacts all a bus ride or bike ride away
- *organisationally*: negative; he experiences pressure rather than comfort or support in his current environment

**Subject Ian** is almost housebound, but takes two brief trips out each week. Having lost his wife some fifteen months ago, he is depressed about his loss and also in constant physical pain from arthritis. An ex-craftsman, surrounded by furniture he has made, it is particularly difficult to accept immobility and inactivity. Days tend to be spent "just sitting". Reminiscing, accompanied by tapes of the old days is a favourite current pastime and perhaps when not so unwell, old hobbies of water colour painting and poetry composition might be tried again. His environment exerts the following influences:

- *physically*: negative; stairs are problematic, reminders of his more functional past are depressing
- socially: neutral to negative; neighbours not depended on, brief visits to local church are just manageable
- *organisationally*: neutral

**Subject Joyce** has a professed and practised positive outlook. Although totally housebound, she fosters and values friendships, with her carers and their families and with younger generation contacts whom she met when still able to get to her local pub. A strong faith sustains her and her sense of humour and enjoyment of a sparky conversation ensures that all visitors are made welcome. A believer in a healthy diet and no pills, indoor mobility is retained although both sight and hearing are very limited. A radio provides entertainment and companionship both day and night, something possibly only acceptable to neighbours because Joyce's home is a bungalow. She would not wish to be anywhere else. Her environment holds strong influences:

- *physically*: positive plus; bungalow is wholly convenient
- *socially*: positive; regular long-time visitors call in
- *organisationally*: positive plus; a comprehensive care package is in place

**Subject Karl** is no longer able to walk out alone but he enjoys his large lounge window, referring to it as "my window on the world". He thinks deeply and reflects on what he has read or seen. He believes in working to do better or to improve one's performance. Frequently he will wait for a particular news bulletin to prompt him to prepare a cup of tea for example. Although Karl says he is not a religious man, he attends church regularly and appreciates the social support and contacts that it provides. It helps him to retain a community presence which he has always enjoyed and he helps with some of the bookwork for the church. Karl likens the concept of any sort of residential living to being "similar to being on a permanent cruise where you have not chosen your companions". His environment exerts the following influences:

- *physically*: positive; house well maintained with stair-lift
- *socially*: positive; at hub of the neighbourhood and church activities
- *organisationally*: neutral

**Subject Lucy** has struggled with severe clinical depression for many years. Now she feels able to manage her own ill health and depression most of the time, but it is a constant battle. Having been an active lady with many interests and a liking for all animals, she finds it particularly difficult that deteriorating eyesight and increased mobility problems, prevent her from accomplishing many things. She has local friendships that she values a great deal and aims to include one social activity each day if she is well enough. Lucy also has a practical interest in her diet. Having given much thought to her future she has opted to go into a residential home, known to her on a respite basis, as a permanent resident when a suitable room becomes vacant, because here she would "never be alone, and if I can't do anything, there is always someone to talk to". Lucy's environment holds the following influences:

- *physically*: positive; ground floor sheltered housing appears ideal
- *socially*: positive; supportive warden and friends
- *organisationally*: neutral to negative; insufficient help when ill

## The common themes defined

Now as we re-examine the twelve case stories and their summaries above, some common themes emerge. They centre around social contacts and relationships, making good use of time and resources and choosing feasible and satisfying pastimes often in line with a healthy lifestyle: all are underpinned by individual aspirations and wishes for personal fulfilment. We note that these themes are remarkably similar to Flanagan's quality of life characteristics, supported also by Anderson and Burckhardt (1999). See Table **3.1** below:

| QUALITY OF LIFE DOMAINS FLANAGAN (1978) | OCCUPATION AS A QUALITY OF LIFE CONSTITUENT (current study) |
|---|---|
| **1.** physical and material well-being | **1.** managing time, resources and health |
| **2.** relations with other people social, community and civic activities | **2.** social contact and relationships |
| **3.** personal development and fulfilment | **3.** aspirations and wishes for personal fulfilment |
| **4.** recreation | **3.** feasible and satisfying pastimes |

**Table 3.1  Comparison of quality of life and occupational domains**

It is now, using the key words from above, that we can name the themes. We can also recognise from the case stories that each theme has a control point of balance or harmony where the subject, within his or her own environment, is most likely to experience a sense of well-being. Lawton and Nahemow (1973) talked about this in their competence-press model. Now we will examine the new themes.

## Definition of new themes

**Using time**  is a control aspect to the day. Representing daylight hours *to be filled*, its two extremes are emptiness where time hangs heavily, and pressure where time is insufficient to accomplish the day's occupations. Resourcing and planning help to create a balanced position here, which is experienced when the day's hours are seen to be comfortably and well-filled.

**Socialising**  represents all human contact and relationships experienced in a day. The two extremes are loneliness and constant presence of non-chosen companions. The balanced position between these two extremes, is experienced when chosen and satisfying social contacts are established.

**Fulfilling aspirations**  represents the subject's driving force, that collection of personal attributes that directs and sustains personal effort during an occupational day. The two extremes are absent or minimal aspirational drive and a strong drive which proves incompatible with capabilities; the position where a subject cannot achieve his/her goals. Here the point of balance or control is experienced when there is a match between held beliefs and accomplishments.

**Range of pastimes**  represents the mixture of daily occupations that are currently undertaken. At one extreme there are insufficient pastimes to compile a day that is viewed as satisfying. At the other extreme an individual may express a need to be *constantly busy*. The tasks here may lack purpose and not be selected for their meaning nor for any sense of satisfaction that arises from involvement. At this extreme the occupations are mere *time fillers*, they consist mainly of *purposeless activities*, and thus do not enhance quality living. The position of harmony is reached when participation in a range of satisfying occupations occurs.

Two examples are given over the next pages. In figure 3(i) themes and concerns are matched for subject Joyce and in Table 3.2 the match between the new themes and the concerns and words of the subjects is demonstrated.

*What the research has taught us*

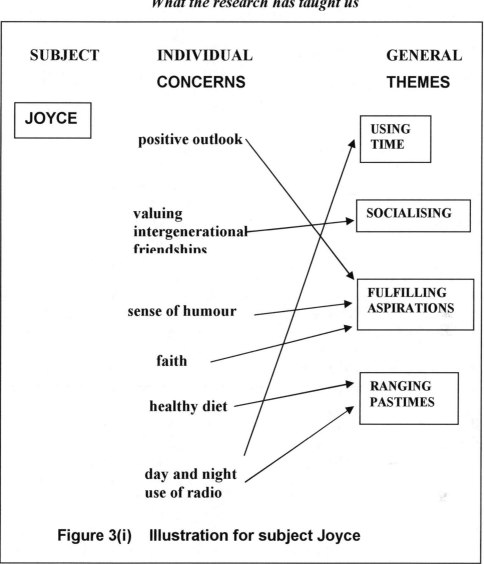

Figure 3(i)    Illustration for subject Joyce

113

| THEME | CONCERNS | STATEMENT |
|---|---|---|
| Using time | Planning | *I like to have one organised activity each day |
| | Pacing | *I don't kill myself, I see how I feel |
| | Structure | *Then I wait for the 6 o'clock News to have my tea |
| | Being resourceful | *I can fill the day without watching the television |
| Socialising | Choice | *I don't see much of the family. I enjoy having a pint with the fellas |
| | Reciprocity | *I helped my neighbour gain qualifications, now I can accept that she cooks my Sunday lunch |
| | Intergenerational | *He's the age my son would have been, now he comes every Friday and we share a can of Guinness |
| | Community involvement | *A church member is coming tomorrow, for me to help with the the books. |
| Fulfilling aspirations | Aspirations | *I always aim to achieve the best; start again if necessary {painting} |
| | Faith | *Oh he's{God} never out of my life, how do you think I manage? |
| | Perpetuity | *I shall give these certificates to my grand-daughter, I don't want them thrown away |
| | Looking on the bright side | *Nobody wants you when you moan do they? I always aim to look on the bright side. |
| Range of pastimes | Adaptation | *I don't get out much now, but this lounge window is my window on the world |
| | Variety | *I have so many lovely things I want to do |
| | Health-related activities | *I eat fish and plenty of vegetables, not so much red meat |
| | Flexibility | *I don't read much, but I like to look through the old photos |

Table 3.2    The relationship between general themes and subject concerns

*What the research has taught us*

In the research stages there next followed a period of testing; to make sure that the newly defined themes accurately represented both the common issues and the individual's concerns which gave rise to them. During this process it became possible to identify the boundary points for each theme; these being *the undesirable positions,* the extremities or end-points where subjects expressed dissatisfaction with their occupational day. At the same time it became possible to locate the area of balance, between the two end points. This *desirable area* is one of harmony where reported factors contribute to the achievement of an occupationally satisfying day.

## Exploring the themes in depth

The themes below are presented in a linear format, purely as a means of representation, suggesting that each theme has two opposite, negative end-points, of "emptiness" and "saturation", whilst somewhere in-between, lies a positive control position of balance or harmony, where a sense of well-being in a particular domain is experienced.

## THEME: USING TIME

x----------------------------------------------x----------------------------------------------x

| **too much time** | **position of balance** | **too little time** |
|---|---|---|
| it "hangs heavily" | time each day is well & comfortably filled | insufficient to accomplish goals |

**Figure 3(ii) Using time**

All study participants made either direct or indirect reference to this theme. Some of the direct references included phrases such as:

> **Gladys**: *"I like to fill my time with something that is meaningful"*

> **Lucy**: *"well I manage to fill my time during the day, without needing to watch the television".*

> **Doris**: *"well I like to go to the launderette twice a week, and that uses up two afternoons".*

For all the subjects then there is a sense of having a number of allocated hours each day, which are available for "filling". Planning and carrying through this theme, constitutes a major task in structuring each day.

For two sets of people the concept of filling time is an uneasy prospect. Those who experience boredom (i.e. the left end of the spectrum in the above figure **3(ii)** have difficulty in filling the daily hours with occupations that hold personal significance. For a variety of reasons, connected with reduced mobility, increased impairment or limited opportunity, some older subjects struggle to find acceptable ways to use their time. Beatrice spoke tentatively about this by saying:

> **Beatrice:** *"I don't say that I am very, very bored"*, then she went on to say: *"I am not a reader. If I read more I am sure the time would go."*

It would be all too easy to take a phrase such as *"sitting around"*, to take a surface approach to interpretation and to assume this phrase indicates boredom, however this is not always so. Karl spends much of his day *"sitting"*, but during many of these periods he is reflecting. He likes to sit and reflect on what he has read in the newspaper, or just seen on the television, and such activities form a valued part of his day:

> **Karl:** *"I put in the washing and have a sit down. Then if there is anything left in the newspaper from the day before I finish that off, then sit and think about what I have read"*.

However, sometimes for others sitting is indicative of boredom or time *hanging heavily*. Clinical factors such as depression, clearly exert a de-motivating influence, so that Ian for instance starts each day with a time use problem, beginning when he wakes thinking:

> **Ian:** *"I would like to get up, but I just lie there"*

and continuing through the day, with many periods of *"just sitting around doing nothing"*.

The opposite position where again study participants experience dissatisfaction with current time use, occurs when there is *insufficient time* to accomplish the many occupations that need fitting into each day (i.e. the right extreme position in figure **3(ii))**. Horace struggles as he tries to maintain a former lifestyle in a large house and experiences frustration, either should he inadvertently take a day-time nap and therefore waste time, or because he has no time for hobbies he would like to pursue, such as playing his keyboard.

**Horace:** *"I bought one {keyboard}, but haven't touched it for three or four years. The amount of work I have to do, it just stays there. There was a time when the washing was piled high, almost to the ceiling and I thought something has to be done".*

## Reaching a harmonious position for using time

There are factors that support the study participants in moving towards a balanced position of satisfaction with regard to time use in a normal occupational day. Planning, coupled with a degree of flexibility is clearly helpful as is the establishment of routine and pacing oneself.

**Beatrice:** *"Then I say to myself 'what shall I do today?' Sometimes I'll say 'I'll just do that little job'. I never kill myself by going like mad all day- doing too much. I just ration myself to a certain point."*

As needs and capabilities change, a flexible approach to time-planning appears helpful. This is noted when Karl who is now mostly confined to his home, talks about scheduling what time he goes to bed. In the dark winter days he has calculated that he needs to go to bed later:

**Karl**: *"I go to bed around half-eleven to 12, on the premise that I am not going to sleep more than about 6 hours anyway. This is just part of me and if it's a winter's morning I can't find anything to think about at that time. But if it is light there is plenty to think about!"*

By way of contrast, Ann has an established routine that is balanced to include at least one activity focus for each day:

**Ann:** *"Wednesday morning badminton, Thursday yoga, Monday evening Scottish country dancing....*

Likewise Lucy also aims to plan one outing or activity each week-day:

**Lucy:** *"Tuesday morning is shopping morning, a little bus comes here to pick us up at 10 o'clock and takes us down to T...for an hour and brings us back. So that is my outing for Tuesday. I find one a day is enough at the moment".*

Then there is Edith who has many projects partly completed and she is able to switch from one occupation to another as the day, the weather, the mood or health dictates:

> **Edith**: *"You see I can put the painting down and go out in the garden if I want a change".*

For Edith choice and challenge bring her much pleasure. She talks too of satisfaction when on retiring for the night, she can "tick off progress made during the day".

A major factor that promotes harmony appears to be a flexible approach to time use and in particular a readiness to switch from unpleasant contexts, as seen in Beatrice's comment about the future: *"well there's only a box and two handles to look forward to!"*, to a more pleasurable time frame, such as the past, with photographs or tapes to trigger happy memories. Fay and Joyce and Ian, who are coping with multiple health problems and restricted mobility, all referred to their enjoyment in reminiscence. Joyce enjoys reminiscing about her past life and spoke of her mother's many accomplishments with pride:

> **Joyce:** *"She used to cook the eels, but she skinned them like that and she dried the skins for sprained wrists".*

and Ian was clearly animated in referring to his pleasurable time spent reminiscing:

> **Ian:** *"I've got a lot of discs...going back to the thirties, people speaking and all that, they are very, very good... the women and when they went to the washing places over in L.... and when they were on the dole and the overhead railway and all the liners and all that".*

It is not possible to generalise with absolute accuracy as to each individual's position on the time use spectrum, however it is possible, considering all the associated factors, to make a reasoned prediction as to each person's position. Equally it is possible to list potential strategies for helping an older person to improve their position and increase their level of satisfaction with daily time that is well spent, as defined in individual terms. For example planning, pacing, flexibility of approach and daily focus, are strategies that some subjects already use successfully to assist them in using their time in a way they experience as occupationally satisfying.

## THEME: SOCIALISING

```
x-------------------------------------------x---------------------------------------------x
```
**insufficient contact**      **position of balance**        **too much contact**
loneliness                    satisfying social contact       **with non-chosen**
                              is established                   **people**

### Figure 3(iii)  Socialising

The case study references to socialising spanned a wide range of interactions, from talks with neighbours to family visits, and from buying chocolate for the little girl next door, to being involved with book-keeping for a local church group. All subjects in the current study spoke on the theme of socialising. Interactions formed part of each daily account and clearly influenced the satisfaction experienced in the day. Accounts of prolonged lack of interaction were frequently linked to described feelings of loneliness, with consequent negative influence over the occupational day. One subject for instance expressed her pleasure in an afternoon spent with a neighbour:

> **Edith:** *"then I went next door at about half past two and started to place The beautiful collection of alpines we had bought, deciding exactly which was the best little pocket for each one…. So time went quickly and every now and then J. would say "Are you ready for a cup of tea yet?"…It was after six when I came home".*

### The negative extremes in relation to socialising

Most people spoke of occasional feelings of loneliness, but for many, living alone did not constitute a problem. Having lived singly for many years and most having no ready recourse to family members as the NLSA results showed (see chapter 4), the study participants described how they had mainly adjusted to being alone. Edith considered herself completely at ease here, although she was aware that she relished conversation and found it difficult to relinquish her visitors because of this. Doris also commented with a degree of sadness:

> **Doris:** *"and with me not having anyone to talk to, I don't discuss anything you see".*

The two people who experienced the greatest problems with loneliness were both also receiving treatment for depression. In addition Ian had also lost his wife just over a year ago, and he still misses her a great deal, but does not like to bother his neighbours:

**Ian:** *"Well I don't know whether its me being pig-headed again. They all say "Ring me any time", but I don't like to. M. is elderly herself and I don't think its fair".*

**Lucy:** *"Sunday is always a dull day here…I find I am very lonely".*

Issues of loneliness and its negative impact become even more prominent when comparative situations are readily visible. Lucy's sheltered housing complex leaves her increasingly aware that many occupants have regular Sunday visits from relatives whilst she has no visitors because she has no family living nearby.

At the other most extreme position, social contacts were anticipated as being equally negative when the element of choice is removed. Karl described why he would not consider entering residential accommodation:

**Karl:** *"it would be like being on a perpetual cruise where you could not choose your travelling companions!"*

Issues of choice are clearly highly significant here and not all study participants viewed the prospect of residential care as a negative move. Lucy has thought through the issues of residential care, has carefully vetted prospective co-residents during holiday admissions, and has now booked her place in a local residential home.

Non-selected or unsolicited social contact is seen to have negative impact in other ways too. Ann talks about the importance of controlling family visits:

**Ann:** *"Well I don't like to see them {the children} too frequently; there's nearly always something wrong with them".*

### Reaching a central position of harmony for socialising

The data reveal several strategies that people use to facilitate relationships and social contacts. Contacts are enhanced by conscious actions as Gladys described when she spoke of going shopping, not necessarily to buy anything:

**Gladys:** *"I go and have a wander around there. Its funny you know, because you nearly always meet someone you know"*

or taking up a new hobby because as Horace commented:

**Horace:** *"it can be a passport to new friendships".*

The fostering of intergenerational links, including an active "liking of children", appears important, particularly in offsetting the alone-ness and "eldest person present" or "only one left" feelings that accompany the death of own age-group friends. We see this in the reports of two nonagenarians; Beatrice who actively cultivates friendships with children:

> **Beatrice:** *"oh yes I've always got time for children, I used to baby-sit, now the children of the children come to visit me!"*

and Joyce who in her seventies fostered a friendship with someone who would have been her son's age. Now twenty years later Joyce has much pleasure and practical support from regular visits which the friend and his wife continue to make:

> **Joyce:** *"oh aye, L. and J. were here yesterday, brought me a lovely little salad tea, all ready"*.

The same friend is there each Friday, to open and share a can of Guinness and to bring a weekly fresh mackerel fillet from the local market. In such cases intergenerational friendships appear very supportive. A converse side is however expressed by Edith when she talks of her concern that she is frequently the oldest person present at social or family gatherings, and *"that is horrid"*.

Whilst a general importance of mixed-age friendships is positively emphasized throughout the interviews, family support is reported with mixed appreciation. Many people expressed issues such as *"they are miles away"* or *"we have nothing much in common"* or they are busy with their own lives, as Gladys commented:

> **Gladys:** *"well my son is a busy line dancer"*.

Even when family visits were made, these were not always entirely welcomed; as seen in Ann's comment on the previous page. There is also a frequently expressed feeling that grown children do not share their parents' values. Both Gladys and Edith talk of "the skip" that will be used to dispose of such valued items as shell collections and books.

> **Gladys:** *"I know what N. {son} will do, if anything happens to me, he'll get one of those big things and just bung everything in and they'll all finish up on B. tip. If I know N., I don't think he ever reads"*.

In general, study participants who spoke of satisfying friendships indicated that these were chosen and mutually fostered. Horace took great pleasure in his regular Thursday evening Union meetings after which:

> **Horace:** *"I go for a few pints with the fellas after the meeting, then come back have my supper, then bed"*.

Gladys also spoke warmly of a group of friends who had first met many years ago at a series of evening classes. They still continue to meet several times a year in local churches where they *"can get a good mid-day meal together"*.

## The positive influence of community presence and support

A strong factor that contributes towards the maintenance of ongoing social contact is an element of community presence. The two major features of *a known environment* and *reciprocity of involvement*, receive frequent mention. Exchange theorists (Rook 1987), would highlight the role of reciprocity and Karl talks about his attitude towards reciprocity in the following way:

> **Karl:** *" yes I have one here {a computer}, but its not mine, belongs to the friend next door, I helped her get some professional qualifications, I helped her research, and it kept me in touch, I thoroughly enjoyed it. Took her four years, and now I don't feel it difficult in accepting some help from her".*

The neighbour now brings Karl a weekly Sunday dinner.

Horace and Edith both enjoy their visits to the Age Concern Mobile Unit, known locally as "the tea-pot bus", for purposes of sharing information and fostering friendships. Horace highlighted the mutual benefits here:

> **Horace:** *"I always have a mug of chocolate on the bus...and I am very friendly with the man on the bus and vice versa".*

and Edith spoke of additional activities that have arisen from this same source, such as shared responsibility for a widely distributed annual crossword competition. Gladys too spoke of reciprocity in community involvement as she can now give time to helping with afternoon church activities, when she herself received much support from church personnel at the time of her husband's death:

> **Gladys:** *"selling some of these books helps to raise some money for church funds, and they were so good to me when N. died".*

Beatrice values the position of her house, because although she no longer makes daily trips to the local village, she still knows all the shop-keepers and "feels a part of the village":

> **Beatrice:** *"I think this is very handy, where we live, for the village, and I think the people are all very nice, there is nobody I don't like going to".*

Horace talks again on the theme of reciprocity as a major theme that drives his weekly occupations. He helps out at a local youth club, having elected to do this because he feels his involvement here may help to repay a somewhat reckless attitude he held during the war whilst others were suffering:

> **Horace:** *"so you see these children had grandfathers who had their guts gouged out during the war ..., and I feel a certain responsibility to do something .... After all they {the grandfathers} had done plenty for me and now I feel as though I am putting something in"*

## What the research has taught us

For those who are housebound, the provision of appropriate community support is essential. Joyce's constancy of carers is vital to her independent living. As she has minimal remaining vision, a change in carers can mean the difference between locating a prepared tea and missing a meal:

> **Joyce:** *"Its difficult if I have to have new carers, I have to tell them where everything is, the washing powder, the tea towel..., and if they put my sandwich in the wrong place, I won't find it!".*

## THEME: FULFILLING ASPIRATIONS

This theme includes personal, moral or ethical codes, spirituality and religious faith, and is supported by personal attributes

```
x---------------------------------------x---------------------------------------x
minimal                 position of balance          High ideals,
mention                 a match between beliefs      incompatible
                        and accomplishments          with capabilities
```

### Figure 3(iv)  Fulfilling aspirations

Most study participants spoke of a personal belief system, philosophy or a set of guiding principles or aspirations that assisted decision-making regarding daily activities. All participants referred either directly or indirectly to some sense of driving force that influenced both the composition of the day and the sense of satisfaction when the occupations were complete. At its least obvious, with minimal directional impact it was referred to as a general and perhaps rather vague principle:

> **Ian:** *"I always look at it like, its no good me feeling sorry for myself and saying 'I've got a problem', and start thinking too much about it- I think one can become a martyr to oneself instead of saying 'Oh for God's sake, shake yourself out of it, there's millions worse off than what you are, but it doesn't make my case any easier.*

Beatrice too expresses a similar general theme that she holds in mind:

**Beatrice:** *"Nobody wants you when you moan do they?...You make the best of each day. I have been very lucky and I always look on the bright side of things".*

At its most influential, there were people who spoke of clear, strong personal strategies that influenced the daily occupational choices and achievements:

**Karl:** *"I have always believed that doing a job today will lead me to do it better tomorrow and if I go on progressing in that way, I am then leading the life I want to live.*

## The negative extremes for fulfilling aspirations

The left hand extreme position for this theme was suggested when a study participant revealed no aspirations to assist the construct of a "good day" and expressed something of a sense of loss because of this. Doris spoke of the fact that she used to attend church regularly but:

**Doris:** *"now it has all changed, now we are only there for marrying or funerals, and I don't like the way they talk to you any more".*

Doris followed this comment by describing herself as *"somewhat restless"*.

At the other extreme were people who held strong moral beliefs about what they should be doing, but found themselves facing obligations now beyond physical endurance or capability. Horace for instance feels a strong moral obligation to assist at a local youth-club as a means to pay back something of his own recklessness during the war. In working with the youngsters he feels a sense of retribution towards their grandparents whom he failed to value. He says of this experience:

**Horace:** *"Now I feel as though I am putting something in. So there is a spiritual action, I feel as though I have got to do something back".*

Horace has been helping at the youth-club for fourteen years, and although now he expresses tiredness and stress, he feels he cannot let them down, so he continues his weekly attendance. Horace now uses a bus for some of his regular excursions, but he still uses his bike to go to the youth club:

**Horace:** *"they seem to expect me on the bike. They would regard me as beginning to crumble, to crack up if I didn't go on my bike".*

## What the research has taught us

**Reaching a central position of harmony for fulfilling aspirations**

Many factors were revealed that appeared to assist individuals towards a balanced approach where they felt able to uphold and fulfil their often long-time held obligations and principles. People in this central position expressed feelings of support or gratitude for these deeply held principles that confirmed self worth. For study participants such as Joyce, a strong faith enables her to carry on. When asked about the relevance of God in her daily life, the reply was almost indignant:

> **Joyce:** *"oh he's never out of it, oh no. How do you think I manage here?"*

Beatrice too expressed a feeling of comfort in her recent return to daily prayer:

> **Beatrice:** *"I say my prayers, thank you for a nice day, and then I try to go to sleep".*

She goes on to describe a sense of gratitude that she is now "back in touch with God". Seven of the twelve study participants referred to the occupation of going to church, but interestingly this number was not connected with the number of people who expressed religious beliefs. The occupation of going to church, holds very different meanings. Beatrice never goes to church because she feels the vicar:

> **Beatrice:** *"will wonder why I haven't been before".*

On the other hand Karl has attended the same church weekly for over 30 years, and readily admits that he has no religious beliefs, but greatly appreciates the friendships fostered there.

Beyond the theme of religious beliefs, some people expressed a strong ethical principle of "doing one's best" or working towards improvement. Edith discounts many television programmes because:

> **Edith:** *"I can learn little if anything from them"*

this is important as she aims to continuously improve both herself and her creative endeavours. Suggesting that she has always experienced this compulsion, Edith refers back to an earlier time:

> **Edith:** *"I did play the piano, but I didn't excel so my heart wasn't in it".*

Karl too is surprised that others may be content to always perform the same job in the same manner, without wanting to improve, as he himself aims to do better each day. Many of the subjects expressed the satisfaction that accomplishment in this area brought; the mothers who were enabled to chat whilst their toddlers ran riot (Gladys helping at an afternoon church group); Fay when able to empathise with the local mayor (who had to read a speech but had forgotten his glasses).

A further factor, prompting a sense of harmony in this theme is the sense of perpetuity. Edith and Fay spoke of beliefs in perpetuity and of the pleasure derived from occupations with a perpetuity theme. Edith's self-made wedding hat incorporated embroidery that Edith unpicked from a dressing gown that belonged to a deceased sister: she was glad that:

> **Edith:** *"something of my sister will be at the nephew's wedding".*

Fay spoke with similar satisfaction about her recently compiled album of certificates for jam-making and preserving:

> **Fay:** *"I thought my grand-daughter might be glad of it, I don't want a lot of it thrown away".*

Personal attributes such as a sense of humour, creativity and empathy and generally having a positive outlook are also helpful. Atchley (1991) reminded us that as a person ages and becomes less competent in physical activities, then the concept of self and self fulfilment may shift so that more value is placed on qualities such as warmth or humour. Atchley quotes a retired school teacher saying: "As you become more like a prune on the outside, you have to become more like a peach on the inside" (p.218). Subjects in the current study demonstrated support for these words. Fay illustrates this with a story about having her handbag stolen in a supermarket and the difficulties on such occasions of being deaf and not knowing how close someone is to you or to your possessions. Following this incident however, a volunteer, herself disabled now accompanies her to the supermarket.

> **Fay:** *"She comes on a Tuesday, she is a wonderful driver and we laugh all the way there. They have threatened to throw us out of Sainsburys, we are such a riot!"*

Sometimes too, a positive outlook is supported when negative stimuli can be avoided. This is seen in Beatrice's case when she actively chooses to avoid the *"doom and gloom"* of a daily newspaper.

## THEME: Having a RANGE OF PASTIMES

```
x--------------------------------------x--------------------------------------x
```

| **paucity of meaningful pastimes** | **position of balance** satisfying occupations are enjoyed | **plethora of meaningless tasks** |

### Figure 3(v) range of pastimes

We saw in Part 2 that our twelve case study participants each described "a set" of pastimes or occupations which they had recently undertaken. In all eighty-five pastimes were mentioned during the Yesterday interviews; these are listed in Part 4, chapter 12. There is great variety here ranging from ten-mile walks to people-watching through a lounge window. There is also diversity in the individual approaches taken to adjustment of both number and type of pastimes that are engaged in, when circumstances necessitate change.

**The negative extremes for having a range of fulfilling pastimes**
At one extreme here there is a paucity of ideas or consideration of occupations. For whatever reason, a day which is free from all occupational intent, or to be more pronounced, a week without any occupational focus, does not bring pleasure to any of the subjects. Ian describes all his days as *"pretty much the same"*, each one beginning with:

> **Ian:** *"Round about 8 o'clock if I want to get up, I can't be bothered, I just lie there..."*

At the other extreme is the position of having a constant need to be occupied throughout the day. There is pressure to be constantly *on the go* or a compulsion to be always *doing something*. Edith expresses a little of this as in when she prepares to go to visit her daughter:

> **Edith:** *I have been sorting out some knitting to take away with me so that I have something to do on those moments when you are left with nothing to do. I must have something...or I would say 'Am I allowed to weed the front garden?'... I have got to be employed.*

Other people also spoke of their need to always have something to do. Cath describes having occasional quiet moments but she never likes to "just sit". Ann too comments that she normally likes to be out, but:

> **Ann:** *"If I have anything to do, I am quite happy staying in"*

For some study participants there is a real fear of *empty time*. Lucy having always been an active person with many hobbies to hand, now finds herself anxious that her increasing eyesight problems will prevent her from being as busy as she needs to be. She speaks of her desperation in contemplating this situation:

> **Lucy:** *"and of course that's [hobbies} all taken from me, so I've got to make something to fill in this. Its taken a lot of thought, so one of them is to go into this Residential Home because I would never be alone. If I can't do anything…there is always someone to talk to".*

## A central position of harmony for fulfilling pastimes

There appears to be a number of factors that assist the individuals towards a balance between the two negative extremes. Included here are personal attitudes about a wide range of occupational issues. Health-related beliefs dictate that healthy eating, preparation of "healthy foods" and learning to manage one's ill-health are positive attributes. The majority of the subjects expressed an interest in healthy eating, with frequent mentions of fish, fruit and vegetables. Cath for instance expresses the interest of many when she says:

> **Cath:** *"I cook a main meal every other day…I eat healthily, lots of fruit and vegetables. I eat chicken and fish, but not so much meat.*

Like several study participants, Cath cooks two main meals at a time, microwaving the second dinner for the following day. The preparation of a daily cooked meal has become a chore for many individuals, although not for all; Horace expresses a different view and enjoys two cooked meals per day:

> **Horace:** *"anything like meals on wheels would be an anathema to me".*

Joyce also refers to meals-on-wheels in conjunction with her diminished appetite as she has aged:

> **Joyce:** *"Well I was getting meals on wheels but I couldn't eat them. I was giving them to the cat and the birds and the pigeons at the back"*

Joyce also sees a healthy aspect to both her nightly tot of whisky and her regular glass of Guinness, although she cannot now cope with the latter except when a friend visits to help out:

> **Joyce:** *"Of course I should have a bottle of Guinness every day but I can't pour it out now, it goes all over the place!"*

## *What the research has taught us*

Many of the people expressed a strong liking for fish, with Edith suggesting that this liking dated from years ago when she and her husband fished at the sea-shore, catching:

> **Edith:** *"dabs, as sweet as honey, a few plaice, but best of all was the bass".*

Likewise Joyce also spoke of her ongoing liking of fish which began in childhood:

> **Joyce:** *"my brothers used to go fishing in the Shropshire Union. We had a great big aquarium at home in the back yard and they used to fetch trout and eels home".*

Beatrice spoke on the same theme too and described trips to the local market where she used to buy fish. She talks more poignantly too of the time many years ago when she was made acutely aware of the necessity of maintaining a healthy eating pattern:

> **Beatrice:** *"I always make sure I have a dinner. I don't make any time when I skip it. I always have my vegetables and make sure that I eat. I have seen so many old people starving themselves. I went to see someone once…and said what did you have to eat today…and she said nothing…just a cup of tea. Now she ended up and her skin and everything went. You have got to eat your meal.*

On a health-related theme too, study participants spoke of the importance of managing their ill health problems, so that impact on daily activities is minimised. For instance Lucy spoke about her recurring depression:

> **Lucy:** *"I have been waking at six in the morning, it's the gremlins you see…So I say to myself, 'you must get up and do something'. I have learnt to manage it now. If I wake up with the gremlins I just say: 'oh go away, shut up, I don't want you'. You see I do now know that it will all pass, I just need to be patient".*

Another way of managing ill health or declining abilities is via adaptation or being ready to actively seek changed occupations as the need arises. Fay has many physical difficulties, but aims for their minimal impact by planning to accomplish one activity per day. She has also been willing to change pursuits in line with capabilities, her most recent pastime being swimming with a disabled club:

**Fay:** *"you see I can only swim on my back and I get scared if people swim underneath me, so I only swim on Fridays with the club".*

As has already been discussed in conjunction with the theme of Using Time, the concept of "having something to do" and of filling time in a meaningful manner, was expressed by all of the study participants. The most harmonious situations arose when a range of possible occupations was to hand, so that individual choice could be exercised and without undue pressure for completion. Edith talks of this, relating it to the context of her bungalow home where she has lived for 48 years:

> **Edith:** *"I am surrounded by lovely things, and I have so much to do…. However it could be managed, I would wish to stay here…until I am no longer anywhere…and I would still hope to do more painting, more shelling, keep the garden better, but I know a lot of that is wishful thinking".*

Having summarised the case study results and identified four common themes, the next chapter will take us on, to see how we can make practical use of this information.

# CHAPTER 9  PUTTING THEORY INTO PRACTICE

## Diagrammatic representation of an occupational day

In the previous chapter, life concerns associated with meaningful occupation were summarised and related general themes were identified. In addition, the study participants gave us ample examples of what constituted a satisfying day for them; where time was seen as well-used, chosen contacts had been enjoyed, selected pastimes had been indulged and personal aspirations were met. In all of these areas a harmonious occupational day occurred when extremes of either under-stimulation or saturation were avoided and the person was able to create a balanced day, which matched current capabilities and resources. It is important to note too that the four general themes are interlinked or *transactive*, so that they each influence the other themes. The task of creating a satisfying day can become complex, particularly when personal situations are themselves complicated or hampered by ill-health or limitations. At these times it becomes necessary to make fine adjustments and compensations in order to regain a position of harmony when a sense of satisfaction and well-being is again experienced. We will take a look now at a series of diagrams that illustrate these points, and they also incorporate the all important aspect of where we live, or environmental impact as it is termed. See now Figures **3(vi) through 3(viii).**

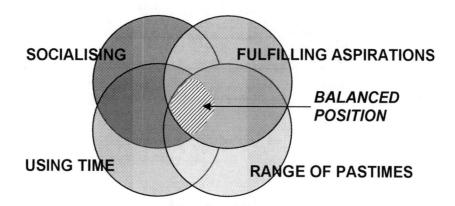

**Figure 3(vi)    Four general themes of an occupational day**

In the figure **3(vi)** we can see that all four themes are being addressed and there is a comfortable and balanced section of overlap in the centre; this is a position of harmony or occupational satisfaction with little or no conflict in any of the areas.

Going back to what our subjects told us; none recounted a story of one, two or three themes; all told accounts of an occupational day that incorporated multiple aspects of all four themes, intermingled and *transactive*, so that each theme influenced and was influenced by the others; the central position of balance needing some careful "tweaking" in order to achieve a day that brought quality and satisfied individual aspirations.

Next let us take a look at what happens to a balanced picture when any one theme is in a position of notable imbalance, either due to negative or over-stimulating influences; see figure **3(vii)** below:

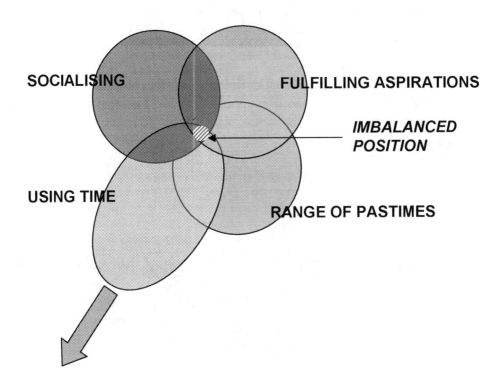

**Figure 3(vii)  General themes of an occupational day:
time usage out of balance**

We can see in the above figure **3(vii)** that when time usage is pulled out of line (for example in Horace's case where he was too busy with essential chores to find time for many of his hobbies), then the whole central area of balanced occupational satisfaction is reduced. The same outcome arises when any of the themes becomes distorted. Horace had described his panic concerning time use; this distortion in turn influenced his perception of a day seen as well spent, as reflected in his VAS score of 3.1 for activity satisfaction. Lucy also demonstrated the same point. Now only able to tackle a very reduced set of pastimes, she found time hanging heavily. This shows in her low VAS score of 2.0, for activity satisfaction and in turn it contributes to her less than average quality of life score of 4.8.

## Impact of the environment

It is also necessary to study the environmental influences over the four general themes. Adding the influence of the environment gives rise to figure **3(viii)** below. Now we get almost a "wobble board effect", so for instance, imagine standing in the centre here, in a known and supportive environment. In this case you have a level playing field and the themes can be addressed with greatest ease. However, if the environment is not supportive, perhaps because it is new and facilities are unknown or perhaps the local environment is not accessible; then in such situations it becomes much more difficult to attain a best position for the four themes, without "wobbling off" out of a comfort zone and into a whole general area where it immediately becomes much more difficult to find a position of balance for any of the four themes.

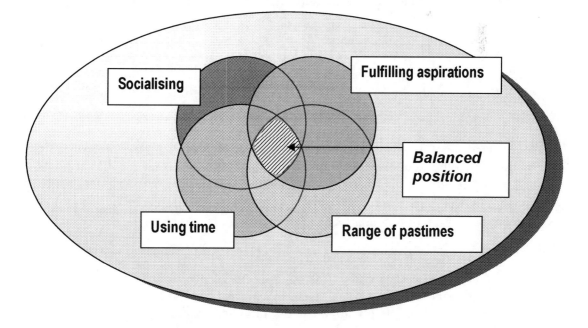

**Figure 3(viii) General themes of an occupational day, influenced by the environmental context**

In figure **3(viii)** the shaded lower boundary illustrates the wobble board effect, so that when the environment changes, this creates a shift in the whole theme composition, so that a harmonious or balanced occupational day may become either more elusive or more readily achievable. For each of the subjects, we saw that strong environmental features (which we will now call: ***physical, social*** and ***organisational)***, have the potential to either enhance the central area of satisfaction, or to diminish it.

For a long time there has been considerable interest in the reciprocal influences between an older person and his or her environment. Lawton and Nahemow (1973) described their competence-press model whereby the level of environmental demands and support can facilitate a positive response in an individual in both psychological and behavioural terms. In the preceding individual accounts, it has been seen that environmental factors, whether of a physical, organisational or social nature, can strongly influence an older person's daily occupations. Let us now remind ourselves of the nature and impact of the environmental influence, is it was seen in the cases of four of our subjects below:

**Beatrice**        collected data suggested that daily occupational satisfaction may be relatively low because loneliness is exacerbated by a lack of ready recourse to companions. However, her quality of life score of 9 is more readily understood when the **positive** influence of the environment is added to the picture:

* 45 years in the same house
* known well to neighbours and local shop keepers
* has thought through a plan for the future, so that even if housebound,
Beatrice feels she can exercise and keep going within the confines of her own home

**Fay**    here we see a situation where theme factors suggest Fay will be experiencing a high degree of occupational satisfaction, but we find she rates her quality of life at 0.9 and her activity satisfaction as 1.7. Whilst poor health undoubtedly has impact here, her situation could also be influenced by the strong **negative** pull of environmental factors:

* local transport is inaccessible
* house stairs are just possible, but will not be so after surgery which is due shortly
* no satisfactory help with house cleaning and gardening
* neighbours are not mentioned
* social contacts and activities are not nearby; all entail either an expensive taxi ride or are dependent upon friends who drive.

Such negative environmental factors, coupled with Fay's current poor health status, indicate that although Fay struggles to overcome the many obstacles and manages to organise days that are generally varied she still perceives her quality of life to be low.

**Gladys**         data suggest that Gladys displays many positive general theme factors. Once again however, as in the case of Fay, their full impact is not realised because of environmental limitations:

  * the road "gets steeper each time I come home"
  * only ground floor rooms can now be accessed
  * preferred activities are all a bus-ride away, and the bus service is not always convenient

Again like Fay, Gladys is experiencing increasing health concerns which will colour her perception of quality of life. However unlike Fay, Gladys has resolved the major concern about her future, as she has located a suitable residential home nearby.

**Joyce**   here as in the case of Gladys above, Joyce perceives her quality of life to be moderate (VAS score of 6). Her data related to the occupational day reveal many limitations but clearly her environment is maximising her quality of life in the following ways:

  * sensitive community support, responsive to need, is implemented and regularly monitored
  * hobbies (radio) are facilitated
  * neighbours and friends visit

As Joyce's needs are complex, environmental balance is of high priority. In such a situation the environmental strengths can enhance quality living. This cannot of course be proven, except by totally unethical means: withdrawal of current environment would possibly remove many if not all elements of quality of life and chance of satisfying occupational engagement for Joyce.

As has been cited on previous occasions, lack of transport can strongly disadvantage older people and marginalize them from involvement in their local environment. The two car owners in the study have described the high value they place on car ownership, Ann declaring: *"oh no I wouldn't go out half as much in the evenings if I didn't have a car"*. Also subjects have spoken nostalgically of the poignant moment when "the car has been taken away". Karl remarked on the "awfulness" of the: *"time my legs went three years ago and the doctor took my car away"*. When personal transport is not available, then the issues around public transport become more crucial. Bus routes that link residential areas with shopping centres are appreciated, and especially valued when the buses are adapted to facilitate entry by wheelchair because then as Edith remarked: *"I can get my loaded shopping trolley on and off"*. Such services that affect general populations involve many decision-makers and frequently the debate can be contentious. Fernie (1991) cites the case of crossing times at traffic lights. Whilst an elderly person may require an extended time period to cross a road in safety, there is pressure to minimise set crossing times in order to avoid traffic congestion.

## Other potential impact factors: health and socio-demography

**Health status** Older individuals who live alone are known to request more support for health-related needs than those who live in partnerships (National Statistics, 2001a). Contact rates for GPs are reported as 8% percent higher (McNiece, Majeed 1999) for older people living alone and pensioner attendance in accident and emergency departments is also reportedly higher when the pensioner lives alone (Hull, Jones, Moser 1997). In recognition that partnership-living can give rise to such different patterns of need and lifestyle pursuit, all the subjects providing our case studies in this instance lived alone and in the community. Health is always recognised as of prime importance when quality of life is assessed. Indeed on some occasions because health is SO important, researchers trying to rank quality of life components for their importance, have removed health from a potential list because it always figures first. Rokeach (1973) did just this and chose to exclude health from quality of life measurement because everybody ranked it as the single most important domain. We chose to look at baseline health of the subjects providing case studies on this occasion because of its potential impact upon occupational involvement and what activities the subjects were able to tackle. We saw in chapter 4 that the SF36 results provided a basic profile of health status for each individual.

Because the yesterday interviews did not specifically ask for information about the impact of health status, there was freedom for each individual to reveal health related limitations to their occupational day, *if they regarded this aspect as influential*. Many subjects referred in passing to reduced mobility, limited choices and new pastimes to replace those that could no longer be managed, but the resulting impact of health impairment upon occupational involvement appeared most strongly influenced, not by the level of impairment, but by other major themes, in particular drives for personal fulfilment plus occupational beliefs. Thus a strong drive for personal fulfilment, as expressed by Karl for example, could go some way towards compensation for the negative impact of greatly reduced mobility and acceptance of an almost housebound status. Cross examination of the SF36 results here reveals that in terms of physical function

Joyce, Lucy, Fay and Karl all have scores of 20% or less. Whilst these scores are reflected in the accounts of their occupational days, they have not always exerted a negative influence over the satisfaction experienced from the day. Joyce and Fay have both indicated high levels of satisfaction here. A more major health impact appears to be the relationship between mental health and satisfaction with the occupational day. Lucy with the lowest score of 36% for mental health, is clearly influenced here. Both she and Ian are currently receiving treatment for depression and both hold the lowest possible SF36 scores of zero in the area of emotional limitations. This score clearly correlates with a level of dissatisfaction with the occupational day for them both. At this point in time however we are left with the unanswered question as to which is the primary cause, occupational deprivation or reduced mental health.

It appears that health status in general exerts a complicated pattern of influence over both perceived quality of life and personal satisfaction derived from daily occupations. Whereas poor health clearly has a diminishing effect upon full activity participation and highly-rated quality of life, subjects in the current case studies have revealed many *adaptive* and *compensatory* skills that in turn act almost as buoyancy aids to support retained engagement in valued pastimes with a consequent sense of on-going well-being.

**Socio-demography**     It is necessary to examine any additional influence on the occupational day that may be attributable to socio-demographic status. In taking the yesterday interview data for the subjects who revealed days that included more negative features than positive ones, we would need to consider Beatrice, Doris, Horace, Ian, Karl and Lucy, with Horace and Lucy presenting with the lowest number of positive factors. Within this cohort of six subjects, four of the ten super profile lifestyles (Brown et al, 1998) are represented, ranging from the second most affluent, lifestyle B group of "thriving greys", to the least affluent lifestyle J group of "have nots". Again Horace and Lucy are representative of two lifestyle profiles, some five groups apart. On this evidence, it appears that amongst the subjects studied this time, there is no significant negative correlation between socio-demographic status and the ability to construct a satisfying occupational day.

In next examining the most positively rated days, we must explore the yesterday interview data of Gladys, Fay and Edith. Use of geodemographic typology indicates that these three subjects again are covered by three different lifestyle descriptors, representing neither the most nor the least affluent. This would suggest that socio-demographic status exerts little or no undue positive influence over the construction of a satisfying occupational day for this group of people. We may anticipate that personal background and upbringing may well have influenced strongly-developed skills of resourcefulness in Gladys, Fay and Edith, but this topic was not investigated as part of this study and cannot therefore be reported.

This short chapter has begun the process of moving research results of earlier chapters into a practical arena, depicted in diagrams and reinforced with further contributions from the subjects. In Chapter 10 we move further into implementing the research results, with the introduction of the *Quality Enhancement through Occupational Satisfaction* Assessment Tool.

## CHAPTER 10 CREATING THE DAY FOR OURSELVES

Grounded in research results we are now in a position to present a tool for practical use which is based on the discovered themes of an occupational day as depicted in Figure 3(viii) of the previous chapter. Such a tool can facilitate the assessment and outcome of personal *quality enhancement through occupational satisfaction,* see figure 3(ix) below. Having resulted from extensive investigations with people aged 75 to 98 years, we are confident that this new tool addresses issues of importance in the daily lives of older people. We will see later how this tool can be used in assessing and targeting occupational interventions when working with vulnerable older people.

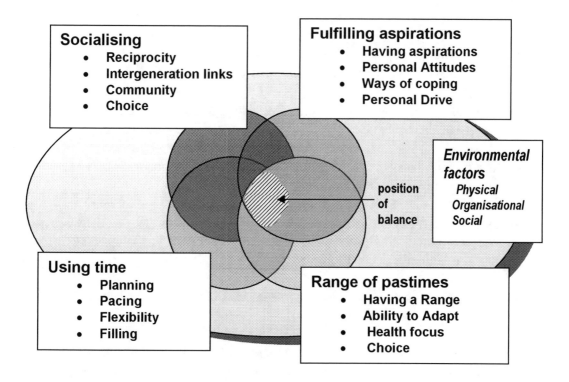

## Figure 3(ix) PRACTICAL ASSESSMENT TOOL:
### *Quality enhancement through occupational satisfaction*
(QETOS)

Each of the tool's four general themes has factors, already described, that contribute towards either a negative position (due to either under or over stimulation) or a positive position of balance. We also discovered that it is possible to *predict* where an individual's position lies between these two extremes. Figure 3(ix) above shows an ideal occupational day, where all themes are balanced, thus the central area is one of harmony and maximum satisfaction. With the addition of a grading system ranging from negative through to balanced, it becomes possible to record individual occupational satisfaction in a quantitative manner. Use of this tool enables achievement of quality and satisfaction in an occupational day to be assessed, and reported in a methodical manner, with progress or regression regularly charted via the same tool. Importantly too, the individuality of each person is expressed and goals can be set to improve the overall balance. As research has indicated there will be a wide variation between completed charts, reflecting individual concerns and strengths. The aim is always to achieve balance which brings personal satisfaction with there being no right or wrong answers. Environmental influences of a structural, organisational or social nature can also be considered if relevant to an individual's situation. The *Quality enhancement through occupational satisfaction* tool is recommended:

- as a tool for therapists with elderly clients who appear to be occupationally dysfunctional or dissatisfied with their daily activities

- as a self-monitoring tool for elderly people who wish to improve the quality of their lifestyle

- as a decision-assisting tool at times of contemplating change, such as a potential move to a new, possibly more protected environment

- as a "ready reference" tool, for use in health promotion with well elderly people, to facilitate discussion of the factors that enhance balance and harmony in daily occupations as age increases

- as a professional assessment tool to record evidence-based practice

The next pages present the complete Assessment Tool: *Quality enhancement through occupational satisfaction (QETOS),* in larger print format, ready for replication and application.

**N.B. The *QETOS* must be copied and used in full, together with the footnote which acknowledges its source.**

# THE ASSESSMENT TOOL: *Quality enhancement through occupational satisfaction (QETOS)(1)*

**AIM:** To assess four main areas of an occupational day
To establish plans for change where necessary
To achieve quality through maximum balance

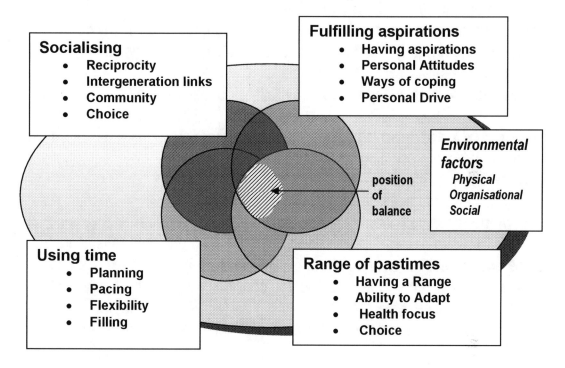

**Socialising**
- Reciprocity
- Intergeneration links
- Community
- Choice

**Fulfilling aspirations**
- Having aspirations
- Personal Attitudes
- Ways of coping
- Personal Drive

*Environmental factors*
*Physical*
*Organisational*
*Social*

position of balance

**Using time**
- Planning
- Pacing
- Flexibility
- Filling

**Range of pastimes**
- Having a Range
- Ability to Adapt
- Health focus
- Choice

# GLOSSARY

**Socialising** concerns all personal interaction with other people:

**Reciprocity:** balancing needs of self and friends/ neighbours, so that you experience both "give" and "take"

**Intergenerational:** studies show that as we grow older our own age friendship circles naturally decrease, befriending some younger people is a healthy and rewarding stance for both parties

**Community:** "No man is an island"- are you content with your interactions within your local community?

**Choice:** are you able to choose with whom you spend time?

1. Green S. (2009) Occupation and Quality in Later Life.

**Fulfilling aspirations** is concerned with your personal belief system that assists decision-making regarding daily activities:

**Aspirations:** represents the spiritual element, ranging from a loose affinity with the world and its resources, through to a strong religious conviction; we all feature somewhere along the spectrum. Do you recognise/ address your own position here?

**Attitudes:** does your general disposition help you through each day?

**Ways of coping:** do you have adequate strategies when things do not go according to plan?

**Drive:** How well motivated are you, to realise your aspirations?

**Range of pastimes** is possibly the easiest theme to identify. It is the most concrete area, representing our knowledge and identification with personal and local activity resources.

**Range:** do you indulge in a full range of possible pastimes?

**Adaptation:** can you adapt favourite pastimes to suit your developing needs?

**Health focus:** research (*1*) has shown that increased personal satisfaction arises when health is considered on a daily basis. Healthy diet, exercise are just two agenda items. How much do you consider your health when you plan your daily activities?

**Choice:** here represents your autonomy, information and ability to select pastimes to suit YOU.

**Using time** represents the 24 hours in a day as a container; when it is used or lies unused, it cannot be regained. Do you use your time effectively?

**Planning:** do you have even a rudimentary plan for each day, so that you can measure achievement?

**Pacing**: are you able to adjust your time use if health needs dictate a slower pace on some days?

**Flexibility**: any rigid plan for time use takes no account of weather, bus timetable vagaries etc., do you have alternative strategies to help deal with such things?

**Filling:** do you feel able to comfortably fill your days with things you wish to accomplish...?

1.Green S. (2009) *Occupation and Quality in Later Life*.

# COMPLETING THE ASSESSMENT (1)

1. First think of whether your **socialising** is satisfying to you at present. You may feel dissatisfied (negative) if you are lonely **or** you have too much association with non-selected companions. Try to rate yourself along the line from negative towards balanced for the sample items under this heading.

2. Next consider your **aspirations**. You may feel negative if **either** you have no aspirations, so you drift through each day and week, **or** you are setting yourself high and unattainable goals to reach unrealistic expectations.

3. Then consider how you **use time** each day. Again the aim is to avoid the negative positions, of **either** racing through the many daily chores, with never having time for the things you enjoy (too little time) **or** finding that time hangs heavily and you are often bored. How balanced is your time use?

4. Next consider your current **range of pastimes.** A negative position may arise because **either** you have an impractical list of pastimes you previously enjoyed, but they are now no longer possible **or** you know of few pastimes which you now enjoy. Rate yourself on the suggested elements here.

5. **Environment (Optional)** People considering possible relocation in later life will want to think about the present suitability of their home environment in supporting their activities. Comment on this if necessary.

Have fun with the assessment, even as you ask yourself some searching questions! Additional criteria may be added to the given areas if these are important to you. Consider the diagram on the previous page and try to relate it to your own daily life. Remember the aim is to achieve a balance that is satisfying to you; all people are different, and there is absolutely no right or wrong answer.

> ➤ **Mark each line at a place between negative and balanced which reflects how you feel today. Remember your aim over time will be to see all areas as balanced as possible**
> ➤ **Reflect on how you have rated yourself**
> ➤ **Decide on one or two areas where you would like to make changes, and write a plan to help you make progress**
> ➤ **Set a date to re-evaluate and assess your progress.**

*If you have reached this point, congratulations! It means you really do have a genuine desire to "add quality to the rest of your life"! Good luck with your implementations.*

1.Green S.(2009) Occupation and Quality in Later Life

# THE ASSESSMENT TOOL: *Quality enhancement through occupational satisfaction (QETOS)(1)*

NAME:......................................................

DATE OF COMPLETION: ............................

**Socialising**    Negative -- -- -- -- -- -- -- -- -- -- Balanced

**Fulfilling Aspirations**    Negative -- -- -- -- -- -- -- -- -- -- Balanced

**Using time**    Negative -- -- -- -- -- -- -- -- -- -- Balanced

**Range of Pastimes**    Negative -- -- -- -- -- -- -- -- -- -- Balanced

**My goal plan is:**

.................................................................................
.................................................................................
.................................................................................

**I will review progress on (date):** .......................................

**Further comments:**

.................................................................................
.................................................................................
.................................................................................

1.Green S.(2009) Occupation and Quality in Later Life.

# THE ASSESSMENT TOOL: *Quality enhancement through occupational satisfaction (QETOS)(1)*

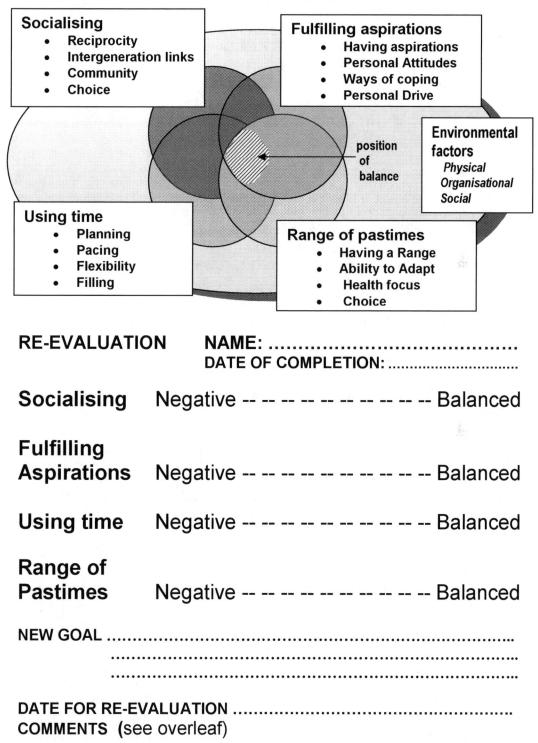

**Socialising**
- **Reciprocity**
- **Intergeneration links**
- **Community**
- **Choice**

**Fulfilling aspirations**
- **Having aspirations**
- **Personal Attitudes**
- **Ways of coping**
- **Personal Drive**

position
of
balance

**Environmental factors**
*Physical*
*Organisational*
*Social*

**Using time**
- **Planning**
- **Pacing**
- **Flexibility**
- **Filling**

**Range of pastimes**
- **Having a Range**
- **Ability to Adapt**
- **Health focus**
- **Choice**

**RE-EVALUATION**     NAME: ...............................................
DATE OF COMPLETION: ...............................

**Socialising**     Negative -- -- -- -- -- -- -- -- -- -- Balanced

**Fulfilling Aspirations**     Negative -- -- -- -- -- -- -- -- -- -- Balanced

**Using time**     Negative -- -- -- -- -- -- -- -- -- -- Balanced

**Range of Pastimes**     Negative -- -- -- -- -- -- -- -- -- -- Balanced

NEW GOAL .........................................................................
.........................................................................
.........................................................................

DATE FOR RE-EVALUATION ................................................
COMMENTS (see overleaf)

*1.Green S.(2009)Occupation and Quality in Later Life.*

# Keeping records

1. It is possible to score the results for QETOS if this is appropriate. This may be so in an ongoing therapeutic setting where progress or regression needs to be recorded in a quantitative manner. Taking the position of balance (B) as the most positive state then this would be recorded as 10. At the other extreme the most negative state (N) would be recorded as 1. For example:

> Socialising          2
> Fulfilling aspirations  8
> Range of pastimes      3
> Using time            7

*The above record suggests a person who is relatively satisfied with a personal use of time and who is also able to address own aspirations in a satisfying way. The quality or amount of socialising is however not satisfying and possibly the range of current pastimes is too small to be satisfying. A goal may then be set to address the latter areas, and a realistic date for re-evaluation recorded.*

2. A record sheet for the client above, using QETOS, may be set up as follows:

## *Tom Smith: QETOS Assessment*

| DATE | SOCIALISING | ASPIRATIONS | PASTIMES | TIME USE | ENVIRONMENT |
|------|-------------|-------------|----------|----------|-------------|
| 6.1.08 | 2 | 8 | 3 | 7 | N.A. |
| 7.2.08 | 3 | 8 | 4 | 7 | N.A. |
| 1.3.08 | 3 | 8 | 5 | 7 | N.A. |
| 16.4.08 | 6 | 8 | 6 | 7 | N.A. |

**Mr Smith was satisfied with the quality of his daily occupations and discharged from further intervention on 16.4.08. Date for review: 9.1.09.**

3. Alternatively individuals may want to use the tool in a more informal manner, simply charting their own position at a given time, reflecting on the positions and establishing a goal to readjust any unsatisfactory area. Even when not recording a quantitative score it is always helpful to make a note of any planned changes or goals and at the same time to make a diary entry to check on any progress. In this way the planned changes get neither forgotten nor subsumed under other pressing tasks!

This chapter has demonstrated how the earlier research can be used in a practical manner, to help older individuals reach maximum occupational satisfaction. Part 4 which follows includes additional material and sample case studies, designed to further assist implementation.

# OCCUPATION AND QUALITY IN LATER LIFE

## PART 4  REFLECTIONS FOR THERAPISTS AND TIPS FOR IMPLEMENTATION

**Synopsis**    *this final section of the book offers additional material.*

*Chapter 11* *provides reflection material, particularly suitable for therapists and researchers in an increasingly accountable environment. Included here are:*

- *Relevance of the research to current therapeutic issues*
- *An examination of the worth of research methods and results*
- *Challenges to earlier findings*

*Chapter 12* *concludes with a selection of tips, sample case studies and lists of occupations gleaned from the present study and additional research conducted with older people across the U.K.*

## CHAPTER 11 THERAPEUTIC APPLICATION AND REFLECTION

In all research study it is essential to look forward and to suggest how the results may be applied. Pierce (2001a) talked of a current *explosive growth in our understanding of occupation.* She goes on to relate this to a more aware health care system which is now valuing functional or occupational outcomes, and she continues by suggesting:

> *A potential time of congruence is approaching if occupational therapy can expeditiously translate an expanding knowledge of occupation into powerful occupation-based practice*

> Pierce 2001a: 249.

Such a *translation* of knowledge into practice as Pierce recommends, necessitates effective tools or application models to direct this process. With this in mind, it has been possible to look forward and make practical suggestions of further use for this study's data-generated thematic model, illustrated earlier in figure 3(viii).

As the model is based on the research results we are now in a position to present a tool for practical use as described and detailed in Chapter 10. Such a tool can facilitate the assessment and outcome of client *quality enhancement through occupational satisfaction*. Having resulted from extensive investigations with people aged 75 to 98 years, we can be confident that this new tool addresses issues of importance in the daily lives of our older clients. Chapter 12 includes case study scenarios of the new tool in use.

## Personal reflections and current therapeutic issues

*When my bones are stiff and aching*
*And my feet won't climb the stair,*
*I will only ask one favor:*
*Don't bring me no rocking chair.*
*....*
*I'm the same person I was back then,*
*A little less hair, a little less chin,*
*A lot less lungs and much less wind.*
*But ain't I lucky I can still breathe in.*

Angelou 1986: On Aging: 48

There is current pressure for therapists, together with other health professionals, to ensure that all work-place endeavours address topical professional and therapeutic issues. Research as well as clinical intervention, needs to be mindful of such interests which are shared by managers, budget-holders and therapists themselves. Issues of *Client-centred practice (CCP)* and *Evidence-based practice (EBP)* are to the forefront. To address them simultaneously is not always an easy task as the two routes towards intervention do not necessarily run parallel. Finlay (2001) describes some of the tensions here as occupational therapists strive to be true to their beliefs in holism, whatever this may mean, within work settings that are increasingly pressured and under-resourced.

This chapter subsection uses personal reflection to explore result implications in relation to such current professional issues. Coupled with words such as Angelou's above, the following statement also served as a stimulus to this book's author as the research began:

*...To add life to the years that have been added to life*

(*Ageing International* 1996:17)

## Therapeutic application and reflection

Such statements act as a spur to all researchers in the ageing field, with the implicit message that increased longevity must be accompanied by ongoing quality of life. Ipso facto, how might this best be achieved? With my own professional concerns and expertise cited in the broad field of occupational science (briefly introduced by Clark *et al.* 1991 as "the systematic study of the human as an occupational being..."p.310), I focused my research here with the intent of increasing the current relatively small knowledge base in this area. I had met elderly patients who expressed Angelou's level of determination as we see in her poem above, but I had many questions that current literature could not answer. In particular what did occupational involvement mean to a vulnerable older person, did it really provide added value to quality living, if so how and what were the means of facilitation particularly in the face of advanced age and deteriorating capabilities?

Hobson (1996) reminded us that **client-centred practice** is a goal towards which all occupational therapists aspire. She informs us that: *the essential element of client-centred practice, having the client actively involved in treatment, planning and implementation, is linked to the concepts of consumerism (CAOT, 1991) and empowerment* (Gage and Polatajko 1995, p.134). Hobson raised issues that have concerned me for a number of years, these include questions such as: *how can you actively involve your client if his/her disability prevents adequate communication?* Hobson proposes graded decision-making and, where necessary, the use of processes that are less cognitively demanding. As I began to be immersed in the current study I became acutely aware that if I was to accurately represent the participant's concerns about occupation I must *be* where they are now, must use words and tools that are familiar, and must listen acutely to their stories. I recorded something of this in field-notes:

> *Rang to book a first appointment, following lead from a local GP. I let the phone ring for a couple of minutes on two occasions, then decided to try again the following day. However, same afternoon, my home phone rang and a voice asked who is there? Suspecting a child with a wrong number, I said my number, and the voice repeated who is it; you have been ringing me. I then realised this was my contact. She then explained that I hadn't given her long enough to get to the phone from the commode, and with the extra hour on the clock, her bowels were all up the creek! We arranged a date for a first interview, in two days time.*

Then two days later, after the first interview, I added the following field-notes:

> *Some key points. A lady with a strong faith and life force, of positive outlook, despite serious sensory deprivation and lack of any living relatives for support. This again raises the question of the value of*

*relative support to some people; is it over-estimated? Her two local friends plus team of carers, appeared to provide genuine support and friendship, clearly valued and fostered by the subject. She exuded warmth and interest in others. A professed 'no pills' lady, she had a liking for simple foods and fish (a common liking amongst the old, elderly I seem to be finding). Pets also figured. Environment was of absolute acute importance. Now with such a small amount of sight, accuracy of positioning of everything from display photographs to ham sandwich in the refrigerator, to glasses and hearing aid and hand or tea towel, were all vital. Any change of carer, could unhinge this so easily. I was aware of this as I made tea, and hoped fervently that I replaced everything exactly. Subject appeared to accept her losses without rancour. She mentioned that she now no longer handles any china- I think she must regret this.*

Field-notes: 019:11.4.

Through naturalistic enquiry with this lady in her own environment, coupled with the use of accessible tools such as the visual analogue scales, I felt I had been able to enter the client's life-world, and to share in the experience of what was important to her. This felt like client-centred practice in action. Through experiences such as this I was made alert to the potential of a visual outcome tool should it arise from the research. The development and use of the assessment tool: ***Quality enhancement through occupational satisfaction* (Figure: 3.(ix))** would seem to be a valid method of rendering research results of practical use in a manner which invites full client participation.

Whalley Hammell (2001) sets the scene in regard to ***evidence-based practice*** when she commented:

> *'Evidence-based practice' has become a contemporary preoccupation for health practitioners, who seek to validate their roles within an increasingly competitive fiscal climate and to assure clients that interventions are informed by a sound knowledge base.*

Whalley Hammell 2001:228.

As a clinical therapist in a fast moving rehabilitation centre in Texas in the mid 1980's I was only too well aware that my practice must be evidence-based and must be worth every cent of the then $68 per hour that my patients were being charged for their out-patient therapy. In the UK the need for such *evidence* has not been quite so obvious until more recent times, particularly at the patient-therapist interface where costs are generally borne by an "invisible" National Health Service payment. Now however, in a climate of increasing accountability, therapy must be seen to be effective by all. Consequently, therapists struggle to find and make public their therapeutic interventions as being *worthy* of ongoing resources. This is particularly difficult in the less concrete areas of practice such as the topic of this study, and auditors may well ask: *Is it cost-effective that occupational therapists spend time in helping elderly clients find meaningful occupations?* This is not an easy question to respond to in monetary terms, but it is possible to proffer some sound comments that support such practice as being worthy in ways which extend beyond altruism.

At a purely practical level, the study of environmental impact upon occupational involvement for vulnerable older people, suggests a potential cost effective outcome because it may lead to retained independence within a community setting. Ergonomists have recognised this for some time. Nayak (1995) commented: *"Design for the young and you exclude the old, design for the old and you include the young"* (p.8). The current study has been able to reinforce and extend knowledge concerning environmental impact at all levels. Through specific enquiry too, it would be possible to take individual findings and explore them further. For example a controlled trial involving low-level busses on a neighbourhood route could produce dual evidence, that of customer satisfaction plus evidence of a reduced need for social service support for elderly shoppers. Nayak's article provided additional evidence as it described how the "Thousand Elder Group" founded at Birmingham University, used focus groups of elderly people to provide valuable feedback to manufacturers on products ranging from door locks to lifts.

On a more esoteric level it is also possible to suggest evidence-based outcomes. Over three decades ago, Englehardt (1977) discussed the important role for occupational therapists of listening to clients and thereby *"helping them create meaning...through engagement in the world"* (p.670). Christiansen (1997) raised Englehardt's comment and develops it by suggesting that when answering the fundamental question of "why do I exist", we need to:

> *"explain the existential importance of everyday activities and the importance of shared meaning within a culture"*

> Christiansen 1997: 170.

In the exploration of shared meanings Christiansen suggests the importance in such ordinary occupations as gardening and letter-writing. In fact all such expressive arts *nourish the soul by providing an opportunity to create meaning.* In terms of this study's results this represents a truism; contentment and opportunity for creative expression were closely linked. It was interesting to find the popularity of poetry-composition amongst the subjects, in addition to painting and other crafts. Earlier writers, for example Mattingly and Flemming (1994), have also suggested that assisting an individual to uncover meaning in life, is therapeutic and beneficial to *engagement and quality of life;* they do however go on to report therapists who fail to document this, because *"it is non-reimbursable"* (p.296).

This study has taken steps to enter the participants' life-worlds, albeit briefly, and to study the essence of meaningful occupation and its links with quality of life for elderly people. Having reflected on the therapeutic justification for interest in the topic, a further point of reflection is valid for all practising therapists, health workers and carers who are considering embarking on a related research project. We must ask whether it is really possible for a therapist to be an unbiased researcher in such instances.

## Researcher versus therapist

From the outset I was aware that just as my interview skills should be honed with each participant I interviewed, there was other professional territory where I may never experience complete ease. I continued to sense the dichotomy of the researcher's need for full and accurate data gathering, versus the therapeutic stance of facilitating change or improvement, or at the very least of "doing no harm". With the latter in mind, I made an early decision that the use of the MST would be inappropriate where there was paucity of occupational involvement. I used the field-notes to record some of the tensions as they were experienced. Subject 019 also serves to illustrate this point:

> *I was let in via intercom buzzer, from the bedroom… … Due to profound deafness and very poor eyesight, interview had to take a non- standard approach and was at times difficult to conduct. Subject however was a willing conversationalist, and clearly loved singing. Again, I felt enormously privileged to be there, and aware of not stressing her; although for me a "subject", I was acutely aware that I wanted her to derive pleasure/ satisfaction from our exchange. For me, this had to be of prime importance. Accuracy remained a key factor for me, but it was secondary to subject's comfort; I was aware there may be some small facets of info. I would leave unanswered, but feel anything vital can probably be solicited afterwards from the Dr contact who knows her well. I was glad this was one of my later interviews, because it seems that my skills have developed over time and I can now glide more quickly into a key area from a*

*subject's lead, even though a standard yesterday interview framework is far from adhered to. This is something akin to a novice versus expert OT assessor I think.*

Data subject 019, field-notes: 11.4.

Despite an ongoing sense of tension between the therapist and the researcher roles, and a lingering, gradual shift on my part, away from the positivist influence of the medical tradition, I suggest that this was a beneficial position. Retained therapeutic strengths in observational detail and medical/ sociological awareness guided a portion of each interview whilst phenomenological principles steered the format for data gathering and analysis. Additionally, although I felt unable to undertake prolonged professional therapeutic intervention, it was possible to meet immediate needs; these were dealt with in a practical manner as follows:

At the close of each interview the researcher stepped from researcher to therapist mode, feeling it would be professionally unacceptable to leave therapeutic needs unmet. Thus the interviews resulted in the following additional interventions:

Ann: ongoing discussion regarding housing alternatives
Beatrice: a bus trip to a local seaside town and fish and chip lunch. This was an activity the subject had previously regularly enjoyed, but lacked confidence to resume after a recent bout of flu.
Edith: two further visits to share garden plans
Ian: referral to community occupational therapist for bath seat and tap turner
Karl: referral to G.P. for re-assessment of poor balance and potential need for mobility aids
Lucy: supply of a long-handled reacher

In reality I had stepped into the position of an "insider" with a few of the participants, not a position I assumed easily as I scrupulously sought ethical precision in terms of information handling. I recorded this in the following manner:

*I have taken to popping in as a neighbour, every 2-3 weeks. I cannot treat {name} as a research subject; I feel enormously privileged that she has accepted me into her lifestyle and friendship circle, and I cannot abuse this. I try to be careful in what I share with others and will of course inform {N} of the official research sessions, whose content will not be shared. A narrow tightrope for any researcher, but truly a position from which to elicit real meaning. Today, our last meeting before my summer holiday, over tea and cakes we had a usual wide-*

*ranging debate and exchanged stories about childhood poverty;
knowing where you were in the order of the classroom, and
frequency of prayer.*

Data subject 011, field-notes: 22.7.

Holliday (2002) supports such a stance:

*Researchers must struggle to pursue the deeper perceptions of
people in their settings*

Holliday, 2002: 195

and writers in educational fields would describe this as naturalistic enquiry (Adelman and Alexander 1982), which in recent past, proved a popular addition to the externally imposed statistical tools for evaluating such complex areas as curriculum change. In-depth involvement gained from an insider's position of natural enquiry, enables the building of a full picture, with maximum light shed into all areas of the scene. With this in mind, I accepted that it was possible to bridge a therapist/ phenomenological researcher/ neighbour role, in a professional manner and to the benefit of all parties.

One further field-note extract, serves to further illuminate this complex area. It is taken from a later interview, and records what happened towards the end of the interview, when talk of disposal of family possessions, as an occupational task, led into a discussion of potential plans for a solution:

*as he talked this afternoon, he asked if he could sound me out
with a new plan he had been forming.... I was readily able to
support his plan, for which he seemed enormously relieved/
grateful. He has strong feelings about fate/ spiritual directional
guidance, some of which are on tape. Like others too he has a
sense of "wanting to pay back" for the good times he had in the
war, of feeling grateful for these times and now wanting to give
something to {his youth work}. A convivial interview, I left
feeling I had not been intrusive, but had acted as a valuable
sounding board.*

Data subject 017, field-notes: 6.9.

The reflexivity described in this section causes me to continue to value the process of reflexive analysis in terms of professional development. The reflections also serve to reinforce and to *add honesty* to the results that have been presented.

## Examining the worth of research methods and results

As any research project draws into its final stages it is essential to discuss issues of worth. This subsection is offered here as an aide memoir to other researchers. It also serves as a source of further information to any readers who want to ask questions about adequacy of methods or results. We must ask how trustworthy our methods have been and address issues of honesty and reliability in the results that have been obtained. Two major subsections follow.

## 1. A critical look at methodology and methods

Plager (1994) reminded us of some of the strengths of using hermeneutic phenomenology. She pointed out that it does not reduce the concerns of human beings to mere characteristics or absolute properties. On the contrary it recognises humans as social beings, each coming from a "meaningful world" and each with his or her own background familiarity. Such pre-suppositions lead a researcher to make naturalistic enquiry where the study of the individual within a familiar environment, aids the understanding and interpretation of a person's concerns. In such situations, individual differences are highlighted and present themselves for deeper investigation.

Denzin and Lincoln (1994) also remind us that a constructivist paradigm "assumes a relativist ontology", or accepts that there are multiple realities and adopts a "naturalistic" set of methodological procedures. Such methodological assumptions have underpinned the current study with the effect that within the identical framework of a "yesterday interview" each of the twelve participants has provided a unique, experiential account, rich in content, and directly related to what is real or meaningful to each individual. Extremes have been noted, from boredom to perpetual action and from the lounge window view of the world, to participation in a 12-mile ramble. Arguably such bare facts could have resulted from a variety of methodological approaches, but the use of hermeneutical phenomenology has enabled a deeper penetration into the significance of the pursuits and related issues, in the daily life-world of the people concerned. At the level of individual case studies, multiple realities have been revealed and at the stage of analysis the phenomenological approach has facilitated a close, intimate examination of the *meaning* behind the everyday occupations as discussed at the beginning of chapter 8. Whilst multiple realities have been recognised and reported, it has been possible to synthesize these, without diluting their individual importance, and to present a smaller set of essences or general themes, that encompass the individual realities.

The phenomenological stance contrasted with many reports of quality of life, as the domains associated with the latter are frequently related in a quantified manner, e.g. number of social contacts, amount of personal choice or autonomy or degree of independence. Whilst overall themes were found to be similar when considered from a phenomenological framework, added value was obtained because subsidiary components were discovered. So social contacts were found to be highly valued again, and we now know relationships in the community can be enriched when reciprocity is present. It is not only the amount of autonomy and choice that is important, but the links with personal aspirations for a satisfying day.

Interviewing in the home meant that the life-world of the individuals could be shared. The researcher was a guest and many meanings such as the home as a repository for memories could be experienced firsthand whilst familiar objects triggered recall of friendships and pastimes. Observation also served to enhance the experiential accounts supplied by the clients.

Two organising systems provided frameworks for the study's methodology. Theoretical frameworks provide focal points, shape and boundaries to study areas. The Rev. Jim Thompson, Bishop of Bath and Wells, on Radio 4, after the Dunblane massacre[3] went further in suggesting that theoretical frameworks bring security, safety and comfort too. He was advocating the use of a spiritual framework of hope and positive attributes, rather than vengeance, greed or retribution at this time. The selection of appropriate theoretical frameworks is a necessary precursor to any major investigation. In the current work, background studies helped in establishing theoretical frameworks to assist relevant data collection and analysis. Two established models emerged as being helpful to the current study.

Hughes (1990) conceptual model of quality of life for elderly people cited eight components and she suggested, "further research could usefully investigate connections and relationships between the different subsystems" (p.55). Her model depicts purposeful activity and quality of the environment as being two adjacent and essential subsystems in supporting quality of life. The current study has been able to probe connections between these subsystems and to provide illustrative examples of the interplay between them. It has shown that environmental circumstances can exert a strong "pull" over the achievement of purposeful activity. In some instances such as the case of Edith, this influence is wholly positive. The positive *organisational element* of environmental influence is particularly noteworthy in the case of the most vulnerable of the subjects. Joyce, aged 98 years, is frail and has very poor sight. Her ongoing ability to fulfil her ambition to continue "living at home" is made possible only because the *organisational element* of her environment is carefully structured to meet her personal needs; a team of three carers is scheduled to assist her three times per day. In other cases, such as that of Doris, environmental pressures of a *structural*

---

[3] BBC Radio 4: Thought for the Day, March 14, 1996.

and a *social* nature, hamper her purposeful activity and her overall quality of life is considerably diminished.

The second model to assist in this study is Law *et al.*'s (1996) Person/ Environment/ Occupation (PEO) Model. Here the interplay between the PEO components is depicted as transactive, in such a way that the satisfactory performance of occupation can be influenced by judicious organisation or manipulation of personal, environmental or occupational factors. The current study accepted occupational factors as given in yesterday interviews, whilst seeking to establish the personal and environmental details that influenced each individual as the occupational day was described. The model's demonstration of the constant interplay between these components greatly assisted the research process and analysis of complex interactions and led to the transactive depiction in the newly proposed assessment tool of Figure: 3(ix.) with its four general themes of an occupational day. For instance, in the case of Fay who presented with major health limitations and an environment which was not supportive, it was apparent that her strong personal attributes of stoicism, humour, planning and adaptation skills, were combining to over-ride the strong negative influences experienced in other domains, and she remained able to construct a day that was experienced as purposeful. The same transactional interplay between personal, environmental and occupational elements was visible in the accounts of all the participants. Had the study taken place over time it would be of interest to note any changing patterns in the interplay. As personal drive and attributes have been seen to play a significant part in creating a satisfying day, it is anticipated that ongoing strength in these areas would stimulate the retention of skills such as adaptation and flexibility which in turn would help to preserve occupational satisfaction.

Methodological tools were sought with pluralism in mind. Kellaher, Peace and Willcocks (1990) suggest that in order to tackle complex fields of study, there is an advantage in multi-methodological approaches as these go beyond the elementary "black box" methods of simple inputs and outcomes. Moss and Lawton's (1982) 'yesterday interview' was selected as the major tool to provide data for phenomenological study, with the anticipation that it would permit the researcher to enter each person's life-world and to hear of real experiences, significant to each individual. It was also the intent that the immediate recall of a "yesterday" would enhance accuracy in the subjects' accounts. In the event it was not always possible to use an exact "yesterday", for instance in Karl's case. He had experienced a most unusual previous day; after normally being housebound, he had been driven out into the countryside for lunch. With hindsight too, interviews conducted on Mondays were not generally viewed as conducive to recalling yesterday as a normal day, because for most subjects Sunday was seen as different. For Lucy, Sunday was a particularly stressful and lonely day as most other residents in her sheltered housing complex had visitors. In all instances the day recalled fell into the category of "a normal day for you, within the past week". Most people were able to recall the day in its entirety; some became considerably side-tracked during the recall, additional material was collected, and as appropriate the researcher used prompts in the story-telling, to return the person to the day in question. Because the subjects were allowed to give accounts in their own ways, the interview content was focussed on real concerns; each concentrated on his or her own life-world and the researcher made no attempt to veer away from this. Whilst individuals told unique stories, it was the general intention that the accounts would enhance knowledge around a range of issues, for example which occupations were seen as purposeful and why and how were these facilitated; what were the greatest impediments to occupational pursuits and were individuals able to overcome such hurdles? Such questions did not form part of the interview process, yet as hoped, most individuals, during their accounts, provided their own in-depth illustrative answers to the unasked questions. Discoveries such as "book-selling" were made and much detail about the meaning of these occupations was gleaned. For example, Gladys takes a few of her large book collection to sell in aid of church funds, at the monthly meetings. In so doing she achieves multiple objectives which she identifies as purposeful to her:

- her son will have less possessions to dispose of on her demise
- the clutter at home is lessened
- it is a means of reciprocation; the church has supported Gladys, now she can return the support by adding to church funds
- reading is facilitated for others, many of whom are themselves elderly and probably read a lot because they share Gladys's disenchantment with current television programming

The yesterday interview, used in this way for the current study, suited the purpose in hand. Perhaps, due to slight change in implementation and absence of quantification in the present work, it is not wholly accurate to title the interview in Moss and Lawton's (1982) original terms.

Additional methodological tools were selected to complement the wholly qualitative data of the yesterday interview. They were not intended to provide data for phenomenological analysis; rather they were sought as subsidiary measures to help in building a fuller picture of all the issues, and to increase the trustworthiness of the resulting report. Two standardised measures, the Nottingham Longitudinal Study of Activity and Ageing Instrument (NLSAA) (Morgan 1998), and the Moss 36-item short-form health survey (SF-36), (Ware and Sherbourne 1992) were used in order to standardise the collection of relevant background information for each subject. The SF-36 proved particularly helpful in facilitating the exploration of links between an individual's state of health and his or her perceptions of a satisfying occupational day. The data from the SF-36 also supported the influence of other themes such as environmental contexts and personal attributes including drive for fulfilment, as exerting stronger influences over a "satisfying occupational day" than even a moderate to severe physical health problem for some of the subjects. Contrastingly the SF-36 supported strong links between an elderly person's state of mental health and occupational satisfaction, and throughout the study its data reinforced the complexities of links between the recognised quality of life domains.

Moss and Lawton (1982), when exploring activity involvement, had indicated difficulty in studying such abstract terms as quality of life and the "meaningfulness" of activities. With this in mind, in attempting to penetrate below the surface of mere occupational involvement, the current study examined (through background studies), then added, visual analogue scales (VAS) to the small battery of methodological tools. The VAS gave individuals the opportunity to record their perceived quality of life (however they interpreted this) and their current satisfaction with activity level. It was then helpful to study the resulting VAS scores in comparison with the collected qualitative data, as reported in Chapter 4. For the people where there was a strong variance, the VAS results helped to explore why this should be, and served to illustrate again the strength of both personal drive and attributes plus environmental support factors.

The final data collection instrument was the multiple sorting task (MST), employed to add rigour to phenomenological data (Sixsmith and Sixsmith , 1987), and chosen to assist individuals further explore their own current experiences regarding occupational involvement. In the event, the MST was used with half of the study participants, and was found to be most productive with the most able people. For those where the MST was not used, the researcher deemed it unethical to re-present a short list of limited occupations to the individuals concerned, in a non-therapeutic context. It was felt that such action could merely highlight an individual's inabilities without potential for therapeutic redress. When many occupations were currently undertaken, the MST facilitated useful ensuing debate about frequency and preferences. Once again the results of the MST served to support some of the brief quotations from the interviews. This was particularly noticeable in the area of contact with family and children. A comment such as Gladys's, "I don't see much of my son, he's a busy line-dancer", was supported and enhanced via the MST where the topic of "visits from children" was invariably placed in the low to medium frequency occurrence categories and in the moderate enjoyment category. Thus the clustering of data, from a variety of sources, added richness to the results as well as reinforcing the trustworthiness of individual comments.

Savin-Baden and Fisher (2002) take the argument regarding trustworthiness further. In referring to the need for researchers to "engage with the messiness and complexity of data interpretation in ways that really do reflect the lives of our participants" (p.192), they suggest that researchers should seek for "honesties", rather than trustworthiness because it avoids the prejudice for similarity in data interpretation. In this study, the subject who followed her own raw data through to final interpretation, was clear that this was an honest representation of her position. The use of multiple data collection tools has yielded data that reflect the complexities of the issues. In relation to the participant group the data illustrate the closely intertwined nature of occupation and quality of life:

- *If you experience poor quality of life, this may be due to a number of domains being affected. In the majority of cases poor health is a contributory factor*

- *If you experience physical health problems and impairments, this does not mean that occupationally satisfying days are unlikely*

- *If you experience days that are occupationally satisfying, you are likely to perceive that your quality of life is good or at least moderate*

- *If you experience days that are not occupationally satisfying, this does not necessarily mean that quality of life is poor*

- *If you experience poor mental health with emotional limitations, it is likely that both quality of life and occupational satisfaction will also be seen to be poor*

Twelve people were recruited to inform the research topic. The use of three intermediary sources in the recruitment process ensured that a spectrum of capabilities was represented in the study. Perhaps such a wide range of ages from 75 to 100 years, and stretching from community active to housebound, could be deemed impractical and to represent too wide a spectrum of need. However as the first studies began, the topic of ageing and its commensurate services covered a population predicted in the UK in 1999 (National Statistics, 2001b) to be 9,294,000, and addressed all people aged 65 years and above, then it can be argued that the study's participant group represents something of the actual diversity of older people living alone in the UK. When those aged 65 to 74 years are removed from the above statistic, those over 75 years still numbered 4,365,000 people.

Purposive sampling, as used in the study, is supported in qualitative studies because it recognises and values deviant cases (Barbour 1999) and it offers researchers a degree of control rather than being at the mercy of any selection bias inherent in pre-existing groups (Barbour 2001). However in her article Barbour (2001) suggests that a criticism can be levelled at purposive sampling when there is a failure to discuss the purposive element at the data analysis stage.

## *Therapeutic application and reflection*

In addition to all subjects living alone in the community, there were two major purposive elements in the selection of the research study group. Firstly a range of three activity levels was sought. At the first level there were those who were active within their neighbourhoods, with three of the four participants here being members of local sports clubs. Generally these people reported the most active lifestyles as may be expected. The two drivers amongst the whole group were found here and the ages of this sub-group were between 75 and 91 years. The range of occupations they described was no greater than that of the second subject sub-group, although the more active pastimes such as rambling and badminton were confined to this group. The second participant sub-group, solicited through a common link with the use of Age Concern's informal support facilities, again encompassed ages from 70's to 90's and they cited regular participation in a wide-range of pastimes. One person here rode a bike and another was an active member of two sports clubs for disabled people, one involving swimming and the other sailing. The third sub-group, recruited via a general practitioner as the most vulnerable group in the study, were mostly housebound and as anticipated had shorter lists of regular occupations. Of particular interest here was the retention of social and community involvement for this group. The theme of *reciprocity* plus skills of *adaptation* ensured that these individuals had sought means to import the community to them. In their retained ability to create meaningful occupational days, despite high levels of physical impairment, these people indicated support for Lawton's suggestion (Birren and Dieckman 1991) that positive and negative quality of life components are at least partially independent of each other. So for instance Karl had a high level of immobility and was prone to falls but satisfactory social involvement and ongoing personal achievement enabled him to rate his quality of life as high. This third sub-group represented a slightly older age range, from 85 to 98 years.

The second purposive element to participant selection was designed to ensure that both sexes were represented. Background results reported in Chapter 4 commented: *although numerically any differences are small, it is interesting to note that in all measures the trend of perceived life quality and satisfaction with activity levels is marginally higher for the female study participants*. In terms of occupational endeavours, the three men made more mention of household chores such as *using the ewbank round where I have my meals,* and using the washing machine. They also placed higher emphasis on cooking and *eating well,* with accounts of cooked breakfasts and *oh I never go hungry*: the female subjects on the other hand emphasised healthy eating and a general desire to minimise the time spent in cooking and meal preparation. In terms of coping without a spouse or life-time partner, male subjects made more mention of aiming to perpetuate standards that their wives had set, again this was particularly noticeable with relation to shopping and meal preparation. On the other hand the women spoke more frequently of *finding something to do* or of effecting change, to fill the vacuum when a partner died, expressing this with phrases such as: *so I took up- (sculpturing, helping with a mother and toddler group, a gym club membership).* An interesting finding, although insignificant in numerical terms, was that all three male study participants were regular attendees at their local churches whereas four out of the nine females indicated some involvement with church activities. In general the women made more reference to creative pastimes such as painting, sewing and reading or composing poetry, whereas the men watched more television. Other pastimes including all aspects of gardening and social activities showed no gender bias, appearing instead to be influenced by personal interests and capabilities. It must be noted that within such a small subject cohort, sex differences noted above are merely observations, with the potential for further investigation.

It is readily acknowledged that in seeking in-depth enquiry with a small, informed study group, it has not been possible to tackle broader issues and variables such as racial or cultural diversity or inner city versus urban living styles. Bearing this in mind, the twelve people accepted into the study, were each able to give a full account of their occupational day and to supply all necessary detail for required additional tests. The overall result was a rich, composite picture of the occupational days of the people concerned.

## 2. A critical examination of results

### *Later life and old age*
Medical doctors, sociologists, economists and others, have been interested in the issues of older people for many years. A short column in *Nature (1999)* reminded readers of such issues that appeared in the journal fifty years previously. At this time there was a symposium on the problems of the rapidly ageing population. The audience heard that the great majority of the elderly are healthy and independent "they outnumber the ailing and decrepit by 30 to 1, and for them the most pressing problem is how to maintain to the end of their days the standard of living of their working lives". (*Nature, 1949)*. It seems that similar issues continue to dominate the ageing scene and attempts to counteract ageism remain important. French (1990) described ageism in the following way: *Ageism defines prejudice against and stereotyping of people because they are old. It is often manifested as age discrimination, which occurs when people are treated differently or unfairly because of their age* (p.179). The National Service Framework for Older People (DOH, 2001) and the later document publishing next steps in implementing the framework (DOH, 2006) are recent key publications that address ageism, and set standards of care for all older people wherever they reside, aiming to integrate services and to help older people to stay healthy and independent.

### *Therapeutic application and reflection*

Study results support the diversity of capacity amongst older people (Wetle 1991), and reject the ageist viewpoint that older age correlates with inactivity. Case studies in the current study clearly illustrate the wide range of diversity in the study sample, with those in advanced old age (over 85years) representing some of the most fulfilled individuals whilst Cath in her mid seventies rated her quality of life as only moderate and told of her daily struggles to battle with low energy levels. The study revealed its own examples of stunning levels of competence and achievement in later life (Carlson 1998); Edith preparing for a one-woman show of her sculptures to celebrate her ninetieth birthday, is one such example. There is some support for Erikson's (1986) work on the topic of interdependency between the ages, as he asserted that being with children could assist an elderly person to find trust and hope. On Lok's (1999) work in fostering intergenerational links is one ongoing proponent of valuable intergenerational links, and subjects in the current study mentioned the high value and pleasure they placed on contact with children and young people. However Erikson's earlier work (1950) with its theme of life's eighth, final psychosocial stage being characterised by a struggle for integrity over despair, without regard for human will or social or cultural influences, was not much in evidence. For one subject, Ian there was a sense of a daily struggle and an ongoing battle to make sense of what life was about. Ian however was the only subject to express such sentiment and he was still suffering bereavement following his wife's death during the previous year. Other subjects spoke of their ongoing ambitions, to learn more, to do better, to accomplish more…There was a general awareness of the "Use it or lose it" principle as Rabbitt (1997) advocated. His large study indicates a strong emphasis on retention of mental capacity when skills are regularly practised, so that crossword puzzle solving is not only an enjoyable pastime; it has a "mental health insurance" element too. The study's subjects took this theme further with an awareness of the need to aim to maintain the status quo, "to walk to the village", etc. so that physical capacity is retained. This aspect of goal-related activity lends support to research concerning social constructionism where as Christiansen (2000) reports: "the accomplishment of personal goals provides building blocks for a lifelong construction of the self". Christiansen goes on to quote Diener (2000) in the discussion of links between achievement of goals and feelings of well-being in suggesting that adaptation and goal flexibility are important components. These features were strongly supported in the current study.

Perhaps the only completely common ground regarding the study's revelations about ageing and vulnerability, was that, in the absence of any diagnosed mental health problems, there was little if any sense of resignation, instead there was almost unanimous ambition. At the least this was expressed as *looking on the bright side* or *aiming to make the most out of each day*, whilst two subjects spoke eloquently of an ambition to achieve more tomorrow than they had achieved today. These discussion comments relating to the elderly subjects must be viewed in context, in that the subjects were all elderly and to varying extents they were vulnerable with a spectrum of ongoing deteriorating health-related issues; however none of the group was at time of interview "ill", or suffering from acute medical problems.

### The environment

As Tickle-Degnen suggests, the environment played a major role in supporting the efforts of the study's subjects:

> *our occupation...is interdependent with our social and physical environment. When that environment is incongruent with our values and beliefs, the manifestation of those values and beliefs in our performance is stifled*

Tickle-Degnen 2001: Foreword

In keeping with earlier literature it appears that *where you live in older age will strongly influence what you can do.* The current study was embarked upon without preconceived environmental questions, but rather with an alertness to detect and explore any indirect or direct references to the influence of the environment.

Because the subject group only included community dwelling elders who lived alone, it was possible to exclude the powerful influences of both partnership and residential living, and to focus specifically on the impact of personal attributes and environmental factors. Lansdown (1994) termed this as "the complex interaction between the characteristics of the individual and his or her environment". Using the conceptual connections highlighted earlier (Hughes 1990 and Law *et al.* 1996), to assist in the data analysis, it became clear that all twelve subjects were undoubtedly influenced a great deal by environmental issues. At a *physical* or structural level, stairs and a hilly approach to the home provided distinct limitations to activities when health and or mobility were reduced, whilst a cul-de-sac positioned bungalow on a bus route, enhanced pursuits. At an *organisational* level a large family home with extensive maintenance needs, considerably restricted time for the pursuit of hobbies, whilst a supportive care package enabled ongoing fulfilling days in a known home environment for another subject. In *social* terms there were strong environmental influences for most subjects, particularly when the home had been occupied in many instances for in excess of forty years. The transactional (Law *et al.* 1996) feature is particularly noteworthy here. For a few subjects the immediate neighbourhood provided ready social connections, however for many subjects the chosen pursuits were a car ride away, and as age and driving restrictions increased, independent pursuit of social activities such as involvement in societies (ranging from gardening to swimming), declined. At this point too, the interaction between personal and environmental influences was highlighted. Karl spoke positively here; now relatively housebound but with retained interest in his local church activities, a personal feeling of *reciprocity* enables him to accept lifts to church and cooked meals, because he had been able to offer support services to others in earlier days, in the same locality and at a time when he was more mobile. In such findings there is considerable support for Kahana's theoretical model of person-environment interactions (Kahana 1980) where well-being arises when personal needs and environmental qualities are matched.

## Quality of life and meaningful occupation

Wilcock (2001a) suggested: "Occupation is so complex yet so fundamental to life" (p.412), in her address which sought to justify why there is a need for a discipline (Occupational Science), to study and articulate the complexities and relevance of occupation in daily life. It is not difficult to find many accounts of the positive associations between health and purposeful occupation and key studies have also demonstrated the occupational needs of very impaired people (Perrin 1997). There is however less record of *how* occupation creates or adds to the sense of well-being; in other words how does occupation fit into an individual's perception of quality of life? There is some writing on this theme, but it is minimal. Law *et al.* (1998) reviewed twenty-three studies that addressed the relationship between occupation, health and well-being, published between 1980 and 1996 and concluded that there was support for links between them, but as most studies were cross-sectional, causal relationships could not be established. Borell *et al.* (2001) in their study of the meaning of occupational engagement for physically impaired, recently-hospitalised older people in Stockholm, commented: "exploration through empirical research of the concept of occupation in relation to people's sense of well-being has just begun" (p311). Writers (Hughes 1990, Bowling 1991, Mayers 1995) along with many others, have accepted that meaningful occupation should have a place in any model of quality of life, whilst other writers (Lawton 1985, Law *et al.* 1998, Anderson and Burckhardt 1999) have suggested that further research is needed. Gill and Feinstein (1994) added to the debate by suggesting that the opinions of patients must be central to further work in this area. Results in the current study have contributed to the debate, and proffered some following key points:

*The use of time* Results in the current study, whilst cross-sectional and therefore unable to offer proof of causal links, have nevertheless indicated a close association between perceived well-being and an on-going capacity to use time in a meaningful way. Gill and Feinstein (1994), supported by Guyatt and Cook (1994) highlighted the subjective nature of quality of life and the importance of harnessing "uniquely personal perceptions" and Law *et al.* 1998 commented in similar vein: "It is important that therapists learn from each client what occupations are important for his or her health and well-being...." (p.90).

Current research has been able to collect such data, to provide quotation and vignettes that indicate *what* and *why* occupations are valued by a group of older individuals. It has been able to move the evidence beyond major concerns of time on task studies (Moss and Lawton 1982, Horgas, Wilms and Baltes 1998) and to penetrate the very essence of occupational involvement for the study's participants.

All participants spoke of the concept of *time being available to fill,* with a general awareness of owning the responsibility for how this was effected. Individual accounts provided in-depth information about how daily lives were led, how time helped the construction of the day and how personal and environmental resources were used. Throughout, there is support for Csikszentmihalyi's work (1993) in the recognition of both a clear link between an inactive mind and unhappiness and a powerful positive feeling as Csikszentmihalyi and LeFevre (1989) described, of "flow" and increased satisfaction when a complex task is tackled and conquered. Edith highlights this when she speaks of *losing herself* in her intense involvement when she is creating shell sculptures.

***Resourcefulness*** is an issue for all and is perhaps strongly emphasised in the study group, due to the participants' past and often prolonged experiences of living through war-time shortages and rationing. Edith talks of not "wasting anything, down to my last wind-fall apple", Gladys talks enthusiastically about "recycling" her books and Joyce graphically described what happened to the eels that her young brother caught. Before they were cooked, Joyce's mother: "skinned them like this", and used the skins for sprained wrists. For some people, time is a precious resource and must be eked out, so that each hour is maximised. Here we find the microwave saving time as two dinners can be cooked together and one re-heated the following day (Edith and Cath). For others there is a need for greater resourcefulness in order to fill the time, so that one planned activity per day (Fay and Lucy) and judicious studying of the television programmes (Beatrice and Karl) helps to produce a day experienced as well-spent.

***Community involvement and the social environment*** The social environment revealed its importance as earlier literature had suggested. Rabeiro (2001) describes this as increasingly important when people are impaired because familiarity promotes support and acceptance. In the current study Karl highlighted the importance of reciprocity within his neighbourhood. This concept of *giving something back* or of *not feeling beholden* was seen to be important to the subjects. In Christiansen's (2000) study of 120 subjects, amongst the older age group of 60-79 year olds, the social significance of projects or occupations was noted to be of major importance. Christiansen describes also the work of Rapkin and Fischer (1992) who found significantly less depression in their cohort of older adults, amongst those whose goals incorporated social engagement.

## Therapeutic application and reflection

The current study showed that all the participants raised the topic of social involvement in some way. As a major theme it had the potential for either a negative or a strong positive influence over the occupational day. People who reported companionable exchanges with chosen contacts suggested that such exchanges rated highly in terms of enjoyment. This result reflects the findings of Snowdon (2001) concerning the fifteen-year study of nuns in Minnesota. Here the nuns, at this time aged between 84 and 106 years have the long-standing support and friendship of others who share their values and interests. They retain active roles in long-standing activities and work-related tasks, such as running the gift shop and an 86 year old nun commented: "I think it is the most fascinating period of your life, intellectually and spiritually you are most alert at this time" (p.19). Snowdon's study also involved post mortem study of 300 brains, and he reported that in addition to heightened well-being, there are clear signs of retained health too: "some of the healthiest, most beautiful brains we have seen are from people over 100" (p.19).

***Family relationships*** The study revealed that in general this group of older people did not spend much time with their children. Often they lived at a distance, but even when living less than ten miles away, meetings were not frequent. Reasons given included children being too busy, having problems of their own or not being interested in the same things. Questions here are raised about future support. National Statistics (2001b) report that the elderly dependency rates continue to rise as people are living longer; there is then a consequent issue around *dependant upon whom?* Evandrou (1997) also reported the reluctance of today's older people to be dependent upon their children, with one older person viewing the concept of moving in with an adult child as little better than going into residential care. In such a climate, community social support becomes increasingly important: known neighbourhoods can be a valuable resource as some of the study's subjects have described.

# Challenges to earlier findings

## What the occupational title signifies

In examining the occupations, it appears that a normal day for a vulnerable elderly person living in the community may incorporate a rich and diverse pattern of activities. The twelve participants in the study revealed eighty-eight discrete occupations (see Chapter 12) that they undertook on a regular basis. The activities are wide-ranging and incorporate a spectrum of more sedentary pastimes, which potentially suggests the influence of advanced age coupled with decreasing mobility and increased health problems. The significance of such activities merits study because the simplicity of an occupation such as *sitting and thinking* belies its individual meaning, from boredom in a certain situation, to a valued and structured period of reflection in another instance. Likewise we can examine the occupation of *going to church*. We have seen that for Karl this occupation fills a long-time social role, and is unconnected with religious beliefs. We then turn to Beatrice who expresses pleasure and comfort in her daily inspirational readings and prayers, yet she does not go to church. A third illustration to highlight the importance of studying the *meaning* of an occupation for an *individual* is the pastime of *having a wander*. Fernie (1991) reminds us that past opinion commonly viewed "wandering" as aimless and undesirable. On the contrary, other opinion (Mace and Rabins, 1981), recognises the exercise value and stimulation which wandering provides. Gladys in the study clearly derives much pleasure from "having a wander". Such examples of stereotypical values that have been allocated to occupations, together with the notion that certain occupations are desirable, whilst others are less so, stultifies the all important personal values that are associated with preferred occupations.

Because the meaning has been teased out of frequently cited occupations such as "sitting around", further challenges are issued to former classifications of occupations. When individuals place their own unique interpretations on what counts in these categories, there becomes a less clear division between the components. CAOT (1997) listed the major categories of occupation as: *self-care, leisure and productivity*, (p.181) and described the type of activities that fit into each of these three categories. The current study reveals that a single occupation may comprise many different aspects of meaning. Gardening (see Chapter 12) is one such example, where a number of sub-activities are incorporated and productivity and leisure become intertwined. Thus recognition of the meaning of gardening for the individual concerned, assumes greater importance than its category allocation.

Kelly (1983) described one of the most severe diseases to be "the hardening of the categories" and it appears that this challenge continues. The study has revealed strong support for Weinblatt *et al.*'s (2000) work in which they too challenge categorisation of occupations for elderly people, viewing this as invalid. Instead the authors suggest it is necessary to listen carefully to the individual narratives, and they illustrate with an account of an elderly lady's trip to a supermarket- as a leisure activity.

### How older people like to spend their time

The current study, with its emphasis on preferences and the meaning of occupational involvement, has revealed challenges to earlier works that have explored time on task, without details of why or whether large chunks of time are spent in pursuits that the elderly people enjoy. A prime example here is television. Horgas, Wilms and Baltes (1998) suggested that of their study sample, 83.3% reported watching television with a mean of 162.7 minutes per day spent in this pursuit. Current research has suggested that many older people do not *like* watching television. It provoked strong reactions such as from Gladys "Enjoy watching television? Corr! I mean it is either violence, sex or bad language or a mixture of all three", and Edith's comment: "I don't enjoy television because I learn little from it." With such reactions in mind, it appears that although the current research is small scale, it has revealed some interesting client-centred points with relevance for service providers. Among these points is the diversionary impact of such devices as television, where as witnessed in residential settings (Green 1995), and continues to be the case whenever programmes are not selected, conversation and meaningful occupational pursuits may be stifled.

## Being simultaneously inactive and occupationally involved

A common assumption, seen in the current encouragement to publish activity programmes as measures of quality assurance in residential settings, is that "sitting around in a quiet room is meaningless and should be avoided". By studying the meaning of *sitting around,* we now know that such an occupation may well be undesirable to some people, but equally it may form part of a programmed, valued and purposeful period of reflection for another individual. Such findings cause us to re-enter the ongoing debate about the nature of occupation. Theoretical discussion continues, and some writers describe inactive states as being occupational. McLaughlin Gray (1997) furthers this idea: "a degree of active participation is evident in all occupations, either by the individual's consent to be a willing participant in a passive activity, or through active and voluntary engagement" (p.15). In terms of passive occupation, Pierce (2001a) also talks of its importance when considering the restoration aspects of occupation. She suggests: "people find waking restoration in different ways; quiet focussed occupations, such as needlework, ...viewing art; listening to music; quiet and solitude..." (p.254). A major challenge here then is for ongoing recognition that occupational involvement does not equate with being active. There are many passive, sedentary occupations, as listed in the following chapter, which bring a great deal of individual satisfaction.

# CHAPTER 12 TIPS, CASE STUDIES AND LISTS OF OCCUPATIONS

This chapter offers fresh material, added to help the reader put the research of earlier chapters to practical use. We could say this is time to "roll up the sleeves" and put ideas into action!

## Tips for getting going

1. Should you want to try out ideas for finding quality and occupational satisfaction in your day, then select any story from Part 2. Each story here represents real life, and is a short, self-contained and non-challenging read. Having read the story you may want to reflect on:

   a. Similar traits here to your own?
   b. Any new coping strategies you may want to try?
   c. Any new ideas or activities you may want to try?

2. If you are a therapist struggling with occupational analysis and links with possible relocation for one of your older clients, check out the stories of Beatrice and Fay, or George and Karl in Part 2. Having read these stories you may want to reflect on:

   a. the differing environmental impact in the two cases
   b. how you can use these factors to help you evaluate environmental impact with your client
   c. would a potential relocation improve environmental impact for your client?
   d. whether sheltered housing would improve environmental impact; here it may be useful also to read the story of Lucy in Part 2.

3. As a researcher wanting to pursue the topic of quality of life and occupational satisfaction for people in later life, begin reading with Part 1, chapter 4 to learn about possible methods you can use. You may then want to reflect on:

   a. your own research question; could this be addressed using any of these methods?
   b. How will you ethically recruit your subjects, avoid bias and establish inclusion and exclusion strategies?
   c. What additional reading do you need to do before going further?

d. This is always a challenging time for any researcher. Temptations to move on too far and too quickly, without completing background study, are always great; you are not alone! Having got this far though, what will you do next?

e. Still not sure? Then check out chapter 11 for a critical evaluation of research methods and results after the study was completed.

4. As a therapist, a researcher or an interested general reader you may wonder whether it is really possible to measure such abstract concepts as quality of life or occupational satisfaction. If so then take a look at visual analogue scales (VAS).
Operationally a VAS is usually a horizontal line, 10 cm. long, with word descriptors at each end; see figure 4(i) below. It is self administered with the client putting a mark on the line to represent how they feel today. The VAS score is determined by measuring from the left hand end of the line to the point that is marked.

|_____|
No quality of life                    Full quality of life

**Figure 4(i) Visual analogue scale indicating quality of life**

You may then reflect on:

a. how you would rate your own quality of life using the 10cm line, ranging from No quality of life at the left to Full quality of life at the right end of the line.

b. whether VAS would be helpful for you in working in another context, maybe with another abstract concept or with another client.

c. how you may use VAS to measure change after intervention.

5. Try putting yourself in your client's place, in your own home environment and experiment with using the model of *Quality enhancement through occupational satisfaction (QETOS)* yourself, by reflecting then answering the points in the simplified self assessment tool in Figure 4(ii) below. Consider a fairly normal day and remember you are evaluating your perceptions of satisfaction with the occupations in your day. As in the VAS above, the ideal here is the right hand end of the line. If you are absolutely satisfied with a category, then you will mark

yourself here, thereby indicating you do not wish to work towards any changes in this area. Most of us however are not satisfied in all aspects of our occupational lives and we like to plan for positive changes we can make. Should you feel negative about any category, due either to under or over-stimulation, then you will mark towards the left hand end of the line, at the farthest point away from balanced.

---

*Having thought about my **Socialising***

I rate myself: zero ———————————————————— Balanced
           negatively                                              or ideal

*Having thought about my **Range of possible activities***

I rate myself: zero ———————————————————— Balanced
           negatively                                              or ideal

*Having thought about my **Time use during the day***

I rate myself: zero ———————————————————— Balanced
           negatively                                              or ideal

*Having thought about Fulfilment of my **Personal aspirations***

I rate myself: zero ———————————————————— Balanced
           negatively                                              or ideal

**Figure 4(ii)   Self assessment of occupational satisfaction**

---

If you want to give yourself a score out of ten, count in from the left and calculate a rating for your mark in each category.

Next consider your personal environment around the home, and think about how it supports your activities at the moment in relation to:

    a.  ***Socialising*** *with people I want to see*         *yes/no*
    b.  ***organising*** *my activities*                  *yes/no*
    c.  ***physically*** *enabling me to do want I want to do*  *yes/no*

*Tips, case studies and occupations*

In relation to your environment, should you find you feel hampered in one or more of the above aspects then you may want to start here in making changes. Here are some suggestions for you to consider:

➢ Would any structural changes (eg acquiring a greenhouse) help to make activities in your current home more satisfying (physical changes)
➢ Have you missed any information (organisational changes) for example bus routes, local learning opportunities that:
  ▪ would give you more choice of activities in your current home area
  ▪ could possibly lead to opportunities to meet new people
➢ Have you meant to introduce yourself to the new neighbour for ages, catch up with old friends (social changes)
➢ Is the current impact of your home environment so negative that you possibly want to plan for relocation in order to improve the environmental influence over your occupational satisfaction?

Finish your self assessment at this stage by adding a goal/ resolution, for example:

**_By the first of next month I will have joined the local wild-life watch group (aiming for positive change in both socialising and personal aspiration categories)_**

then make a note of the date when you will check on your progress. Place this note in a conspicuous place!

6. Having possibly examined your own occupational satisfaction and considered the impact of your personal environment, reflect on the crucial increased impact of the home environment as we age. We hear accounts of people fulfilling a life-time ambition of a move to the country "when we retire". Yet without prior careful evaluation of the environmental impact such a move can bring there is a strong possibility of:

➢ Loneliness due to diminished social contacts,
➢ Less organisational resources such as an infrequent bus service
➢ Possibly even such a negative physical influence as a home in a beautiful location, but on a hillside.

7. Perhaps as a therapist you are now feeling ready to test out the new assessment tool with a group of older people? Overleaf is a sample Self-Help Leaflet which can be used to provoke discussion and/or to introduce the

assessment tool. The leaflet is in 16 point type, and in ready format for free copying. Backed by an introduction from an informed speaker, this leaflet can be shared with a lay group of older people. Before you embark on this, you will need to be well acquainted with the assessment tool itself, see Chapter 10, and be prepared to answer questions should they arise. If you do invite the group members to fill out the assessment tool, you will need to be available to assist as necessary. You could introduce the assessment to your lay group in the following way:

***Self Assessment*** *You may want to carry this out if for example:*

  ➢ *You have been ill recently and can no longer manage former hobbies*
  ➢ *You feel lonely, unfulfilled or bored*
  ➢ *You have changed accommodation and are unsure about launching into a new environment*
  ➢ *You are trying to adapt to living by yourself*

   *By filling out an assessment you will see whether you are organising your daily activities to give you the best possible quality of life. Your leader will have copies of the assessment with diagrams which show how the important factors fit together.*

**N.B. The Self Help Leaflet on the following two pages: "Activities and Quality of Life at 75, 85, 95 plus" should be used in full, together with the footnote which acknowledges its source.**

# Activities and Quality of Life at 75, 85, 95 plus

We know that our quality of life is improved when we can do what we want, when we want. We feel better when we can get out and meet friends, tidy the garden, join a community project, complete a tricky crossword etc. There is a positive buzz of satisfaction or achievement on such occasions and our quality of life is enhanced. However, on cold, wet days when our joints might ache, our mood is low, or the local bus isn't running, then just how can we motivate ourselves? Can we work out how to regain an activity pattern that will once again make us feel good?

This self-help leaflet arises from the findings of a research study(1), carried out to explore some answers to these questions.

**What we found out: Some things help people feel better about their daily occupations:**

**DO**  **Have a choice of available pastimes**
**Ensure there is a social element- even just a phone call**
**Aim to fulfil a personal aspiration- however simple, such as to complete one more puzzle clue than yesterday**
**Plan each day so that the hours are comfortably filled in a way that holds meaning**
**Take every opportunity to make new friends**

**AVOID**  **Time hanging heavily, or feeling pressure that time is too short to do everything planned**
**Setting a daily goal which is too high to reach**
**Being inflexible or not trying new activities**
**Neglecting your health**

*(1) Green S. (2009) Occupation and Quality in Later Life*

# Some examples

Ann 75yrs. talking about planning, *"I like to have one organised activity a day".*

Beatrice 90yrs. and aspirations, *"Nobody wants you when you moan do they? I always aim to look on the bright side".*

Ian 85yrs. talks about adapting pastimes, *"I don't get out much now but this lounge window is my window on the world"*

Joyce, 98yrs. talking about making a new friend ten years ago in the pub, *"He's the age my son would have been, now he comes every Friday and we share a can of Guiness".*

Fay, 83yrs. and her aspiration of perpetuity, *"I shall give these certificates to my grand-daughter, I don't want them thrown away".*

Edith, 88yrs. talks about her range of activities, *"I have so many lovely things I want to do; even grow chives on my windowsill if gardening becomes too difficult.*

## Some of factors that help to make a satisfying and balanced day

➢ *Planning and pacing oneself*
➢ *Having a basic structure for the day and the week*
➢ *Being flexible and resourceful*
➢ *Reciprocity; accepting help where you previously gave it*
➢ *Health-related activities, such as healthy diet & exercise*

**ADDITIONAL NOTES ABOUT THE RESEARCH (1)** The study was carried out by: In-depth Yesterday Interviews (Moss and Lawton 1982), The Moss 36-item short form health survey (SF36) (Ware and Sherbourne 1992, Jenkinson *et al.* 1996), Visual Analogue Scales (VAS) (Tiplady *et al.* 1998) to self-rate quality of life and activity levels, The Multiple Sorting Task (MST) (Sixsmith and Sixsmith 1987) to self-rate activities for enjoyment etc. **ACKNOWLEDGEMENTS** Thanks are due to A and J Sixsmith and B Acheson Cooper for mentorship and to: Ann, Beatrice, Cath, Doris, Edith, Fay, Gladys, Horace, Ian, Joyce, Karl and Lucy, ** for taking part in the study to self-rate quality of life and activity levels. ** Pseudonyms are used to protect privacy.
*Green S.(2009) Occupation and Quality in Later Life.* www.trafford.com/08-1384

## Sample Case Studies

Ten case study synopses are presented on the next pages. For each case, the assessment *Quality Enhancement through Occupational Satisfaction* (QETOS) as illustrated in figure 3(ix) Chapter 10, has been completed and there is a plan of action designed to help the individual work towards a more satisfying occupational day.

---

### 1. ELEANOR aged 72 years

Eleanor moved into her local hospice last month, when her husband could no longer cope at home. She is realistic about her poor prognosis and her energy is limited. With a wide circle of friends she has almost constant visitors, which she appreciates, but they tire her. She would like to complete the scrapbook she began for her grandchildren earlier this year. The occupational therapist sits with Eleanor as she completes QETOS with the following results:

| *QETOS* | | |
|---|---|---|
| SOCIALISING | 2 | (negative because of no choice) |
| FULFILLING ASPIRATIONS | 2 | |
| RANGE OF PASTIMES | 5 | |
| USING TIME | 1 | |

With unrestricted visiting hours Eleanor was attempting to socialise with several well-meaning visitors each day. With no choice or fixed visiting times she is becoming frustrated and tired, having accomplished little of what she would like to achieve.

*Plan: Eleanor's key worker at the Hospice will hold a diary and visitors will be encouraged to ring to book a visiting time agreed by Eleanor. Specific time slots will be kept free for Eleanor's own use. Key worker and occupational therapist will be available to assist with scrapbook completion as required.*

*Re-evaluation: Two week's time.*

## 2. JACK aged 69 years

Jack retired from a busy working life 4 years ago. Having a manual job, Jack had plenty of overtime but this left him little time or energy in latter years, to cultivate hobbies. He had thought he would perhaps take up travelling, but his wife died suddenly just six months after he retired and since then he lost all interest in travelling alone. He has taken to staying at home with his television for company. A friend suggested that he should pop into the local Age Concern Mobile Advice Unit, to see if he can "sort himself out". A male volunteer helps him fill out QETOS.

In chatting to the volunteer Jack talks about having few friends and feeling lonely with the time passing slowly. He also feels he has put on weight and neglected himself a bit.

| *QETOS* | | |
|---|---|---|
| | SOCIALISING | 2 |
| | FULFILLING ASPIRATIONS | 1 |
| | RANGE OF PASTIMES | 2 |
| | USING TIME | 1 |

*Plan: In studying the completed QETOS Jack realises he could make changes in most areas, to help himself feel better. The volunteer suggests Jack may like to go along to a weekly Men's Group, meeting in a local church hall. Just a walk away and running "Cooking for One" each Monday lunch-time, Jack could learn some healthy cooking tips, meet others in similar situations and could check out other activities on offer.*

*Re-evaluation: No formal date set, but Jack agreed to give the plan a try and pop in again to the Age Concern Unit in a month's time to let the volunteer know how things are going.*

## Case 3     FREDA aged 94 years

Having just had her 94th birthday, for a first time Freda acknowledges to her family that she is "beginning to feel her age". She has slowed down, and has considerable pain from osteo-arthritis. The supportive family want her to move into sheltered accommodation but Freda is determined to remain in the large family home with her lovely garden. She will however accept a visit from a community occupational therapist to discuss possible bathing aids.

Whilst making the home visit, the community occupational therapist suggests there may be other areas where Freda could be helped to achieve her ambition to "stay put". Freda agrees to pursue this and begins by completing QETOS.

**QETOS**    SOCIALISING                3
             FULFILLING ASPIRATIONS     4
             RANGE OF PASTIMES          8
             USING TIME                 7

        ENVIRONMENT
             ***Socialising*** *with people I want to see*          *No*
             ***Organising*** *my activities*                       *Yes*
             ***Physically*** *enabling me to do want I want to do*  *Yes*

***Plan:*** *Whilst QETOS revealed positive areas, with the environment supporting her chosen pastimes, Freda agreed there were areas of change which could be made which would leave her with more time to pursue her pastimes. Family agreed to find a gardener, lunches to be delivered three times per week and Freda would try a once weekly visit to a local day centre, to increase her social contacts. The occupational therapist will call again to check on progress, to fit a shower seat and to discuss having a ramp to the garden.*

***Re-evaluation:*** *In one month.*

## Case 4      Arthur aged 84 years

Arthur moved into residential care two years ago when his wife died. Following a stroke 20 years ago which left weakness in his left arm and leg, he had learnt to cope with the associated difficulties. However care staff at the Home now report Arthur has become withdrawn and reluctant to do anything for himself. The staff realise they know little of Arthur's previous life and he has no children or close relatives to provide information. The visiting consultant occupational therapist was called in to advise. An initial assessment indicated that completion of QETOS could be a helpful next stage.

| **QETOS** | | |
|---|---|---|
| | SOCIALISING | 0 |
| | FULFILLING ASPIRATIONS | 2 |
| | RANGE OF PASTIMES | 1 |
| | USING TIME | 1 |

ENVIRONMENT

| | |
|---|---|
| ***Socialising*** with people I want to see | *No* |
| ***Organising*** my activities | *No* |
| ***Physically*** enabling me to do want I want to do | *Yes* |

Arthur offered that he had lessened his aspirations to "just getting through each day", which he was just about managing. He was completely mobile within the Home, but unaware of things he could do any more, so "just sat" and "let the time pass". He could not remember when he last had a visitor and was not interested in "women's talk", so kept himself to himself. Further discussion revealed that Arthur used to enjoy both his garden and classical music; he used to be a pianist. When he first entered the Home a twice weekly volunteer had played the piano and Arthur enjoyed these sessions a great deal. No-one had explained why the volunteer no longer came. After liaising with the care staff over possible options, the following plan was agreed.

*Plan: Arthur would be encouraged to use another lounge, where two men usually sat. One of the domestic helpers had a husband who was a keen pianist and missed the piano they had to sell when moving to a small bungalow; he would be delighted to come in one evening a week to see if the residents enjoyed his music. The recreational therapist would investigate incorporating a weekly gardening session into the programme and would encourage Arthur to join in.*

*Re-evaluation: The visiting occupational therapist would call again in 6 weeks to assess progress.*

## Case 5        Susan aged 65 years

Susan lives alone at home and has received community support since she was found confused and wandering in the street 12 months ago. She tells her support worker that some days "go OK", but others are "awful, with nothing to do". The support worker and Susan complete QETOS together.

| *QETOS* | | |
|---------|---------------------|---|
| | SOCIALISING | 2 |
| | FULFILLING ASPIRATIONS | 1 |
| | RANGE OF PASTIMES | 2 |
| | USING TIME | 1 |

QETOS completion and ensuing discussion indicated that Susan lacked resources both personally to decide what she wanted to do and in a practical way because she had little idea of what her community could offer her.

*Plan: Community support to be increased to twice per week, to introduce Susan to the local library where she could view classes on offer. She also agreed to a referral to an adult mental health day centre with a view to accepting counselling as a means to pursue personal development.*

*Re-evaluation: set for two month's time when Susan hopes to have sampled at least one new group to discuss.*

## Case 6    Peter aged 61 years

Peter was diagnosed with early onset dementia six years ago. He and his wife coped at home until his admission to residential care 4 months ago. Peter communicates little and presents as either wandering and withdrawn or angry and abusive. Peter, his wife Patricia and the occupational therapist complete QETOS together.

| *QETOS* | SOCIALISING | **0** |
| | FULFILLING ASPIRATIONS | **0/1** (an estimation by Patricia) |
| | RANGE OF PASTIMES | **0** |
| | USING TIME | **4** always "on the go/restless" |

The higher score for time use was related to Peter's early morning waking then restless wandering, plus abusive outbursts which together meant most of his days were filled, but with meaningless activity. Peter's wife revealed him to be a "health addict", with cycling and early morning gym attendance figuring regularly in his former life-style. His sedentary leisure time had been little, but Peter always enjoyed art galleries and exhibitions and had a passion for the bold colours of modern abstract works on display.

*Plan: From the above QETOS completion and ensuing discussion, a plan was drawn up and agreed with Patricia and Peter's care home staff. A structured day would incorporate an early morning track-suit circuit of the grounds during the current summer period, to be increased or reduced depending on Peter's reactions. Peter would be asked if he would like to chose two art reproductions for his room and he would be introduced to the sensory room in the Home, with its tranquil atmosphere and its coloured themed areas.*

*Re-evaluation: two week's time.*

**Case 7      Patricia, Peter's wife, aged 55 years**

Patricia is helped to fill out her own QETOS following her presentation to care home staff as highly anxious, stressed and very upset each time she visits Peter in the Home. Patricia told the occupational therapist at the outset that she would just have to give up her job, and agreed with the occupational therapist that she would complete her own QETOS to help her determine what she could do to decrease her stress and anxiety and regain some personal quality time.

| *QETOS* | | |
|---|---|---|
| | SOCIALISING | 1 |
| | FULFILLING ASPIRATIONS | **"don't know any more"** |
| | RANGE OF PASTIMES | 1 |
| | USING TIME | 9 |

As she completed QETOS Patricia was alerted to the fact that she raced through each day, to be with Peter each hour she was not at work, with no thought to any "outside world". Although she recognised there would be a day when Peter was "no longer there", she could not bear to think of it.

***Plan:*** *aware that Peter had his own new plan to try out (see previous case study), Patricia agreed to:*

1. *Visit Peter 5 days per week instead of every day*
2. *Discuss reducing to part-time work with her employer*
3. *Re-establish contact with one or two local friends*
4. *Contact the occupational therapist again if and when necessary.*

**Case 8      Trudy aged 73 years**

Trudy has lived alone since her partner died six months ago after a short illness. They had long-held plans to retire together to the country and had moved to a cottage in the Lake District when her partner retired some four years previously. Having been busy sorting out the new house and garden, they had never found time to meet local neighbours or to make new friends. Trudy is now very lonely and depressed, and is referred to the occupational therapist attached to her G.P practice. The completed QETOS reveals:

| QETOS | | |
|---|---|---|
| SOCIALISING | **0** |
| FULFILLING ASPIRATIONS | *feels "cheated", unable to score* |
| RANGE OF PASTIMES | **2** |
| USING TIME | **3** |
| ENVIRONMENT | **Negative** |

Overall when Trudy studies her scores, she realises that her new environment offers her little now that she is alone. She feels it impractical for her to try to make new friends and both the remote location of the cottage and its large garden will always cause her problems. Trudy opts to discuss moving back to her former location where she has several good friends and contacts for groups she previously enjoyed; the Ramblers and local Gardening Society always figured regularly on Trudy's schedule.

***Plan:*** *The occupational therapist will call in 6 weeks to check on progress, Trudy may request an earlier visit if she feels it necessary.*

## Case 9      Hilda aged 88 years

Hilda visits her General Practitioner for her annual health check. She asserts that she is fine, with just one problem, her tiredness. Some days she just cannot fit in all she wants to do, and there are things Hilda would really like to do whilst she "has her health". The full check up reveals no physical problems, and the Practice Nurse takes over to complete QETOS.

| *QETOS* | | |
|---|---|---|
| | SOCIALISING | 1 |
| | FULFILLING ASPIRATIONS | 1 |
| | RANGE OF PASTIMES | 6 |
| | USING TIME | 2 |

Hilda elaborates on her scores, adding that she is too busy to go out any more, so meets few people, hence her unsatisfying social score. She has always been full of aspirations, always wanted to do better, but time is too short and "it just doesn't work". Whilst she has a good range of pastimes, she cannot find time to paint or write any more; housework seems to take all her time and energy.

*Plan: Hilda will try a twice-weekly home help. If this works out, she would like to try the local weekly water-colour painting class to meet like-minded people and develop her own skills.*

*Re-evaluation: in two month's time when Hilda is next due to visit the chiropody clinic at the surgery.*

**Case10      Ken aged 63 years**

Ken is spending a few days in hospital following surgery for knee replacement. The occupational therapist sees him for a routine assessment and recognises his low mood, coupled with a reluctance to go home. Ken agrees to continue his assessment by completing QETOS.

| *QETOS* | | |
|---------|---|---|
| | SOCIALISING | 1 |
| | FULFILLING ASPIRATIONS | 1 |
| | RANGE OF PASTIMES | 2 |
| | USING TIME | 1 |
| | ENVIRONMENT | *unsatisfactory in all respects* |

Ken reveals low scores in all areas and is particularly anxious about his home environment. Eight years ago he was rehoused from his old terrace into a new apartment. At the time he felt he had been lucky in his allocation of a fifth floor apartment with a view right over the city. However the neighbourhood has increasing problems with noise, rubbish and teenage gangs who congregate around the lifts. Ken has become reluctant to leave his flat unaccompanied and has given up most of his previous hobbies. It is clear that the environmental situation is having a negative impact on all other areas.

*Plan:   Ken agrees to discuss his situation with the social worker, in order to find out housing options open to him. He expresses an interest in a local sheltered housing scheme where he could feel safe again, and free to come and go without worrying about his property.*

*Re-evaluation: Ken can contact the occupational therapist again if he feels the need to pursue his occupational satisfaction once his housing is sorted out.*

**The final case study example overleaf, again uses Case 1- Eleanor and demonstrates how her assessment would look in diagrammatic form**

## CASE 1    *Eleanor*

Eleanor moved into her local hospice last month, when her husband could no longer cope at home. She is realistic about her poor prognosis and her energy is limited. With a wide circle of friends she has almost constant visitors, which she appreciates, but they tire her. She would like to complete the scrapbook she began for her grandchildren earlier this year.

**ASSESSMENT TOOL:** *Quality enhancement through occupational satisfaction*
**DATE OF COMPLETION:** *1.3.2009*

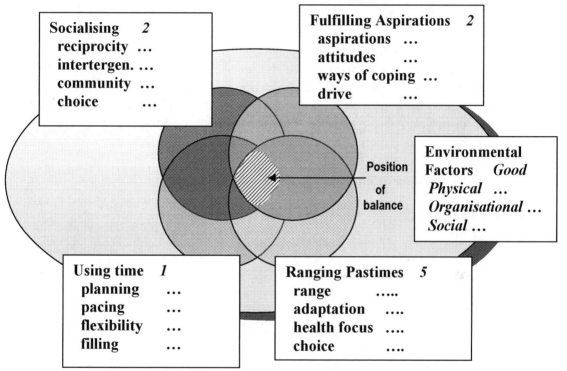

Socialising    *2*
   reciprocity  ...
   intergen. ...
   community  ...
   choice       ...

Fulfilling Aspirations    *2*
   aspirations  ...
   attitudes       ...
   ways of coping  ...
   drive            ...

Environmental
Factors    *Good*
   *Physical*  ...
   *Organisational* ...
   *Social* ...

Position of balance

Using time    *1*
   planning    ...
   pacing       ...
   flexibility   ...
   filling        ...

Ranging Pastimes    *5*
   range        .....
   adaptation   ....
   health focus  ....
   choice        ....

**Assessment reveals:** with unrestricted visiting hours Eleanor is attempting to socialise with several well-meaning visitors each day. With no choice or fixed visiting times she is becoming frustrated and tired, having accomplished little of what she would like to achieve. Whilst environmental factors are supportive and positive, all other areas are being pulled away from a central position of balance and occupational satisfaction.

*Plan: Eleanor's key worker at the Hospice will hold a diary and visitors will be encouraged to ring to book a visiting time agreed by Eleanor. Specific time slots will be kept free for Eleanor's own use. Key worker and occupational therapist will be available to assist with scrapbook completion as required.*
*Re-evaluation: 15.3.2009.*

The next pages contain lists of actual occupations undertaken by older people at the time of survey. These may serve to generate interest amongst others who want to consider expanding or changing their own occupational profiles.

## Occupations mentioned in Yesterday Interviews

The following occupations were all mentioned as part of the study participants' accounts of their normal, regular weekly activities. People tended to highlight the occupational tasks that absorbed either time or effort, so that some spoke of "getting up", whereas others took this activity for granted. It is not possible to divide the occupations into any classic structure such as self-maintenance, productivity and leisure, because each occupation held its own relevance for the individual. For instance the work of gardening for one person was seen as a creative leisure pursuit by another. The occupations are therefore presented in a small number of alphabetically ordered categories. Numbers in brackets indicate how many participants mentioned the occupation; otherwise there is no hierarchical significance.

**Creative pursuits:**

knitting (2)

embroidery (3)

crochet

flower pressing

photography

poetry (4) (composition & reciting)

photography

painting (water colour) (3)

sewing clothes (2)

hat-making

shell sculptures

car maintenance

playing a keyboard

**Friendships/social activities:**

having relatives for a meal (2)

day centre

"having a wander"(2)

having a visitor (2)

Salvation Army teas

receiving a letter (2)

going out for pension (2)

spending time with children (4)

dancing (2)

re-selling books

Weight watchers

ladies afternoon group

visiting charity shops (2)

Age Concern's mobile resource
unit(3)

Church-related activities (7)

using a bus or taxi (6)

going to the launderette

Union meeting and having a pint

going shopping with a friend

window shopping

# Tips, case studies and occupations

**Games:**

| | |
|---|---|
| cards (2) | crosswords (3) |
| table tennis | scrabble (2) |
| lottery | |

**Gardens:**

| | |
|---|---|
| garden design | gardening (3) |
| picking soft fruits | jam making (2) |
| growing vegetables (2) | tending cut flowers (2) |
| feeding birds & squirrels | sitting there (4) |

**Home maintenance:**

| | |
|---|---|
| tidying (5) | housework (5) |
| washing | checking the shopping list (2) |
| checking the house | closing the curtains |
| meal preparation (10) | cooking (7) |
| shopping -local (7) | shopping –supermarket (5) |
| sorting out (7) | buying fish (3) |
| home decorating (2) | |

**Personal care:**

washing and dressing (3)

**Sedentary activities:**

| | |
|---|---|
| television (7) | sitting and thinking or reflecting (2) |
| sitting around/dreaming (3) | making long distance phone calls (2) |
| reminiscing/ sharing memories (4) | planning (3) |
| listening to radio (3) | saying prayers (2) |
| singing | having a snooze (2) |
| reading books (3) | reading newspapers (4) |
| inspirational reading | looking out of the window/ people |
| having a cup of tea (7) | watching (3) |
| having a glass of wine/ whisky/ Guiness (4) | |

**Sports:**

| | |
|---|---|
| Scottish country dancing | badminton |
| walking (2) | yoga |
| going to the gym (3) | swimming (2) |
| riding a bike | table tennis |
| sailing | |

**Travel:**
     driving (2)                           day trips (3)
     taking a holiday (2)

## Occupations referred to during the Multiple Sorting task

Although due to its probing nature it was deemed insensitive to use the Multiple Sorting Task (MST) with all study participants, in particular those who had few occupations they could currently manage, the MST was used with six of the twelve participants, and revealed the occupations which were most enjoyed and those that provoked less enjoyment.

**High enjoyment activities**: having a cup of tea, crosswords (2), going to the village, poetry(4), sitting in the garden(3), playing cards, seeing friends (5), charity shops, gardening, painting, creative sewing (2), reading the *Echo* to keep in touch, time with children (2), having a wander and meeting people, Age Concern's mobile resource unit (3), having a meal with a friend (3).

**Medium to Low enjoyment activities**: cooking (4)- takes too long and is gone too quickly! I am fed up with this, not much fun for one. Seeing the children- there is usually something wrong with them! Sorting out (3). Housework (3). Sitting and thinking- I have no choice, I do plenty of this. Reading the newspaper (2)- its too depressing. Shopping- "this has recently become a chore, I have to take my trolley just for a pint of milk now; its something to hold on to". Television because there are only a few programmes enjoyed (2), (travel, archaeology, period drama),

*Tips, case studies and occupations*

## Additional UK Survey

Following an open letter published in a national magazine for seniors, 121 people wrote letters in response. The request was made to older people living alone at home, and asked for details about their current occupational pursuits

**KEY**

| | | |
|---|---|---|
| **M/F** | **=** | **sex of respondent** |
| **MS** | **=** | **marital status** |
| **Factors =** | | **additional points mentioned by respondents, as influencing their activity involvement** |
| **Other =** | | **additional related information** |

## STATISTICAL SUMMARY

| | |
|---|---|
| **Age range:** | **75-100 years** |
| **Males :** | **12** |
| **Females :** | **107**    **Unknown sex=2** |
| **Widowed :** | **86** |
| **Single :** | **7** |
| **Divorced:** | **2** |
| **Married:** | **2**    **Unknown partnership status=24** |
| **Partner in Nursing Home:** | **1** |
| **Loneliness is cited by:** | **7** |
| **Religion is cited by:** | **22** |
| **Group Participation cited by:** | **35**    **(excluding church activities)** |
| **Volunteering is cited by:** | **19** |
| **Crafts are cited by:** | **20** |
| **Pet owners:** | **35**    **(cat, dog, budgie, fish, hens, tortoise)** |
| **Involvement in garden activity:** | **33** |

## Occupation and Quality in Later Life

| ID | M/F | MS | Age | Occupations | Factors | Other |
|---|---|---|---|---|---|---|
| 46 | F | ? | 87 | volunteers (Oxfam 4/7); garden; phone calls; cooks apples, club (lunch club with friends) | | driver (car) |
| 47 | F | ? | 82 | craft (Costume maker for dance group); crosswords; garden; TV | | Mid-week service reader; phone calls; types |
| 48 | F | W | 80 | reads (newspaper); crossword, Dickens Fellowship | | |
| 49 | F | ? | 85 | craft (Knits bedsocks/charity); reads, TV (Countdown); watches birds; writes letters | housebound | |
| 50 | F | W | 76 | pet (dog); garden; club (WI); | bereaved; lonely | |
| 51 | F | W | 76 | pet (cat); volunteers (mail); day centre; religion (Church); club (Widows group in town) | | "lifeline"; bus campaigner |
| 52 | F | ? | 87 | club (Bingo); club (lunch) | | |
| 53 | F | D | 77 | pet (3cats); crosswords in bed; sport (swims in sea; walks); craft (sewing) | fighting spirit | coffee out |
| 54 | F | W | 80 | church; typing; reads (newspaper); crossword; garden centre & bit of gardening); TV (Countdown etc) | | v accessible environment; shops; library; trams |
| 55 | F | W | 79 | volunteers (Oxfam) – uses bus; religion (church); clubs | | Walks to local shops; uses train; |
| 56 | F | W | 81 | garden (flower arranging); club (bridge); religion (evening mass) | | Rheumatoid Arthritis |
| 57 | F | W | 80 | religion (Prayer groups); crossword; club (WI Treasurer) | | driver |
| 58 | F | W | 81 | garden; crosswords | Faith | driver; types; WI Treasurer |
| 59 | F | W | ? | reads (newspaper); TV (countdown) | | son local |
| 60 | F | ? | 78 | pet (budgie); club (history club with friends); TV; craft (embroidery) | lots of rests | 3 heart attacks; Osteoarthritis |
| 61 | F | ? | ? | volunteers (Oxfam); likes the garden | aches & pains | free bus pass; types |
| 62 | F | W | 75 | friends & charlady; shops | | |
| 63 | M | W | 100 | home brew; IT (computer) | tires quickly | new electric typewriter |
| 64 | M | W | 78 | radio (day & night) | | catches any bus & talks to all; family visit |
| 65 | F | W | 81 | church (computing); pub shandy; village cricket; home organ | | bus reduced to local shops |
| 66 | F | W | 77 | sport (swimming); gardening (garden & hanging baskets); craft (sewing for charity; embroidery) | | driver; children phone |
| 67 | F | W | ? | U3A (science & tech lecture) | | |
| 68 | F | W | 76 | crossword; religion (church lunch helper, choir); records; TV | | |
| 69 | F | W | 79 | sport (swims @ leisure centre); (club) rumikit & bridge | | good neighbours; family meals |
| 70 | F | W | 86 | | | active in retirement club |

# Tips, case studies and occupations

| No. | Sex | Status | Age | Occupations | Trait | Notes |
|---|---|---|---|---|---|---|
| 71 | F | W | 76 | club (bakes for over 60's club); volunteers (play-school) | | driver; visits daughter |
| 72 | F | W | ? | sport (keep fit; swimming; badminton); garden | | |
| 73 | F | W | 75 | cleaning; baking; religion (church for 5pm prayers); craft (knitting); TV (Countdown); reads Bible | | |
| 74 | M | ? | 89 | religion (Baptist church a.m; Methodist p.m) | | S.A. evening - ea Sun for 14 years; uses bus |
| 75 | F | W | 77 | swimming; garden (greenhouse) | Sense of humour | 7 years after stroke; home & power chair user; driver |
| 76 | F | W | ? | club (Chair of community centre); runs lip reading classes | | |
| 77 | F | W | 89 | light gardening; TV (Countdown) | Is content | driver |
| 78 | M | ? | 81 | gardens; reads (newspaper); TV (Countdown & 15:1); old dance music | | conservatory; family |
| 79 | F | W | 79 | pet (dog); U3A writing group; craft (tapestries) | | driver; lost dog recently-using Internet to find a new dog |
| 80 | F | W | 76 | crosswords; light gardening; volunteers (Victim Support Office worker) | | first trip in Shopmobility scooter |
| 81 | F | W | 83 | church (choir); voluntary (lunch club helper); | long lonely evenings | |
| 82 | F | W | 86 | sport (keep fit; swims;) crosswords; writes letters | | driver |
| 1 | F | W | 74 | crosswords | Sense of humour | |
| 2 | F | ? | 80 | pet (3 birds); IT; garden (greenhouse/veg) | | Voluntary treasurer twice |
| 3 | F | W | 79 | garden (cuts lawn); holidays | | |
| 4 | F | W | 78 | holidays (caravans); male friend | | 4 children |
| 5 | F | ? | 80 | crosswords; craft (crochet); TV (news) | very active; takes no naps | Is a Reverand |
| 6 | F | W | 90 | craft (painting); reads; | | |
| 7 | F | W | 81 | shopping; | | driver (outdoor 4 wheeler), recently widowed |
| 8 | F | W | 78 | TV (soaps); memoir writing; pet (dog) | | |
| 9 | F | W | 78 | gardening & vegetable growing; baking; painting plates | | e-mail granddaughter in Australia; has a caring family |
| 10 | M | ? | 80 | craft (writing) | lonely | |
| 11 | F | W | ? | pet (dog); TV (soaps); voluntary (Age Concern Shop); friends | Faith is important | driver (car) |
| 12 | F | W | 84 | club (Elder Tree Club; bingo) | | |
| 13 | F | ? | 77 | crosswords; pet (fish); craft (knitting); reads; | | polyarthritis; bed 1a.m - 6 am; dial-a-ride library & shops |
| 14 | F | W | 84 | garden (sits) | | |
| 15 | F | W | 78 | religion (choir); volunteers (Alzheimer's Group); gardening | | ? |
| 16 | F | W | 79 | day centre - lunch & whist; crosswords; gardens (pot plants) | | |

## Occupation and Quality in Later Life

| ID | Sex | Status | Age | Occupation | Wellbeing | Notes |
|---|---|---|---|---|---|---|
| 17 | F | W | 86 | pet (2 cats); club (Over 60's); craft (crochet); reads / religion (Bible) | | sleeps well 10p.m - 6a.m |
| 18 | F | W | 80 | | | Canada coach tour - family gift |
| 19 | F | W | 75 | pet (3 cats); volunteers (RSPCA shop) sport (swims); voluntary (charity shop); TV (countdown); religion (church to meet sister) | Is lonely | late house move; misses free buses |
| 20 | F | W | 79 | pet (budgie); club (lunch club; bingo) | | family; sheltered flat |
| 21 | F | ? | 80 | religion; dancing | | |
| 22 | F | ? | 82 | betting; club (bingo); TV (countdown) | | |
| 23 | F | W | 79 | wallpapering/decorating; crosswords; club (art class); IT; family phone calls | | |
| 24 | F | W | 77 | club (TLC Group); club (British Legion) | | twice widowed; appreciates free bus |
| 25 | F | W | 80's | volunteers (patient support group); club; | Is lonely | |
| 26 | F | W | 83 | films; | alone | |
| 27 | F | W | 82 | gardens & vegetable growing; seeing people | busy | |
| 28 | F | S | 79 | TV (countdown) | housebound (temporarily) bereaved; depressed | window with view; good neighbours |
| 29 | M | W | 93 | craft (writes); talks to self | | took a bus trip |
| 30 | F | ? | 94 | sport (exercises); TV (countdown); day centre | healthy eating | |
| 31 | F | W | 84 | volunteers (charity shop); TV (countdown); | | driver (car); family links |
| 32 | F | W | 86 | pet (2 cats, tortoise); religion (Bible & chapel); volunteers (Charity Shop); crosswords | | |
| 33 | F | W | 82 | pet (cat); day centre - plays piano; | Evenings lonely | |
| 34 | F | W | 84 | garden (pot plants) | lots of rests | Arthritic; Electric buggy |
| 35 | F | ? | 83 | pet (cat); enjoys garden | | Cycles 1.5m to village; has a window over A6 |
| 36 | F | W | | 87 year old man friend; tidying | | Sunday roast with family if there is a bus |
| 37 | F | W | 79 | Milking Jerseys; pet (cat); garden; Meals on Wheels; sits in garden; does competitions; writes to MPs; craft (tapestries) | Fighting | Arthritic but fighting |
| 38 | F | W | 92 | | | "tubes & pipes in working order"; 6 children Sheltered housing - 60 ladies; lunches; hairdressing |
| 39 | F | ? | 86 | club (Bingo) | | Bus to library |
| 40 | F | S | 81 | TV (quizes); crosswords | | |
| 41 | F | W | 76 | pet (cat); crosswords; reads (newspaper) | | |
| 42 | f | W | 87 | Line dancing | | a "holy cluster" |
| 43 | F | W | 76 | volunteers (League of Friends at Hospital); garden | | |
| 44 | F | W | 76 | pet (dog); garden; local village shop; club (WI) | | |

194

# Tips, case studies and occupations

| No. | Sex | Status | Age | Occupations | State | Notes |
|---|---|---|---|---|---|---|
| 45 | F | W | 80 | garden (Courtyard with plants); pet (cat); shops; art & literacy classes, sewing, religion (chapel) | | local son |
| 83 | F | W | 75 | pets (2 cats); sport (rambling); religion (choir); shops with daughter | | chats to neighbours when drying washing |
| 84 | F | W | 80 | reads (newspaper & codeword); religion (church meetings); garden | | driver (pensions enable a small car) |
| 85 | F | S | 75 | religion (walks to 8am communion; walks to country church tea & cakes) | | collects papers for 3 neighbours |
| 86 | F | W | 82 | club (Bowls; bingo); library by bus | | son rings daily; has a travel card |
| 87 | F | W | 84 | reads; cards with friends | | son comes to lunch Sundays; bus user |
| 88 | F | W | 75 | U3A walking group | | |
| 89 | F | W | 81 | reads (newspaper puzzles); patience; sport (swims); TV (sport) | | Has 4 meals a day |
| 90 | M | M | 76 | TV (Countdown); crossword; home brews | | wife has alzheimers in a nursing home; visiting |
| 91 | F | S | 78 | pet (dog); volunteers (3 hrs work/day); crosswords; garden/vegetables, TV club (Out & about club); U3A (writing as "insurance" & calligraphy); puzzles; cross-stitch | Is content | |
| 92 | F | W | 75 | sport (6 mile walks); club ("Brains Trust"); coffee a.m church; garden (9th floor views & pots) | | TWG; visits friends |
| 93 | F | W | 83 | pet (cat); garden (cuts wild flower grass); craft (embroidery); makes xmas gifts | | |
| 94 | F | W | 79 | pet (cat); feeds birds; reads (talking newspaper tapes) | | |
| 95 | F | S | 80 | crosswords; TV | | sleeps in chair & walks; has Carewatch scheme |
| 96 | F | W | 84 | pet (dog); feeds ducks; friends; enjoys garden; TV | | 15 min walk to shops; no car/bus; meal prep |
| 97 | ? | ? | 85 | voluntary; religion (church); garden | | |
| 98 | F | W | 80 | gardens (tiny garden); sequence dancing; club (over 60s) | Is content | driver |
| 99 | F | W | 84 | reads | reminisces | sometimes sees family |
| 100 | F | W | 80 | pet (dog); (club) Age concern lunch; TV (Countdown); reads (book tapes) | vigilant | diabetic; shops with trolley; phones daughter |
| 101 | F | W | 81 | day centre attendee | | daughter phones |
| 102 | M | ? | 73 | day centre attendee | | |
| 103 | M | ? | 77 | day centre attendee | | |
| 104 | M | ? | 78 | pet (hens&birds); garden; friends; cooking; religion (prayers) | | |
| 105 | M | ? | 95 | voluntary (chair of community club); | | |
| 106 | F | W | ? | reads (newspaper & puzzles); potters in garden; craft (knits); religion / club (Chapel lunch club) | same routine | recent location change, lack of money, same routine |
| 107 | F | W | 87 | U3A writing group; garden, | | |
| 108 | F | W | 77 | sport (Easy exercise group); TV; radio; house tasks | ? | driver; gardens with difficulty; sees friends |
| 109 | ? | ? | 75 | | | |

## Occupation and Quality in Later Life

| # | Sex | Status | Age | Occupation | | |
|---|---|---|---|---|---|---|
| 110 | F | ? | 79 | sits on Sea Front; TV | often "feels like a young girl" | smokes; stocks & shares |
| 111 | F | W | 75 | IT (computer); competitions; dancing; crosswords | | helps disabled neighbours (flats) |
| 112 | F | W | 77 | volunteers (charity shop); TV (soaps) | | types |
| 113 | F | W | 78 | garden; volunteers (hospital charity work); TV (15:1); sport (walks; dances) | | Visits elderly neighbour |
| 114 | F | W | 75 | garden; craft (knitting) | | wife alzheimers, in a home, visits often |
| 115 | M | M | 87 | TV (15:1; Countdown) | | friend drives her |
| 116 | F | W | 82 | religion / social (supportive house groups with hymns; communion service); TV; | | collects pension & gossips |
| 117 | F | W | 77 | brushes teddies; sport (swims); club (hard of hearing) | fears dependence | |
| 118 | F | D | 70 | voluntary work & Quakers; hears children read | | ex principal lecturer (retired 10 yrs); holidays walks to village; ex-nurse; no family; brother abroad |
| 119 | F | S | 80 | night time radio | | |
| 120 | F | S | 95 | social (friends come for scrabble afternoons); crosswords; reads | housebound, very lonely; sleeps poorly | |
| 121 | F | W | 81 | lunch club; reads (large print books) | | friends & sister dead |

## CONCLUDING COMMENTS

Are you one of those readers who always opens a new book at the last page......?

Whether you are a curious new retiree wondering how to fill and organise the newly empty days stretching ahead of you, or a busy therapist wondering how to assist an older patient to increase quality of life through occupational satisfaction, then here are a few final top tips:

1. Mental health is of supreme importance; having aspirations, developing a daily goal will help you.
2. Finding balance in a day lessens frustrations and brings harmony.
3. Four key areas, whatever your age or health status:

> ❖ Socialising
> ❖ Having a range of possible pastimes
> ❖ Using your time in a meaningful way
> ❖ Staying mindful of your aspirations; what *you* would like to achieve

If your appetite is now whetted, please turn to the earlier sections of the book where you will find all you need to know to help you achieve.

***Bon courage!***

# REFERENCES

Abell S (1998) The lifelong preservation of the self: integrating the contributions of Erikson and Kohut. *Journal of Aging and Identity, 3(2),* 87-98.

Adelman C, Alexander R (1982) *The Self-evaluating Institution.* London: Methuen.

Age Concern, England (2006) *Fact Sheet 45, Staying healthy in later life*

*Ageing International* (1996) The Journal of the International Federation on Ageing. Transaction Periodicals Consortium, New Brunswick NJ. *23(2),* 17, 38.

American Occupational Therapy Association (1995) Position paper: occupation. *American Journal of Occupational Therapy, 49(10),* 1015-1018.

Anderson K, Burckhardt C (1999) Conceptualisation and measurement of quality of life as an outcome variable for health care intervention and research. *Journal of Advanced Nursing, 29(2),* 298-306.

Angelou M (1986) *And Still I Rise.* London: Virago.

Angevaren M'Aufdemkampe G'Verhaar HJJ'Aleman A'Vanhees L (2008) Physical activity and enhanced fitness to improve cognitive function in older people without known cognitive impairment *Cochrane Systematic Review.* John Wiley & Sons, Ltd. http://dx.doi.org/10.1002/14651858.CD005381.pub2. Accessed 29.5.08.

Aronson K (1997) Quality of life among patients with multiple sclerosis and their caregivers. *Neurology, 48 (1),* 74-80.

Atchley R (1991) The influence of aging or frailty on perceptions and expressions of the self: theoretical and methodological issues. In: JE Birren, JE Lubben, JC Rowe, DE Deuchman, eds. *The Concept and Measurement of Quality of Life in the Frail Elderly.* San Diego: Academic. 209-225.

Baltes M, Baltes P (1986) (eds.) *The Psychology of Control and Aging.* Hillsdale, New Jersey: Lawrence Erlbaum.

## *References*

Barbour R (1999) The case for combining qualitative and quantitative approaches in health services research. *Journal of Health Service Research Policy, 4,* 39-43.

Barbour R (2001) Checklists for improving rigour in qualitative research: a case of the tail wagging the dog? *British Medical Journal, 322,* 1115-1117.

Batey P, Brown P (1995) From human ecology to customer targeting: the evolution of geodemographics, in *GIS for Business and Service Planning,* eds. P. Longley and G. Clarke, Cambridge: Geoinformation International.

Baum C (1995) The contribution of occupation to function in persons with Alzheimer's disease. *Journal of Occupational Science Australia, 2(2),* 59-67.

Bennet K (2002) Low level social engagement as a precursor of mortality among people in later life. *Age and Ageing, 31,*165-168.

Bing R (1981) Occupational therapy revisited: a paraphrasistic journey. *American Journal of Occupational Therapy, 35,* 499-518.

Birren J, Dieckmann L (1991) Concepts and content of quality of life in later years. In : JE Birren, JE Lubben, JC Rowe, DE Deuchman, eds. *The Concept and Measurement of Quality of Life in the Frail Elderly.* San Diego: Academic. 344-359.

Blair A (2007) Teachers taking early retirement up nearly 50%. *The Times, January 16, 2007*

Boeing H, Dietrich T, Hoffmann K, Pischon T, Ferrari P, Lahmann PH, et al (2006) Intake of fruits and vegetables and risk of cancer of the upper aero-digestive tract: the prospective EPIC-study. *Cancer Causes Control. 2006; 17(7),* 957-969.

Borell L, Lilja M, Andersson Sviden G, Sadlo G (2001) Occupations and signs of reduced hope: an explorative study of older adults with functional impairments. *American Journal of Occupational Therapy, 55(3),* 311-316.

Bowling A (1991) *Measuring Health.* Buckingham: Open University Press.

Bowling A, Dieppe P (2005) What is successful ageing and who should define it? *British Medical Journal, 331,* 1458-1551.

Bowling A, Iliffe S (2006) Which model of successful ageing should be used? Baseline findings from a British longitudinal survey of Ageing. *Age and Ageing, 35(6),* 607-614.

Brown P, Hirschfield A, Batey P (1998) Working Paper 56: *Adding Value to Census Data: Public Sector Applications of the Super Profiles Geodemographic Typology.* Liverpool: The Urban Research and Policy Evaluation Regional Research Laboratory (URPERRL)

Bultena G, Wood V (1969) The American retirement community: bane or blessing? *Journal of Gerontology 24,* 209-217.

Canadian Association of Occupational Therapists (1991) *Occupational Therapy Guidelines for Client-centred Practice.* Toronto: CAOT Publications.

Canadian Association of Occupational Therapists (1997) *Enabling Occupation: An Occupational Therapy Perspective.* Ottawa: CAOT Publications.

Carlson M, Clark F, Young B (1998) Practical contributions of occupational science to the art of successful ageing: how to sculpt a meaningful life in older adulthood. *Journal of Occupational Science, 5(3),* 107-118.

Carpenter I, Gladman J, Parker S, Potter J (2002) Clinical and research challenges of intermediate care. *Age and Ageing 31,* 97-100.

Christiansen C (1997) Acknowledging a spiritual dimension in occupational therapy practice. *American Journal of Occupational Therapy, 51(3),* 169-172.

Christiansen C (2000) Identity, personal projects and happiness: self construction in everyday action. *Journal of Occupational Science, 7(3),* 98-107.

Clark F, Parham D, Carlson M, Frank G, Jackson J, Pierce D, Wolfe R, Zemke R (1991) Occupational science: academic innovation in the service of occupational therapy's future. *American Journal of Occupational Therapy, 45(5),* 300-310.

Clark F, Azen S, Zemke R, Jackson J, Carlson M, Mandel D, Hay J, Josephson K, Cherry B, Hessel C, Palmer J, Lipson L (1997) Occupational therapy for independent-living older adults. *Journal of the American Medical Association, 278 (16),* 1321-1326.

## References

Cochrane Review (2001) Validation therapy for dementia. Neal M, Briggs M. http://www.cochrane.org/cochrane/revabstr/ab001394.htm (Accessed 25.9.2001).

College of Occupational Therapists (COT) (1993) *Curriculum Framework for Occupational Therapy. Standards, Policies and Procedings 161.* London: COT.

Coyne I (1997) Sampling in qualitative research. *Journal of Advanced Nursing, 26,* 623-630.

Creek J (ed.) (1990) *Occupational Therapy and Mental Health.* Edinburgh: Churchill Livingstone.

Creek J, Hughes A (2008) Occupation and Health: A Review of Selected Literature. *British Journal of Occupational Therapy, 71(11),* 456-468.

Creswell J (1998) *Qualitative Inquiry and Research Design. Choosing among five traditions.* 2nd. edition. Thousand Oaks, California: Sage.

Csikszentmihalyi M, Lefevre J (1989) Optimal experience in work and leisure. *Journal of Personality and Social Psychology, 56,* 815-822.

Csikszentmihalyi M (1993) Activity and happiness: towards a science of occupation. *Occupational Science Australia, 1(1),* 38-42.

Cumming E, Henry W (1961) *Growing Old: The Process of Disengagement.* New York: Basic.

Cunningham W, Brookbank J (1988) *Gerontology: The Psychology, Biology and Sociology of Aging.* New York: Harper and Row.

*Dementia UK: summary of key findings – a report into the prevalence and cost of dementia (2007),* Personal Social Services Research Unit PSSRU, (LSE) and Institute of Psychiatry (King's College London), for the Alzheimer's Society. at:www.alzheimers.org.uk (Accessed 28.02.2007)

Denham M (ed.) (1997) *Continuing Care for Older People.* Cheltenham: Stanley Thornes.

Denzin N, Lincoln Y (eds.) (1994) *Handbook of Qualitative Research.* Thousand Oaks: Sage.

Department for Communities and Local Government (2008) *Lifetime Homes, Lifetime Neighbourhoods – A National Strategy for Housing in an Ageing Society*. London: DOH.

Department of Health (2001) *National Service Framework for Older People*. London: DOH.

Department of Health (2006) *A new ambition for old age: Next steps in implementing the National Service Framework for Older People*. London: DOH.

Department of Health (2009) *Living well with dementia: A National Dementia Strategy*. London: DOH.

Diener E (2000) Subjective well-being: the science of happiness and a proposal for a national index. *American Psychologist, 55(1)*, 34-43.

Dietch J, Hewett L, Jones S (1989) Adverse effects of reality orientation. *Journal of the American Geriatric Society, 37*, 974-6.

Englehardt HT Jr. (1977) Defining occupational therapy: the meaning of therapy and the virtues of occupation. *American Journal of Occupational Therapy, 31*, 666-672.

Erikson E (1950) *Childhood and Society*. New York: W.W Norton and Company.

Erikson E, Erikson J, Kivnick H (1986) *Vital Involvement in Old Age*. New York: W.W Norton and Company.

Evandrou M (1997) Social care today and beyond. In M Evandrou, ed. *Baby Boomers: Ageing in the 21$^{st}$ Century*. London: Age Concern. 119-141.

Extracare Charitable Trust (1997) *Organisational Flyer*. Coventry: Extracare Charitable Trust.

Farquhar M (1995) Elderly people's definitions of quality of life. *Social Science and Medicine, 41(10)*, 1439-1446.

Feil N (1993) *The Validation Breakthrough*. London: Jessica Kingsley.

Fernie G (1991) Assistive devices, robotics and quality of life. In: JE Birren, JE Lubben, JC Rowe, DE Deuchman, eds. *The Concept and Measurement of Quality of Life in the Frail Elderly*. San Diego: Academic Press,142-167.

## References

Finlay L (1999) Applying phenomenology in research: problems, principles and practice. *British Journal of Occupational Therapy, 62(7),* 299-306.

Finlay L (2001) Holism in occupational therapy: elusive fiction and ambivalent struggle. *American Journal of Occupational Therapy, 55(3),* 268-276.

Flanagan J (1978) A research approach to improving our quality of life. *American Psychologist, 33,* 138-147.

Fletcher A, Dickinson E, Philp I (1992) Review: audit measures: quality of life instruments for everyday use with elderly patients. *Age and Ageing, 21,* 142-150.

Ford H, Gerry E, Johnson M, Tennant A (2001) Health status and quality of life of people with multiple sclerosis. *Disability and Rehabilitation, 23(12),* 516-521.

Frankl V (1984) *Man's Search for Meaning.* Washington: Washington Square Press.

Freeman B (1997) Seniors on the internet. *OT Practice,* May, 43-48.

French S (1990) Ageism. *Physiotherapy, 76(3),* 178-182.

Gage M, Polatajko H (1995) Naming practice: the case for the term client-driven. *Canadian Journal of Occupational Therapy 62,* 115-118.

Gentile K (1991) A review of the literature on interventions and quality of life in the frail elderly, In: JE Birren, JE Lubben, JC Rowe, DE Deuchman, eds. *The Concept and Measurement of Quality of Life in the Frail Elderly.* San Diego: Academic Press, 74-88.

George LK & Bearon LB (1980) *Quality of Life in Older Persons: Meaning and Measurement.* New York: Human Sciences.

Gill T, Feinstein A (1994) A critical appraisal of quality of life measurements. *Journal of the American Medical Association, 272,* 619-626.

Glass TA, de Leon CM, Marottoli RA, Berkman LF. (1999) Population based study of social and productive activities as predictors of survival among elderly Americans. *British Medical Journal, 319,* 478-483.

Golledge J (1998) Distinguishing between occupation, purposeful activity and activity, part 1: Review and explanation, *British Journal of Occupational Therapy, 61(3),* 100-105.

Gray A, Fenn P (1993) Alzheimer's Disease: the burden of the illness in England. *Health Trends 25,* 31-7.

Green S (1995) Elderly mentally ill people and quality of life: who wants activities? *British Journal of Occupational Therapy, 58(9),* 377-382.

Green S, Acheson Cooper B (1998) Occupational choices of elderly residents in sheltered housing, Abstract 883, *Conference Proceedings, World Federation of Occupational Therapists,* Montreal, June.

Green S, Acheson Cooper B (2000) Occupation as a quality of life constituent: a nursing home perspective, *British Journal of Occupational Therapy, 63(1),* 17-24.

Green S, Sixsmith J, Ivanoff SD, Sixsmith A (2005) Influence of occupation and home environment on the well-being of European elders. *International Journal of Therapy and Rehabilitation, 12(11),* 505-509.

Grimley Evans J (2002) National initiatives in ageing research in the United Kingdom. *Age and Ageing, 31,* 93-94.

Guyatt G, Cook D (1994) Health status, quality of life, and the individual, *Journal of the American Medical Association, 272(8),* 630-631.

Habu H, Saito N, Sato Y, Takeshita K, Sunagawa M, & Endo M (1988) Quality of post-operative life in gastric cancer patients seventy years of age and over. *Internal Surgery, 73,* 82-86.

Hagedorn R (1997) *Foundations for Practice in Occupational Therapy,* 2nd. edn. Edinburgh: Churchill Livingstone.

Halling S, Kunz G, Rowe J (1994) The contributions of dialogal psychology to phenomenological research. *Journal of Humanistic Psychology, 34(1),* 109-131.

Hayes V, Morris J, Wolfe C, Morgan M (1995) The SF-36 Health Survey Questionnaire: is it suitable for use with older adults? *Age and Ageing, 24,* 120-125.

## References

Heidegger M (1927) *Sein und Zeit*, translated: John Macquarrie and Edward Robinson (1962), *Being and Time*, Oxford: Blackwell.

Hobson S (1996) Being client-centred when the client is cognitively impaired. *Canadian Journal of Occupational Therapy 63(2)*, 133-137.

Holliday A (2002) *Doing and Writing Qualitative Research.* London: Sage.

Honigsbaum M (2003) 90,100, 130 who's counting? *The Guardian Weekend, 15.2.03.* 106-111.

Horgas A, Wilms H-U, Baltes M (1998) Daily life in very old age: everyday activities as expression of successful living. *The Gerontologist, 38(5),* 556-568.

Hughes B (1990) Quality of Life, in *Researching Social Gerontology*, ed. SM Peace, London: Sage.

Hull S, Jones I, Moser K (1997) Factors influencing the attendance rates at accident and emergency departments in East London: the contribution of practice organisation, population characteristics and distance. *Journal of Health Service Research and Policy, 2,* 6-13.

Husserl E (1950) *The Paris Lectures* (transl. P. Koestenbaum). The Hague: Martinus Nijhoff.

*International Federation on Ageing* (1999) http://www.ifa-fiv.org/page3p.htm (Accessed 5.2.1999).

Ilott I (2008) A present of evidence for everyday activities. *British Journal of Occupational Therapy, 71(12),* 509.

Jenkinson C, Layte R, Wright L, Coulter A (1996) *The U.K. SF-36: an Analysis and Interpretation Manual.* University of Oxford: Health Services Research Unit, Department of Public Health.

Kahaner E (1980) A congruence model of person-environment interaction. In M P Lawton, P Windley, T Byerts, eds. *Aging and the Environment: Directions and Perspectives.* New York: Garland STPM.

Keith R (1995) Conceptual basis of outcome measures. *American Journal of Physical Medicine and Rehabilitation, 74,* 73-80.

Kelly GA (1983) The psychology of personal constructs. *Rehabilitation, Supplementry Readings.* Milton Keynes: Open University Press.

Khaw K-T (1997) In search of the clues to a healthy old age. *MRC News,* Autumn, 10-13.

Kielhofner G (1995) (ed.) *A Model of Human Occupation: Theory and Application* (2nd. edition), Baltimore: Williams and Wilkins.

Kingston P, Bernard M, Biggs S, Nettleton H (2001) Assessing the health impact of age-specific housing. *Health and Social Care in the Community, 9(4),* 228-234.

Kirkwood T (2001) Reith Lecture 1. Radio 4 Online: downloaded from www.bbc.co.uk/radio4 March 2001.

Kirsh B (1996) A narrative approach to addressing spirituality in occupational therapy: exploring personal meaning and purpose. *Canadian Journal of Occupational Therapy, 63(1),* 55-61.

Kohut H (1977) *The restoration of the self.* New York: International Universities Press.

Krefting L (1990) Rigor in qualitative research: the assessment of trustworthiness *The American Journal of Occupational Therapy , 45(3),* 214-222.

Kupfer B, Weyerer S (1995) Physical activity and mental health among the elderly. Theoretical background and possibilities of intervention. *Verhaltenstherapie, 5(1),* 21-29.

Lamb KL, Brodie DA & Roberts K (1988) Physical fitness and health-related fitness as indicators of a positive health state. *Health Promotion, 3,* 171-82.

Lansdown R (1994) Living longer? Qualitative survival. Meeting report. *Journal of the Royal Society of Medicine, 87,* October, 636.

Lau A, McKenna K (2001) Conceptualizing quality of life for elderly people with stroke. *Disability and Rehabilitation, 23(6),* 227-238.

Law M, Cooper B, Strong S, Stewart D, Rigby P, Letts L (1996) The person-environment-occupation model: a transactive approach to occupational performance. *Canadian Journal of Occupational Therapy, 63(1),* 9-23.

Law M, Steinwender S, Leclair L (1998) Occupation, health and well-being. *Canadian Journal of Occupational Therapy, 65(2),* 81-91.

# References

Lawton MP (1985) The elderly in context: perspectives from environmental psychology and gerontology. *Environment and Behaviour*, *17*, 501-519.

Lawton MP (1991) A multidimensional view of quality of life in frail elders. In: JE Birren, JE Lubben, JC Rowe, DE Deuchman, eds. *The Concept and Measurement of Quality of Life in the Frail Elderly.* San Diego: Academic Press, 3-27.

Lawton MP, Nahemow L (1973) Ecology and the aging process. In C. Eisdorfer and MP Lawton, eds. *Psychology of Adult Development and Aging.* Washington DC: American Psychological Association.

Lawton MP, Moss M, Glicksman A (1990) The quality of the last year of life of older persons. *Milbank Quarterly, 68,* 1-28.

Letts L, Law M, Rigby P, Cooper B, Stewart D, Strong S (1994) Person-environment assessments in occupational therapy. *The American Journal of Occupational Therapy*, *48(7)*, 608-618.

Levin H (1938) Occupational and recreational therapy among the ancients. *Occupational Therapy and Rehabilitation 17(5).*

Le Clerc D (1699) Translated: Drake J, Baden A. *The History of Physick.* London: Printed for D Brown, A Roper, J Leigh.

*Lifetime Homes. Lifetime Neighbourhoods: A National Strategy for Housing in an Ageing Society* (2008). London: UK Government.

Link L (1996) Add purpose to exercise. *OT Week, July 11$^{th}$,* 16-17.

Lucksinger M (1994) Community and the elderly. *Journal of Housing for the Elderly, 11(1),* 11-28.

Mace N, Rabins P (1981) *The 36-hour Day.* Baltimore: Johns Hopkins University Press.

Mahony P, Rodgers H, Thomson R, Dobson R, James O (1998) Is the SF-36 suitable for assessing health status of older stroke patients? *Age and Ageing 27,* 19-21.

Massey V (1995) *Nursing Research*, Second edition, Pennsylvania: Springhouse Corporation.

Mattingly C, Fleming M (1994) *Clinical Reasoning: Forms of Inquiry in a Therapeutic Practice*. Philadelphia: FA Davis.

Mayers C (1995) Defining and assessing quality of life. *British Journal of Occupational Therapy, 58(4)*, 146-150.

McAuley E, Rudolph D (1995) Physical activity, aging and psychological well-being. *Journal of Aging and Physical Activity, 3(1)*, 67-96.

McKay E, Ryan S (1995) Clinical reasoning through story telling: examining a student's case story on a fieldwork placement. *British Journal of Occupational Therapy, 58(6)*, 234-38.

McLaughlin Gray J (1997) Application of the phenomenological method to the concept of occupation. *Journal of Occupational Science: Australia, 4(1)*, 5-17.

McNiece R, Majeed A (1999) Socio-economic differences in general practice consultation rates in patients aged 65 and over: prospective cohort study. *British Medical Journal, 319*, 26-28.

Mendola W, and Pelligrini R (1979) Quality of life and coronary artery bypass surgery patients. *Social Science and Medicine, 13A*, 457-61.

Metz D (1997) Growing old gracefully. *MRC News*. Autumn. 8.

Meyer A (1922) The philosophy of occupational therapy, *Arch Occup Ther 1*, 1-10. reprinted from *The Collected Papers of Adolf Meyer*, Baltimore: The John Hopkins Press, 1952, pp 86-92 in Engelhardt H. (1977) Defining Occupational Therapy: The Meaning of Therapy and the Virtues of Occupation. *American Journal of Occupational Therapy, 31(10)*, 666-672.

Meyer A (1977) The philosophy of occupational therapy, *American Journal of Occupational Therapy, 31*, 639-642. (original work published 1922).

Milligan C, Bingley A, Gatrell A. Cultivating health. *End of Project Research Report Oct 2003*, Institute for Health Research, *Lancaster University*

Montazeri A, Milroy R, Gillis CR, McEwen J (1996) Quality of life: perception of lung cancer patients. *European Journal of Cancer, 32A (13)*, 2284-2289.

Morgan K (1998) The Nottingham longitudinal study of activity and ageing: a methodological overview. *Age and Ageing, 27-53*, 5-11.

# References

Moss M, Lawton MP (1982) Time budgets of older people: a window on four lifestyles. *Journals of Gerontology, 35,* 576-582.

Mounter C, Ilott I (1997) Occupational Science: a journey of discovery in the United Kingdom. *Journal of Occupational Science, Australia. 4(2),* 50-55.

National Statistics (2001a) (eds. C Griffiths, J Fitzpatrick) *Geographic Variations in Health I DS No.16.* London: The Stationery Office.

National Statistics (2001b) (eds. D Pearce, P Goldblatt) *United Kingdom Health Statistics 1 UKHS No.1.* London: The Stationery Office.

*Nature* (1999) 50 Years Ago, Volume 397, 4 February 1999, 393.

*Nature* (1949) 5 February, cited ibid.

Nayak U (1995) Elders-led design. *Ergonomics in Design, January.* 8-13.

Nelson D (1997) Why the profession of occupational therapy will flourish in the 21st Century, *American Journal of Occupational Therapy, 51(1),* 11-24.

NIACE (1998) Older and Bolder response to "The Learning Age". http://agenet.ac.uk/ (Accessed 28.7.1998).

Niemi M-L, Laaksonen R, Kotila M, Waltimo O (1988) Quality of life 4 years after stroke. *Stroke, 19(9),* 1101-1107.

*On Lok News* (1999) From Kelley's notebook: tributes to a friend at Generations, Spring, 7.

Parker S, Peet S, Jagger C, Farhan M, Castleden C (1998) Measuring health status in older patients. The SF-36 in practice. *Age and Ageing, 27,* 13-18.

Patterson W (1975) The quality of survival in response to treatment. *Journal of the American Medical Association, 233,* 280-1.

Peloquin S (1997) The spiritual depth of occupation: making worlds and making lives. *American Journal of Occupational Therapy, 51(3),* 167-168.

Perrin T (1997) Occupational need in severe dementia: a descriptive study. *Journal of Advanced Nursing, 25,* 934-941.

Phillipson C (1997) Employment and training for 2020 and beyond, in *Baby Boomers, Ageing in the 21ˢᵗ Century*, ed. Maria Evandrou, London: Age Concern.

Pierce D (2001a) Occupation by design: dimensions, therapeutic power and creative process. *American Journal of Occupational Therapy, 55(3),* 249-259.

Pierce D (2001b) Untangling occupation and activity. *American Journal of Occupational Therapy. 55(2),* 138-145.

Pischon T, Lahmann P, Boeing H *et el.*(2006) *Journal of the National Cancer Institute, 98(13),* 920-931.

Plager K (1994) Hermeneutic Phenomenology, in: Benner P (1994) (ed.) *Interpretive Phenomenology.* Thousand Oaks, California: Sage. 65-84.

Pope C, Ziebland S, Mays N (2000) Analysing qualitative data. *BMJ, 320,* 114-116.

Power M, Quinn K, Schmidt S and WHOQOL-OLD Group (2005) Development of the WHOQOL-Old Module *Quality of Life Research 14 (10).* Netherlands, Springer.

Rabbitt P, Lunn M, Ibrahim S, Cobain M, McInnes L. (2008) Unhappiness, health and cognitive ability in old age. *Psychological Medicine, 38(2),* 229-36.

Rabbitt P (1997) *MRC News,* Spring No.73, 25-27.

Rabeiro K (2001) Enabling occupation: the importance of an affirming environment. *Canadian Journal of Occupational Therapy, 68(2),* 80-89.

Rapkin B, Fischer K (1992) Framing the construct of life satisfaction in terms of older adults' personal goals. *Psychology and Ageing, 7(1),* 138-149.

Reilly M (1960) Research potentiality of occupational therapy, *American Journal of Occupational Therapy, 14,* 208, cited in West 1984.

Reilly M (1962) The Eleanor Clarke Slagle Lecture: occupational therapy can be one of the great ideas of 20ᵗʰ century medicine. *American Journal of Occupational Therapy, 16(1),* 1-9.

# References

Riboli E, Kaaks R (1997) The EPIC Project: rationale and study design, *International Journal of Epidemiology, 26*: S6-S1.

Richards S (1998) The Casson Memorial Lecture 1998: Occupation for health- and wealth? *British Journal of Occupational Therapy. 61(7)*, 294-300.

Rokeach M (1973) *The Nature of Human Values*. New York: Free Press/ Macmillan.

Rook R (1987) Reciprocity of social exchange and social satisfaction among older women. *Journal of Personality and Social Psychology, 52*, 145-154.

Rowe J, Kahn R (1998) *Successful Aging*. New York: Pantheon.

Royal College of Nursing (1975) *Improving Geriatric Care in Hospital*. London: RCN. 11-29.

Royeen C (2002) Occupation reconsidered. *Occupational therapy international, 9(2)*, 111-120.

Rudman D, Cook J, Polatajko H (1997) Understanding the potential of occupation: a qualitative exploration of seniors'perspectives on activity. *American Journal of Occupational Therapy, 51(8)*, 640-650.

Sabonis-Chafee (1989) cited in: Occupational terminology: interactive dialogue. *Journal of Occupational Science (2001), 8(2)*, 39.

Sartre J (1943) *Being and Nothingness*. Translation of "L'etre et le neant". Paris: Gallimard, 1943. First published in English, 1958, London: Methuen.

Savin-Baden M, Fisher A (2002) Negotiating 'honesties' in the research process. *British Journal of Occupational Therapy, 65(4)*, 191-193.

Scherer M and Cushman L (2001) Measuring subjective quality of life following spinal cord injury: a validation study of the assistive technology device predisposition assessment. *Disability and Rehabilitation, 23(9)*, 387-393.

Schreiber H (1996) Limits in geriatric surgery: indications, ethics, economy. *Langenbecks Archiv fur Chirurgie, s2*, 457-466.

Seshamani M, Gray A (2002) The impact of ageing on expenditures in the National Health Service. *Age and Ageing, 31*, 287–294.

Shin D, and Johnson D (1978) Avowed happiness as an overall assessment of the quality of life. *Social Indicators Research, 5*, 475-92.

Sixsmith J, Sixsmith A (1987) Empirical phenomenology: principles and method. *Quality and Quantity, 21*, 313-333.

Skevington SM, (1999) Measuring Quality of life in Britain: an introduction to the WHOQOL-100, *Journal of Psychosomatic Research, 4(5)*, 449-459.

Slovick D, Fletcher A, Daymond M, Mackay E, Vandenburg M, Bulpitt C (1995) Quality of life and cognitive function with a diuretic compared with a beta-blocker. A randomized controlled trial of bendrofluazide versus dilevalol in elderly hypertensive patients. *Cardiology in the Elderly, 3(2)*, 139-145.

Snowdon D (2001) Aging with Grace: What the Nun Study Teaches us About Leading Longer, Healthier, and More Meaningful Lives, extract in *The Universe*, Sept. 9, 19.

Spirduso W, Gilliam-MacRae P (1991) Physical activity and quality of life. In: JE Birren, JE Lubben, JC Rowe, DE Deuchman, eds. *The Concept and Measurement of Quality of Life in the Frail Elderly*. San Diego: Academic. 226-55.

Stenhouse L (1975) *An Introduction to Curricular Research and Development*. London: Heinemann.

Strong S, Rigby P, Stewart D, Law M, Letts L, Cooper B (1999) Application of the Person-Environment-Occupation Model: a practical tool. *Canadian Journal of Occupational Therapy, 66(3)*, 122-133.

Tickle-Degnen (2001) in: Law M, Baum C, Dunn W (eds.) *Measuring Occupational Performance*. Thorofare, New Jersey: Slack Incorporated.

*Times* (July 5, 2000) Queen to pay for 100th birthday cards.1.

*The Time of Our Lives! 2007 - 2010 - draft consultation* (2007) E. Sussex; http://www.eastsussex.gov.uk/yourcouncil/consultation/2007/qualityoflife/ (Accessed: 27.11.2007).

Tiplady B, Jackson S, Maskrey V, Swift C (1998) Validity and sensitivity of visual analogue scales in young and older healthy subjects. *Age and Ageing, 27*, 63-66.

## References

Tomassini C (2006) *The Oldest Old in Great Britain: change over the last 20 years*. Population Trends 123, Newport: Office for National Statistics.

Tout K (1992) International perspectives on ageing and marginalisation; Paper presentation. International Conference: Marginalisation of elderly people, Liverpool, 13-15 May 1992, page 3.

Turner A, Foster M, Johnson S (eds.) (1992) *Occupational Therapy and Physical Dysfunction, 3$^{rd}$. edition*. Edinburgh: Churchill Livingstone.

U.S. Bureau of the Census. International Programs Center. International Data Base, December 1999.

U3A Annual Report (2006) University of the Third Age, website: http://www.u3a.org.uk. (Accessed 14.11.2007).

Wagg A, Denham M (1997) Ethical dilemmas in continuing care, in *Continuing Care for Older People*, ed. M Denham. Cheltenham: Stanley Thornes Ltd. 45-57.

Wallymahmed M, Baker G, Humphris G, Dewey M, MacFarlane I (1996) The development, reliability and validity of a disease specific quality of life model for adults with growth hormone deficiency. *Clinical Endocrinology, 44(4)*, 403-411.

Ware J jnr, Sherbourne C (1992) The Moss 36-item short-form health survey (SF-36).1. Conceptual framework and item selection. *Medical Care, 30*, 473-83.

Weinblatt N, Ziv N, Avrech-Bar M (2000) The old lady from the supermarket – categorization of occupation according to performance areas: Is it relevant for the elderly? *Journal of Occupational Science, 7(2)*, 73-79.

Wenger N (1988) Quality of life issues in hypertension: consequences of diagnosis and considerations in management. *American Heart Journal, 116*, 628-632.

Wertz FJ (1983) From everyday to psychological description: analysing the moments of a qualitative data analysis. *Journal of Phenomenological Psychology, 14(2)*, 197-241. Cited in Finlay (1999).

West W (1968) Professional responsibility in times of change. *American Journal of Occupational Therapy, 22*, 9-15.

West W (1984) A reaffirmed philosophy and practice of occupational therapy for the 1980's. *American Journal of Occupational Therapy, 38(1),* 15-23.

Wetle T (1991) Resident decision-making and quality of life in the frail elderly. In: JE Birren, JE Lubben, JC Rowe, DE Deuchman, eds. *The Concept and Measurement of Quality of Life in the Frail Elderly.* San Diego: Academic. 279-296.

Whalley Hammell K (2001) Using qualitative research to inform the client-centred evidence-based practice of occupational therapy. *British Journal of Occupational Therapy 64(5),* 228-234.

WHOQOL Group (1996) People and health: What quality of life? *World Health Forum (17),* 354-356.

Wilcock A (2001a) Occupational science: the key to broadening horizons. *British Journal of Occupational Therapy, 64(8),* 412-417.

Wilcock A (2001b) *Occupation for Health, Vol. 1.* London: British Association and College of Occupational Therapists.

Wood W (1996) Legitimising occupational therapy's knowledge. *American Journal of Occupational Therapy, 50(8),* 626-34.

Wood W (1998) Nationally speaking: the genius within. *American Journal of Occupational Therapy, 52(5),* 320-325.

Woods B (2002) Reality orientation: a welcome return? *Age and Ageing, 31,* 155-156.

Yerxa E (1998a) Health and the human spirit for occupation, *American Journal of Occupational Therapy, 52(6),* 412-418.

Young J, Robinson J, Dickinson E (1998) Rehabilitation for older people: at risk in the new NHS. *British Medical Journal, 316,* 1108-1109.

Zanetti O, Oriani M, Geroldi C, Binetti G, Frisoni G, Giovanni D, De Vreese L (2002) Predictors of cognitive improvement after reality orientation in Alzheimer's disease. *Age and Ageing 31,* 193-196.